Contents

List of Tables and Figures

Tables

Figures

Acknowledgements

I feel very grateful to my colleagues from the Bank of Greece, George Hondroyiannis, Stelios Pantazidis and George Zombanakis, for reading various parts of the manuscript with particular care and for making essential comments. I would like also to thank George Stubos (also from the Bank of Greece) for providing me with all the available material he had on the particular countries; and he had plenty! Finally I would like to thank Maria Pitta, a doctorate student at Panteion University, for her assistance with Chapter 9. Needless to say, the author is responsible for all the remaining errors.

CHRISTOS PAPAZOGLOU

List of Abbreviations

ATPs	autonomous trade preferences
BH	Bosnia and Herzegovina
CE	Central Europe (Czech Republic, Hungary, Poland, Slovak Republic and Slovenia)
CLI	Cumulative Liberalization Index
CMEA	Council for Mutual Economic Assistance
CPI	Consumer Price Index
EBRD	European Bank for Reconstruction and Development
ECE	Economic Commission for Europe
EU	European Union
FDI	Foreign Direct Investment
FTAs	Free Trade Agreements
FYROM	Former Yugoslav Republic of Macedonia
GDP	Gross Domestic Product
GIR	Gross International Reserves
GNFS	Goods and Non-Factor Services
GNP	Gross National Product
IMF	International Monetary Fund
LI	Liberalization Index
MEBOs	Management–Employee Buy-Outs
PPP	Purchasing power parity
RS	Republika Srpska
SEE	South Eastern Europe (Albania, Bosnia and Herzegovina, Bulgaria, Croatia, Former Yugoslav Republic of Macedonia, Romania, and Serbia and Montenegro)
SFR	Socialist Federal Republic
SITC	Standard International Trade Classification
SM	Serbia and Montenegro
UN	United Nations
WIIW	The Vienna Institute for International Economic Studies
WTO	World Trade Organization

This page intentionally left blank

1
Introduction

The region of South Eastern Europe (SEE) has been among the least developed in Europe, at least as far as modern history is concerned. This has been especially true for those countries in the region that were operating under central planning after the end of the Second World War, primarily reflecting the fact that the process of industrialization did not rely on market criteria. Investment decisions, in particular, were to a large extent the result of arbitrary assessments on the part of central planners, instead of reflecting comparative advantage and expected market returns (United Nations/Economic Commission for Europe, or UN/ECE 1999). Economic viability in these countries was mostly preserved through their close cooperation with other communist countries, forming, as a result, a largely closed system. Due to their 'economic isolation', therefore, when the economies of these countries came to face the competition of the world markets following the break-up of the communist regimes, most of the existing capital stock turned out to be economically non-viable.

Thus for most of these transition economies, the last decade of the twentieth century was a period of economic degradation. As a matter of fact, the transition process towards the market system revealed a number of problems and challenges which were not only related to economic reconstruction and development but also to issues concerning the establishment of democratic rules and the need for major institutional reforms. This was particularly true for the countries of SEE, in which the lack of democratic tradition and the surfacing of ethnic disputes and armed conflicts led to extensive political instability, which, in turn, affected their economic performance quite adversely.

This chapter takes a brief look at the region of SEE, pinpointing the issues that we shall focus on in this book. Furthermore, we will present an overview of the structure of the book and a short summary of each chapter.

A snapshot of the issues of the region

The region of SEE consists of the following transition countries: Albania, Bosnia and Herzegovina (BH), Bulgaria, Croatia, Former Yugoslav Republic of Macedonia (FYROM), Romania, and Serbia and Montenegro (SM). Table 1.1 presents some basic data for the countries of the region from 2003 and denotes their economic lagging relative to both the region of Central Europe (CE), and the 15 member states of the European Union (EU). More specifically, with respect to per capita income and in terms of purchasing power parity (PPP), the region's average stood at about 57 and 28 per cent of CE and EU averages respectively in 2003.[1] Thus, from the basic data in Table 1.1 it becomes clear that by the end of 2003 the region of SEE still remains largely underdeveloped, particularly when compared to more advanced European regions.

The economic consequences of transition were particularly severe for the countries of SEE, contributing, as a result, to an increasing disparity between

Table 1.1 Basic data for the region of SEE in 2003

	Area in km²	**Population (millions)**	**GDP (in US$ mil.)[a]**	**GDP per capita (US$ at current exchange rate)**	**GDP per capita (in euro at PPP)**
Albania	28,748	3.1	6,100.0	1,950.0	3,740.0
Bosnia and Herzegovina	51,129	3.9	7,050.0	1,850.0	6,030.0
Bulgaria	110,994	7.8	19,855.0	2,545.0	6,830.0
Croatia	56,538	4.4	28,400.0	6,400.0	9,890.0
FYR Macedonia	25,713	2.0	4,670.0	2,280.0	6,340.0
Romania	238,391	21.7	56,950.0	2,620.0	6,730.0
Serbia and Montenegro	102,173	8.3	19,570.0	2,360.0	n.a.
SEE[b]	*613,686*	*51.2*	*142,595.0*	*2,785.0*	*6,790.0*
CE	*553,871*	*65.9*	*432,215.8*	*6,560.0*	*11,985.0*
EU-15	*3,154,000*	*383.0*	*10,476,298.0*	*27,360.8*	*24,235.0*
SEE as percentage of CE		*77.7*	*33.0*	*42.5*	*56.7*
SEE as percentage of EU		*13.4*	*1.4*	*10.2*	*28.0*

n.a. = not available
[a] Calculated using the current exchange rate.
[b] The GDP per capita in euro at PPP does not include SM due to the unavailability of data.
Sources: The Vienna Institute for International Economic Studies (WIIW); European Bank for Reconstruction and Development (EBRD) (2003); and European Economy (2003).

them and their counterparts in CE. The adverse initial conditions (reflecting their inherited economic distortions) and their relative geographical isolation as a result of their location on the periphery of Europe were among the major factors explaining their economic underdevelopment. Furthermore, the lack of tradition with respect to both democratic rule and market economy institutions has been of considerable importance and has contributed to persistent institutional gaps in the specific countries. To make matters worse, for the majority of the transition period, there has been a reluctance on the part of governments to make a firm commitment to macroeconomic stabilization and structural reform.

The process of disintegration of the former Socialist Federal Republic (SFR) of Yugoslavia and the ensuing conflicts, initially in Croatia and BH and latterly in Kosovo, had a major destabilizing effect on the region and constituted another important reason for slow economic development. Armed conflicts and the resulting political instability have been a major restraining factor on Foreign Direct Investment (FDI) inflows, thus depriving the countries of the region of important sources of foreign finance that would have been vital to their growth prospects.

Despite the similarities of these economies, primarily stemming from the fact that they have all embarked on a course towards the market system, there are significant differences as well. In particular there are differences with respect to their degree of development since, according to Table 1.1, the per capita GDP in 2003 ranged from less than US$2,000 in Albania and BH to US$6,400 in Croatia, which is about the CE average. With respect to size, Romania is by far the largest country of the region in terms of population and area, while together with Bulgaria they account for more than 50 per cent of the region's GDP.

An interesting question to tackle at this point refers to whether SEE can be considered as a region or not. A complete answer must rely on political, historical and economic criteria. First, with respect to political and historical criteria, the answer is possibly negative. In fact, after the break-up of the Ottoman and Habsburg empires following the end of the First World War, the countries of SEE followed different alliances (European Bank for Reconstruction and Development, or EBRD 2004a). After the end of the Second World War, although all these countries were drawn into the communist bloc, they followed relatively different paths as well. The Socialist Federal Republic of Yugoslavia followed a more independent route, being less influenced by the Soviet Union. However, the extent of cooperation among the constituent republics of the country was quite limited. This was manifested by the eruption of wars and ethnic conflicts as soon as the break-up of the country took place in the early 1990s. By contrast, Bulgaria and Romania remained firmly loyal to the Soviet Union until the end of the communist regime. Finally, Albania chose the road of almost complete isolation from the rest of the world.

Turning to economic criteria, the particularly low trade links among the countries of the region (combined, at least until recently, with a variety of very substantial restrictions and impediments to mutual trade) constitute significant evidence that the particular countries do not consider themselves as part of a coherent regional entity (see Anastasakis and Bojicic-Dzelilovic 2002; EBRD 2004a). Nevertheless, the European perspective, as is expressed through their ultimate aim of EU accession, has put them on the same course and this refers to both political as well as economic developments. First, with respect to the former, it facilitated their process of democratization considerably, contributing to the establishment of political stability and to greater willingness for a peaceful settlement of tensions and ethnic differences. Second, with respect to economic developments, it enhanced the willingness of the South East European countries to cooperate with each other by encouraging bilateral free trade agreements that could eventually turn the region into a free trade area.

Despite the problems and challenges faced by the countries of the South East European region, particularly during the first decade of transition, the prospects for future growth and prosperity remain quite positive. In particular, since the end of the Kosovo War the region has made remarkable progress. The firm commitment to macroeconomic stabilization and to the acceleration of structural reforms has led to strong output growth and to steadily declining inflation rates. In addition, the progress in establishing the democratic rule in all countries and the resulting political stability reduced investment risk significantly. This, in turn, together with the acceleration of the privatization progress, has led to the substantial recovery of FDI inflows. Finally, regional cooperation has become an important policy objective in all countries of the region. Undoubtedly, the region has started catching up with the countries of CE and this process, to the extent that the political consolidation turns out to be a truly lasting situation, could end up being quite effective.

An overview of the book

The previous section touched upon different issues that largely affected the economic performance of the region since the start of transition and which constitute the primary focus of this book. In particular, our aim has been to analyse the broad factors that largely determined the course of the countries of SEE during transition, particularly with respect to economic performance. Thus issues concerning macroeconomic stabilization and structural reform, as well as trade and FDI developments, are at the heart of our analysis.

The book consists of two parts. The first part, which extends from Chapters 2 to 7, primarily concentrates on the broad determinants of economic performance of the South East European countries during transition. These broad determinants basically refer to the initial conditions that these countries had to face at the start of the transition process, to the effectiveness of macroeconomic stabilization and to the extent of progress with respect to structural reforms. More specifically, our analysis starts in Chapter 2 by presenting the stylized facts of transition as these were experienced by the countries of SEE during the first decade of the transformation process. It clearly highlights the degree of harshness that was imposed on the economic performance of the region, particularly in comparison to the corresponding experience of the countries of CE. Next, Chapter 3 examines the importance of initial conditions and thus the extent to which economic performance was adversely affected by the economic distortions inherited from central planning.

While initial conditions may considerably affect economic performance early on in the transition period, it is the effectiveness of macroeconomic and structural reform policies that gain in importance as transition progresses. Chapters 4, 5 and 6 focus on the effectiveness of these particular policies in these countries. More specifically, Chapters 4 and 5 concentrate on macroeconomic policies and performance. Chapter 4 examines the period prior to the Kosovo conflict (end of 1998), while Chapter 5 considers the period after the war, (i.e., from 1999 onwards), proceeding as far as the availability of data allows. As we shall explain in more detail below, the transition for BH and SM started much later in relation to the other countries of the region, so our analysis in Chapter 4 focuses only on the five early starters, while Chapter 5 refers to all seven states of the region. Next, Chapter 6 examines the extent of the progress made regarding structural reform by the countries of the region, relying on the structural indicators developed by the EBRD. Finally, in Chapter 7, we attempt an empirical investigation of the relative importance of the broad determinants examined in the preceding chapters on the economic performance of the South East European countries. What we do, in other words, is try to quantify the contribution of these broad factors to the output performance in the specific countries.

The second part of the book examines issues that stem from the external economic relations of the region of SEE *vis-à-vis* the rest of the world. It consists of three chapters which focus on developments regarding international trade relations and FDI inflows, as well as on the role of the euro with respect to the exchange rate arrangements of the countries of SEE. Thus, Chapter 8 examines the trade patterns of the countries of SEE with respect to geographical distribution as well as sectoral composition. Moreover, the low level of intra-regional trade represents an issue that will be considered in more detail in this chapter. Next, Chapter 9 concentrates on the performance of the South East European countries in attracting FDI inflows. In particular, the performance of both individual countries and the region as a whole is examined and compared with that of the Central European countries. Furthermore, we attempt to identify the most important factors that have been responsible for the weak performance of the South East European economies, particularly during the first decade of transition. The last chapter focuses on the euro and on how it may affect the exchange rate policies followed by the countries of the region. By considering the economic conditions and the policy objectives of each country, the analysis assesses the implications of the euro for the sustainability as well as the effectiveness of the current exchange rate arrangements of the countries of SEE.

Some clarifying remarks

One point that we should mention refers to the fact that our analysis in Chapters 2, 3, 4 and 7 relies on five countries in the region, namely Albania, Bulgaria, Croatia, FYROM and Romania, instead of seven. This is due to the fact that, as we have pointed out, BH and SM started their transition process at a much later date. More specifically, in BH the Dayton Accord was signed in December 1995 and the political change in SM occurred in October 2000. Thus, in essence, the transition process in these two countries started in the years following these two events (i.e., 1996 and 2001 for BH and SM respectively). As a result, the particular chapters which focus on issues concerning the first decade of transition rely essentially on the five early starters. Note that for the purpose of our analysis the first decade of transition extends until the period prior to the Kosovo conflict (i.e., end of 1998). This coincides with the end of a rather 'unpleasant' period characterized by conflicts, economic backwardness and limited progress in stabilization and reform. The end of the war in June 1999 constituted a turning point for the South East European countries and signalled the beginning of a new era for their prospects of growth. This was primarily the result of a renewed commitment of both the international community to monitor more closely the progress being made in the transition process and the governments of the particular countries to take firmer steps towards stabilization and reform.

Another remark refers to the fact that in most instances of our analysis we compare the performance of the South East European countries with that of the Central European ones. The countries of CE include the following: Czech Republic, Hungary, Poland, Slovak Republic and Slovenia. For these countries the transition process has almost been completed and this was manifested by fact that they became full members of the EU in 2004. Our analysis uses the particular countries as a point of reference in order to evaluate the extent of progress or lagging of the South East European countries relative to a group of countries that largely constitute a success story.

A final point worth mentioning concerns the major data problems. The quality of the data has been a serious impediment that almost all studies on transition economies acknowledge. Particularly with respect to output, official data is more likely to underestimate output as well as growth rates because of the emergence of the private sector, which initially was not fully covered by statistics, but also because of the development of a large unofficial economy.[2]

Part I

The Transition Experience of the South East European Countries

This page intentionally left blank

2
The Stylized Facts of Transition in South Eastern Europe

The countries of the SEE region to a large degree experienced the stylized facts that characterized the transition process in most of these economies, primarily during the first decade of transition: that is, basic economic variables to a certain extent displayed the same or similar trends as in other countries or regions in transition, such as the countries of CE. At the same time, however, they exhibited significant variations. These variations can be attributed to substantial differences in several factors such as the economic circumstances at the onset of transition, the effectiveness of policy and reform measures and the political conditions, particularly the emergence of wars and ethnic conflicts.

Two more profound facts refer to the massive decline in the level of economic activity, primarily reflecting the sudden dismantling of a cumbersome and highly integrated economic system, and the substantial spike of inflation, which was the result of the immediate price controls removal. The pattern followed by the variables involved, however, displayed significant differences across the South East European and the Central European countries. These differences concerned the initial severity and persistence as well as subsequent trends.

Additional stylized facts that characterized the transition process and refer to the pattern of other important economic variables also exhibit significant variations across the two groups of countries. These facts include trends in variables such as industrial production and the extent of change in the economic structure, employment, productivity, registered unemployment and capital formation.[1] The trends followed by these variables may not exhaust all the economic aspects of transition, but they do effectively reveal some of its economic consequences as well as the extent of its severity for the region of SEE, particularly when compared to CE. The behaviour of these variables, together with output and inflation developments, provides important insights about the economic conditions of the region at the outset of transition as well as about the effectiveness of the transformation process. These insights, in turn, allow us both to evaluate the overall performance and also to compare it with the performance of other transition counties, such as the ones in CE.

When analysing the pattern of these stylized facts and comparing the performance of the South East European region relative to CE for the transition period under consideration, one can separate the trend of the particular variables into two phases. The first refers to the initial stages of transition and involves the initial response of these basic economic variables to the transformation process. This is primarily associated with declining trends in output and in the other variables as well as with rising inflation. These developments reflected the initial impact of transition on these economies and, as a result, were largely affected by the initial conditions that prevailed in each country. The second phase follows as soon as recovery gets under way while inflation starts to decline. It is the impact and the effectiveness of stabilization and reform policies, the building of market institutions as well as the increasing integration of these economies into the world markets that primarily affected developments during the second phase. The analysis below will reveal that the performance of SEE was much worse than that of CE during both phases.

Output and inflation trends

Although output fell everywhere across the transition economies, it is generally agreed that the depth and length of the decline, as well as the course of the subsequent recovery, varied significantly across countries.[2] This has also been true in the case of the South East European and Central European regions where there are notable differences between them regarding the corresponding patterns of output as well, as highlighted in Figure 2.1.[3] In particular, the South East European countries experienced a much deeper and more persistent output decline than the countries of CE.[4] The lowest GDP figure in CE was 83 per cent of its 1989 level, attained in 1992, while for SEE the corresponding point was 72 per cent, achieved in 1993. Furthermore, by the end of 1997, the countries of the CE region had recovered all of their output loss and the GDP index stood at 103 per cent of its 1989 level. By contrast, the output recovery in the case of the South East European region was quite slow and as a result it was still about 25 percentage points below the 1989 level at the end of 1998.

The most striking difference between the two regions has been associated with the course of output following the early recovery: while output followed a U-shaped pattern in CE, the South East European region experienced a severe setback in output growth. In particular, the recovery in CE following the initial recession was sustained throughout the period and, as a result, output growth displayed an increasing trend. In SEE, by contrast, the initial output recovery was short-lived and a major growth reversal occurred in 1996. As we shall see in more detail in Chapter 4, this was due to the output

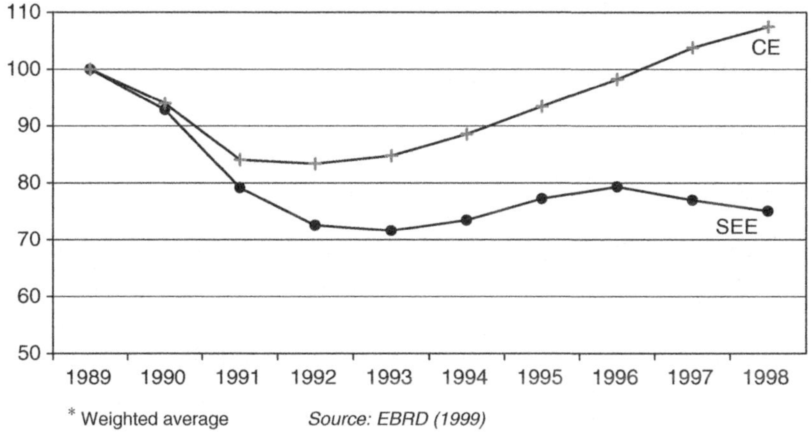

Figure 2.1 Real GDP index (1989 = 100)*

declines encountered in Albania, Bulgaria and Romania. Output in the other two countries of the region, Croatia and FYROM, followed the U-shaped trend but appeared to recover rather slowly. There are two things, however, that one must keep in mind with respect to the two states of the former SFR of Yugoslavia. The first is that transition started in 1992, rather than in 1990, since that was their first full year of independence which, in turn, meant that prior to that year the fall of output was not related to the transition process. Second, in the case of Croatia, the output decline during the period under consideration was exacerbated by armed conflict.

Almost all transition economies experienced an initial spike in inflation at the beginning of the transition process as price controls were removed. However, as in the case of output, the initial increase as well as the subsequent course of disinflation differed considerably among the transition economies. Figure 2.2 shows the inflation trend for the period 1990–98 in SEE and CE.[5] As was the case with output, the course of inflation followed different paths in the two regions. In the Central European economies, after the initial spike, inflation rates have been steadily declining. By 1993 the annual average inflation rate of the region was below 40 per cent (27 per cent), which was the case for all five individual countries as well. SEE was less successful in curbing inflation. In particular, besides a much larger initial increase, the declining trend after the early spike was disrupted by a major inflation reversal.

As Figure 2.2 indicates, the unweighted mean inflation rate for the SEE region almost converged to the respective Central European average in 1995, falling to 24.5 per cent. This decline in inflation, however, was not sustained and SEE experienced a resurgence of inflation. The inflation reversal, like the growth reversal, occurred in Bulgaria and Romania (and, to a much lesser

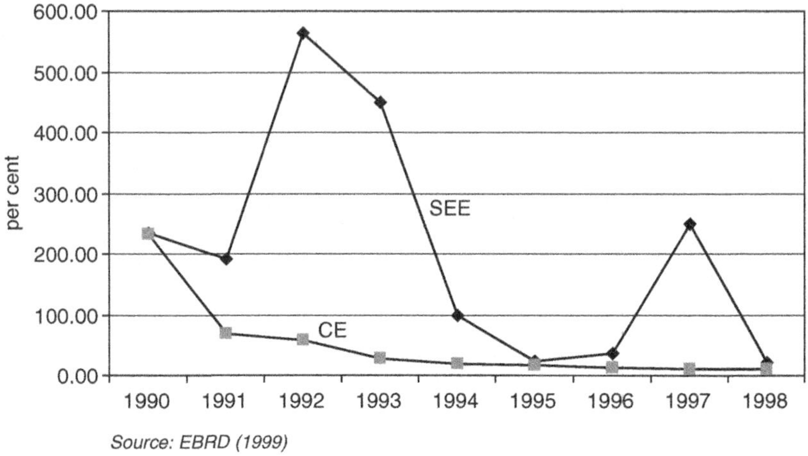

Figure 2.2 Annual inflation rates (period unweighted average in retail/consumer price level)

extent, in Albania). As we shall see below, the growth reversal was to a considerable extent related to the limited success of the particular countries to effective disinflation.

Table 2.1 includes some additional information regarding output and inflation developments in the countries of SEE.[6] FYROM experienced six years of consecutive output decline, the longest in the region. The cumulative output decline (weighted average) for the entire South East European region since 1989 was almost 30 per cent, with Croatia and Albania seeing a percentage fall in activity of about 40 per cent. On the other hand, the region's cumulative growth between the year with the lowest output level and 1998 was only 4.8 per cent, as opposed to almost 30 per cent for CE. Albania and Croatia were the two countries with the fastest growth, while the performance of the remaining three countries was rather disappointing. Turning to inflation performance, Table 2.1 confirms the fact that inflation peaked twice in three countries (i.e., Albania, Bulgaria and Romania), which is reflected in the unweighted inflation average for the entire region. The second peak was not as high in the case of Albania while the same cannot be said in the case of Bulgaria and, to a lesser extent, Romania. Finally, as a result of the two peaks, the average inflation for the region fell to moderate levels (below 40 per cent) twice, in 1995 and 1998. Albania was more successful in bringing inflation down to such levels (1994), while Bulgaria and Romania did not succeed in doing so until 1998 and 1999 respectively. Croatia and FYROM appeared to have done remarkably well since they were able to bring inflation to moderate levels in 1995 down from the hyperinflation rates that occurred in 1993 and 1992 respectively.

Table 2.1 Output and inflation performance until 1998

Countries/ regions	Years of output decline	Cumulative output decline since 1989 (%)	Real GDP, 1998 (1989 = 100)	Cumulative output growth between lowest level year and 1998 (%)	Year(s) of peak inflation	Maximum average inflation rates	Year at which inflation fell below 40%	Inflation in 1998
Albania	3.0	39.6	86.44	43.1	1992/1997	226.0/33.2	1994	20.6
Bulgaria	4.0	26.7	65.90	3.5	1991/1997	338.4/1,058.4	1998	18.7
Croatia	4.0	40.5	77.77	20.6	1993	1,500.0	1995	6.4
FYROM	6.0	32.0	71.60	5.3	1992	1,664.4	1995	0.5
Romania	3.0	21.0	76.10	1.8	1993/1997	255.2/154.8	1999	59.1
SEE[a]	*4.0*	*28.4*	*75.06*	*4.8*	*1992/1997*	*563.6/250.3*	*1995/1998*	*21.1*
CE[a]	*3.2*	*16.6*	*107.46*	*28.9*	*1990*	*233.9*	*1993*	*10.3*

[a] Weighted average for output, unweighted average for inflation.
Sources: EBRD (1999) and Fischer and Sahay (2000).

Changes in output structure

The overall drop in output initially reflected the decline of activity in almost all sectors of the economy. However, the output decline was above all the result of a large drop in industrial production. The fact that the old regime favoured the development of (heavy) industry, since it was believed to be the key determinant to rapid economic growth, led most transition economies to end up with relatively large manufacturing sectors. Thus it was rather expected that the fall in output would primarily be the result of an enormous decline in industrial production reflecting the considerable shrinking of the artificially large manufacturing sector, as indicated in Figure 2.3. As expected, the drop in industrial output was in excess of the overall output decline. Particularly for the South East European region, the drop was around 50 per cent of the 1989 level, in comparison with 30 per cent for the Central European countries. The large fall in production in Bulgaria and Romania, the two states with very large industrial sectors, was primarily responsible for the corresponding decline in the entire region. Furthermore, in the South East European area, the recovery of industrial output after the initial decline was not sustained. This growth reversal primarily reflects the corresponding trends in Bulgaria and Romania, and has been responsible for the respective reversal in the total output trend.

The overall shrinking of industry constituted an important aspect of the transition process since it reflected the extent of structural change of the particular economies and the movement towards an economic restructuring on the basis of market incentives. As indicated, industry was the largest sector at the beginning of the transition. In fact, according to Figure 2.4,

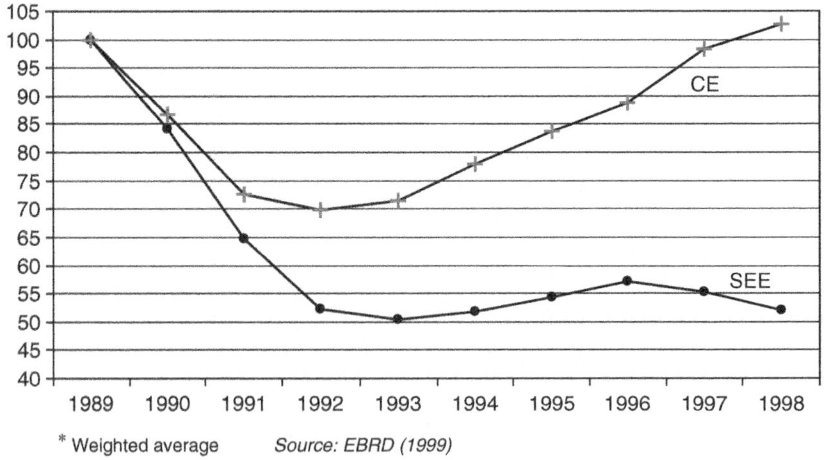

Figure 2.3 Index of industrial production (1989 = 100)*

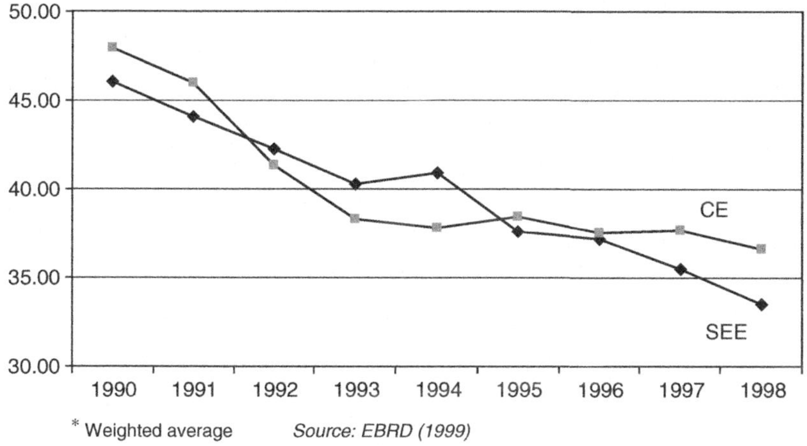

Figure 2.4 Industry, value added (% of GDP)*

when comparing the shares of value added by industry as a percentage of GDP between CE and SEE, we see that in 1990 they were about the same level (48 per cent and 46 per cent respectively). Then the figures in both cases followed a declining trend, and in 1998 the value added of industry stood at around 36.5 per cent of GDP in the Central European countries and 33.5 per cent in the SEE. In the South East European region the initial high share of industry was mainly due to the large manufacturing sectors established in Bulgaria and Romania. Croatia, on the other hand, was a country which, at the beginning of the transition process, had an output structure rather similar to market economies: that is, it combined a relatively small industrial sector with a significant services sector and a much smaller agricultural one.

The decline of the share of industry was quite significant in the SEE region and similar to the experience of the Central European region. With respect to the share of agriculture, however, the situation in the two regions was rather different. To begin with, as Figure 2.5 indicates, the share of agriculture in the South East European region was about twice as much that of CE in 1990 (18.5 per cent of GDP in SEE and about 9 per cent in CE). Furthermore, while in CE the share of agriculture declined steadily by almost 50 per cent during the period 1990–98, the corresponding share in SEE did not show a significant change. More specifically, after an initial drop in 1991, it increased steadily until 1997, displaying only a modest decline in 1998. As a matter of fact, with the exception of Romania, the share of agriculture in the other countries of the region either increased or remained at the same level.

Thus while the pattern of structural change in the Central European region approached that of developed countries as the shares of both industry and

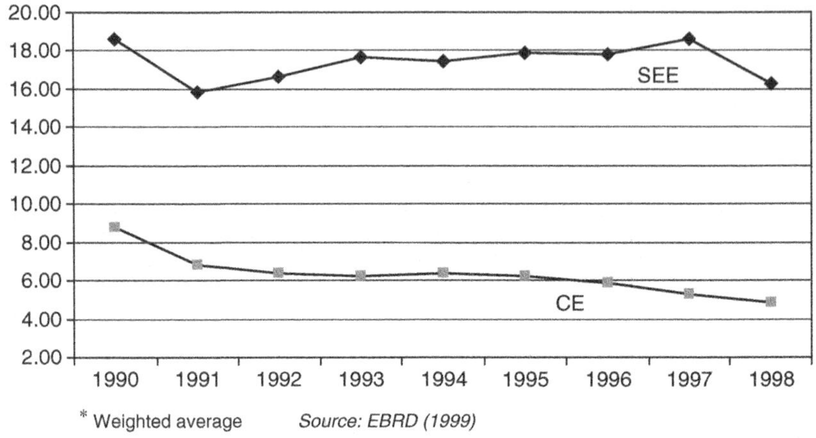

Figure 2.5 Agriculture, value added (% of GDP)*

agriculture declined in favour of services, the corresponding trend in the South East European region was not as clear or uniform. More specifically, Romania and Bulgaria experienced a significant increase in services which was largely the result of the reduction of industry. Croatia and FYROM started with a relatively large services sector. The former did not exhibit significant structural change, while the fall in the share of industry in the latter was combined with increases in both services and agriculture. Finally, Albania represents a rather special case where the main feature of the structural change was the significant increase in the share of agriculture (from 36 per cent of GDP in 1990 to almost 55 per cent by 1993). This was primarily the result of a considerable reduction in industry since the share of services remained about the same.

Trends in employment, productivity, registered unemployment and investment

The initial decline in output was also accompanied by falls in employment and productivity, rising unemployment and declining investment. Trends in employment are shown in Figure 2.6. As expected, employment initially declined less than output but then it fell by considerably more.[7] The decline in employment for SEE extends over the entire period in contrast to CE where, as in the case of output, it follows a U-shaped pattern. As a matter of fact, until 1994 employment in CE followed a more profound falling trend than in SEE, whereas, during the same period the decline in output was much larger in the latter region. Thereafter, while employment started recovering in CE, it continued its declining trend in the South East European region.

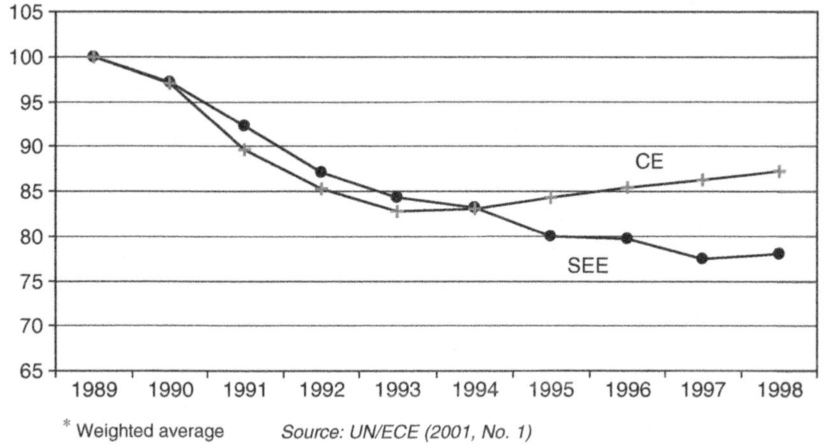

Figure 2.6 Total employment index (1989 = 100)*

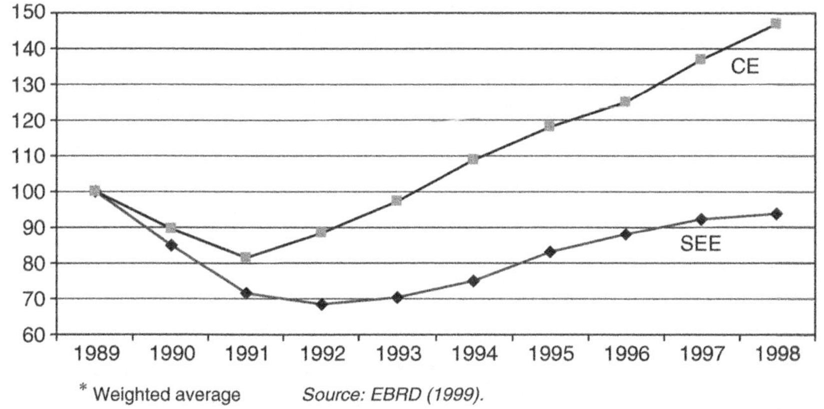

Figure 2.7 Productivity index (1989 = 100)*

The difference between the two regions regarding the trends in employment *vis-à-vis* that of output led to important implications for the trend in labour productivity (Figure 2.7). More specifically, while in both regions output initially fell faster than employment (implying an initial decline in labour productivity), in the case of CE this was reversed as output recovery started in 1993, suggesting a rise in productivity as well. By contrast, output decline in SEE persisted, largely reflecting the much slower recovery in the level of labour productivity. The low productivity for the South East European economies, coupled with the disappointing output performance, constituted a strong indication that the shedding of labour and the implied imposition of hard budget constraints lagged considerably in those countries relative to the Central European economies.

The evolution of registered unemployment rates is shown in Figure 2.8. Unemployment initially increased sharply and then it declined gradually in both regions. In CE, the strong productivity performance was primarily responsible for the slow retreat of unemployment mirroring the gradual employment recovery. In SEE the registered unemployment rate was higher than in CE. The persistent output decline was the main reason for the worst unemployment outlook. Furthermore, the declining trend of unemployment was disrupted reflecting the impact of the output reversal. Finally, as Blanchard (1999) pointed out, registered unemployment may not be a very good measure for unemployment since the incentive to register may differ over time and across countries. It was, however, the only measure available from the start of transition.

The drop in investment constitutes a stylized fact as well. In both regions investment fell more than GDP and thus, as Figure 2.9 shows, the investment to GDP ratio initially declined. This to a large extent was expected given the fact that investment under central planning was high but inefficient. However, in both regions the initial decline was rather mild. This was primarily true for the Central European region, where the ratio of fixed investment to GDP, after the initial small decrease, recovered significantly following an increasing trend throughout the entire period. This, however, was not the case for the South East European region. In particular, the South East European countries experienced a reversal in the upward trend in 1996. This reversal in the investment to GDP ratio took place after three consecutive years of increase (1994–96), and it was in sharp contrast with the behaviour

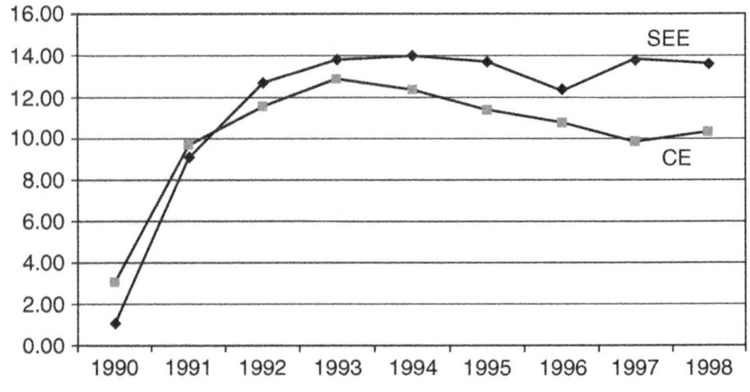

* Weighted average *Source: UN/ECE (2001, No. 1)*

Figure 2.8 Registered unemployment (% of labour force)*

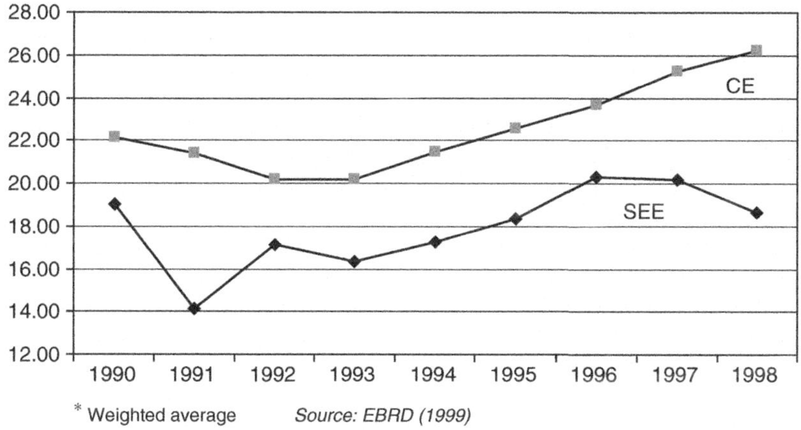

Figure 2.9 Gross fixed capital formation (% of GDP)*

of the corresponding ratio in the Central European region. Thus, it appeared that higher investment was sustained only in countries where output had entered a consistent path of growth.[8] FDI constituted a very significant part of the investment that played a substantial role in the growth prospects of transition economies. However, as we shall see in Chapter 9, its distribution was highly uneven with only a small portion being directed towards the South East European countries, and thus it was not able to have a sufficiently strong impact on the rate of investment in the regions.

Some concluding remarks

The analysis has clearly shown that economic performance during transition varied considerably between the two regions. The economic consequences of transition for the economies of SEE were much more severe. This refers both to the initial response as well as to the subsequent trend in basic economic variables. The analysis in the remaining chapters of Part I will undertake the task of tracing the main reasons behind the poor economic performance of the South East European region. As indicated in Chapter 1, the analysis will concentrate on three factors which constitute the basic determinants of the transition process, and will try to pinpoint their relevance to the rather disappointing economic performance of the region.

The first factor refers to the role of the initial conditions, which differed widely across transition economies. The initial conditions primarily concern the extent of structural and macroeconomic distortions at the start of transition, thus constituting important determinants (particularly in explaining economic performance during the early period of transformation).

However, while initial conditions are more likely to have affected performance during the first phase of transition, they become less relevant in the later stages of transition. The remaining two factors refer to the effectiveness of policy measures that were implemented in order to facilitate the shifting towards the market system and which were, as a result, primarily responsible for the economic performance during the second phase of transition. In the preceding analysis we noted a wide disparity in inflation performance between the two regions, largely reflecting the effectiveness of macroeconomic stabilization. Thus the second factor deals with the timing and the scale of launching comprehensive stabilization programmes. In other words, the introduction of credible macroeconomic policies to curtail inflation and generate favourable conditions for economic growth constituted a critical factor that greatly affected economic performance.

The third key factor, which has been crucial to economic performance during transition as well, refers to the extent of structural and institutional reforms. Structural policies, such as the extent of progress in privatization and liberalization measures, for instance, as well as the building of the required supporting institutions, were essential in making the markets an effective mechanism for allocating resources and thus paving the way for economic growth and development.

3
The Impact of Initial Conditions

Despite the similarities in their economic systems, the economic characteristics of the transition economies at the starting point of the transformation process differed widely because they inherited different degrees of structural and macroeconomic distortions, their integration into the world market was at varying levels and there were also significant differences in income levels. Furthermore, some countries had already introduced some market reform measures, while others had kept intact the rigid rules of central planning up until the end of the communist regime.

The importance of initial conditions is twofold. The first refers to the fact that they were very closely linked to the degree of initial decline in economic activity and thus had a major direct impact on economic performance, particularly during the early stages of transition, which means that countries which had already had some experience of market-oriented reforms prior to transition and were somewhat exposed to the nature of market institution were in a better position to implement more effectively fully-fledged market reforms. This, in turn, would diminish the negative impact on economic performance. Second, as Coricelli (1998) and Murrell (1996) pointed out, the extent to which some of these countries already had in place some rudimentary form of market functioning may have been crucial to the choice and effectiveness of market-based policies, which primarily affected the extent as well as the sustainability of the subsequent recovery.

The extent of initial distortions in South Eastern Europe

The breakdown of the old regime found the South East European economies at different starting points but, overall, in a much worse state than their counterparts in Central Europe. The common characteristics of the South East European countries that contributed to the adverse initial conditions primarily include the low level of development, particularly relative to the countries of the Central European region, the unfavourable 'natural' characteristics, such as their physical distance from Western European markets, as well as the existence of adverse structural, macroeconomic and institutional characteristics which primarily reflected the practices of central planning.

There were, of course, country-specific distortions and/or circumstances, which were also responsible for the less favourable conditions in particular countries at the start of the road to a market economy. In particular, the two largest independent states, Bulgaria and Romania, were until the end very loyal to the legacies of planning and to heavy industrialization, and as a result the extent of economic distortions was substantial. At the other end of the spectrum, the successor states to the former Republic of Yugoslavia had made significant progress, particularly with respect to the public controls of prices, private ownership of small firms and the structure of external trade. These favourable circumstances, however, were largely undermined by the lack of national institutions, as well as by negative political developments such as civil strife and ethnic conflicts. Finally, Albania, the poorest state in Central and Eastern Europe, was a rather peculiar case. In particular, a very strict implementation of the communist principles of central planning was combined with an exceptionally high degree of isolation from the outside world and a very large agricultural sector, the latter two being largely in contrast with the experience of most communist states.

Tables 3.1 and 3.2 include a number of indicators which describe the initial conditions that prevailed in SEE and CE at the outset of the transition process. The analysis heavily relies on the indicators developed by De Melo *et al.* (1997) and, following the methodology of World Bank (2002), we divide them into two broad categories which refer to the nature of the distortions imposed on these economies. In particular, Table 3.1 includes mostly structural distortions, while the ones included in Table 3.2 are of a macroeconomic and institutional nature.

Structural distortions

The degree of urbanization and industrialization constitute indicators of development. However, high levels of urbanization and situations of overindustrialization are indicative of the degree of bias towards the development of heavy manufacturing as opposed to services by the old regime. The extent of urbanization and industrialization are captured by columns 1 and 2 respectively in Table 3.1. Furthermore, column 3 (which measures the deviation from the average level of industrialization) gives an idea of the extent of structural distortion. Bulgaria and Romania are the two states of the region with the highest degree of industrialization (together with the Slovak Republic they have the highest level in all Eastern and Central Europe). Next, according to column 4, the share of agriculture was about 10 per cent of GDP for the majority of the South East European economies. Albania constituted a notable exception with the share of agricultural sector there being in excess of 25 per cent of GDP.

Table 3.1 Initial conditions: structural distortions

	(1) Urbanization (% of population) 1990	(2) Degree of Industrialization	(3) Deviation from average industrialization	(4) Share of agriculture	(5) Private sector share in GDP prior to transition	(6) Degree of liberalization prior to transition	(7) Share of CMEA trade, 1990	(8) Location
Albania	37.0	37.0	−7.4	26.0	5.0	0.0	2.0	1
Bulgaria	68.0	59.0	14.6	11.0	7.2	0.1	15.0	0
Croatia	62.0	35.0	−9.4	10.0	10.0	0.4	6.0	1
FYROM	59.0	43.0	−1.4	12.0	14.0	0.4	6.0	0
Romania	53.0	59.0	14.6	14.0	12.8	0.0	3.0	0
Czech Rep.	65.0	38.0	13.6	10.0	12.3	0.0	10.0	1
Hungary	62.0	36.0	−8.4	14.0	14.9	0.3	10.0	1
Poland	62.0	52.0	7.6	13.0	28.6	0.2	17.0	1
Slovak Rep.	57.0	59.0	14.6	7.0	6.0	0.0	10.0	1
Slovenia	62.0	44.0	−0.4	5.0	11.0	0.4	5.0	1
SEE[a]	*55.8*	*46.6*	*2.2*	*14.6*	*9.8*	*0.2*	*6.4*	
CE[a]	*61.6*	*45.8*	*5.4*	*9.8*	*14.6*	*0.2*	*10.4*	

[a] Unweighted average.
Sources: De Melo *et al.* (1997) and Davidson Institute (Data on Transition Economies).

Table 3.2 Initial conditions: macroeconomic distortions and institutional characteristics

	(1) PPP adjusted GNP per capita (US$, 1989)	(2) Average growth 1985–89	(3) Repressed Inflation 1987–90	(4) Black market premium, 1990 (%)	(5) Foreign debt prior to transition (percentage of GDP)	(6) Openness (percentage of GDP)	(7) Years under central planning	(8) Independent state prior to transition	(9) Democratic rights index 1989[a]
Albania	1,400	3.6	4.3	434	36.9	32.0	47.0	2	0
Bulgaria	5,000	2.7	18.0	921	50.6	32.0	43.0	2	0
Croatia	6,171	0.2	12.0	27	74.7	37.0	46.0	1	42
FYROM	3,394	0.2	12.0	27	0.0	9.0	47.0	1	42
Romania	3,470	–0.8	16.8	728	2.9	25.0	42.0	2	0
Czech Rep.	8,600	1.6	–7.1	185	12.2	42.0	42.0	1	17
Hungary	6,810	1.6	–7.7	47	64.0	64.0	42.0	2	58
Poland	5,150	2.8	13.6	277	63.4	38.0	41.0	2	58
Slovak Rep.	7,600	1.6	–7.1	185	6.8	22.0	42.0	0	17
Slovenia	9,200	–0.4	12.0	27	0.0	11.0	46.0	1	42
SEE[b]	*3,887*	*1.2*	*13.6*	*427.4*	*33.0*	*27.0*	*45.0*		
CE[b]	*7,472*	*1.4*	*0.7*	*144.2*	*29.3*	*35.4*	*42.6*		

[a] Index in which 100 is the maximum.
[b] Unweighted average.
Sources: De Melo *et al.* (1997); Davidson Institute (Data on Transition Economies); and Murrell (1996).

The existence of some form of private sector as well as the extent of liberalization constitute significant indicators which capture the extent to which some elements of market-based reform were introduced before the collapse of the communist regime. Following Table 3.1 and columns 5 and 6 respectively, we see that Romania has a high level of private sector involvement although this was confined to the agricultural sector, while, at the same time, the extent of liberalization was nil. The two states of the former Republic of Yugoslavia combined the existence of private sector together with some significant degree of economic liberalization, largely reflecting the steps taken towards reform prior to transition. Bulgaria also appeared to have introduced some very limited measures of reform. Finally, Albania was the country with the smallest share for the private sector and with no progress in liberalization.

Trade dependence on the other communist states, measured by the ratio of Council of Mutual Economic Assistance (CMEA) exports and imports to GDP, represents another structural distortion with respect to the external trade of these economies, which largely reflected the intention of the old regime to boost intra-communist trade flows. The extent of trade dependence for the SEE region was much lower than the corresponding one for the CE region, with the majority of the countries having a share of CMEA trade well below 10 per cent of GDP in 1990 (column 7, Table 3.1). Bulgaria was the only country where the share of CMEA trade stood at 15 per cent in 1990. It will be pointed out below, however, that the countries of SEE were much less open economies than their counterparts in Central Europe.

Finally, another form of structural weakness for the region has to do with a 'natural' characteristic, which refers to geographical proximity to the developed markets of Western Europe. Thus, according to column 8, we use a dummy variable to indicate that a particular country has a thriving market economy as a neighbour.[1] Undoubtedly, the countries of CE must have been in a more favourable position *vis-à-vis* their counterparts in SEE due to better access to Western markets.

Macroeconomic distortions

The macroeconomic distortions are reported in Table 3.2. It is with respect to these distortions that there is significant diversion between the two regions. A large enough degree of divergence refers to the level of development of the particular economies (column 1). In particular, GNP per capita levels, measured in US dollars for 1989 and adjusted for PPP, differed significantly between the two regions. Albania appeared to be the poorest country and only Croatia had an income level of a little over US$6,000. On average, the economies of CE had income levels almost twice as high as those in SEE. Looking at the pre-transition growth, 1985–89 period, it is clear that most countries were experiencing stagnation and facing low rates of growth (column 2). Albania – and, to a lesser extent, Bulgaria – were the exceptions, while Romania faced negative growth. The situation was quite similar in the Central European region.

The next three variables measure macroeconomic imbalances. The first one, column 3, refers to the extent of repressed inflation, measured here as the difference between the increase in real wages and real GDP (De Melo *et al.* 1997). Repressed inflation was much higher in the economies of SEE, particularly in Bulgaria and Romania. Albania was the country with the weakest inflationary pressures in the region. The black market exchange rate premium, column 4, reflected the difference between the black market exchange rate and the official exchange rate. This indicator measures the extent of rationing of foreign exchange which operated, at the same time, as a subsidy to imports and tax on exports. Bulgaria and Romania (and, to a lesser extent, Albania) presented especially high exchange rate premia, primarily reflecting the strictness of communist rule, while countries that had begun some reforms, such as the former Yugoslav republics of Croatia and FYROM, had much lower ones. The extent of foreign indebtedness prior to transition constitutes the third indicator, column 5. Croatia and Bulgaria (and, to a lesser degree, Albania) were the most indebted countries of the region. Romania's very low foreign debt was the result of the communist regime's effort to repay it during the second part of the 1980s.

The existence of significant degree of openness prior to transition, particularly when it extents beyond the CMEA trade, would count as a favourable condition since it could give some leverage to these countries against the negative effects of transition on performance (column 6). The countries of SEE were relatively closed economies and this was not as helpful. More specifically, Romania's openness was exceptionally limited, while Bulgaria and Albania were quite closed economies as well. The low degree of openness of FYROM to a large extent is due to the fact that it was a part of a much larger state.

The next two indicators capture institutional characteristics that prevailed in these countries just prior to transition. The first one, column 7, refers to years under central planning. More years under a communist regime meant considerable lack of familiarity with market institutions. As we see, there is not much difference between the countries of the two regions with respect to this variable. The next one, shown in column 8, refers to whether the particular states were independent states prior to transition. This is important since, in the case of emergence of new states, there is complete lack of national institutions. Following De Melo *et al.* (1997), the countries that were independent states prior to 1989 take the value of 2, members of decentralized states such as the former Yugoslav republics take the value of 1, and new nation states take the value of 0. As we see in SEE, the two former Yugoslav republics take the value of 1 while the others are given the value of 2.

Finally, political conditions prior to transition were important since the existence of some form of democratic rights under the communist regime would help to facilitate the transition to economic liberalization and the establishment of democratic rule. Column 9 captures an index for democratic rights in 1989 (Murrell 1996). There is a striking difference between the three independent states of SEE, (i.e., Albania, Bulgaria and Romania) and the other transition countries. The index for democratic rights stood at zero for these three countries prior to transition, reflecting the imposition of solid communist rule, while some rudimentary form of democratic rights appeared in the other countries, particularly the successor states of the former Yugoslav Republic.

Overall, the analysis indicates that the countries of SEE faced much more unfavourable initial conditions than the countries of CE. In particular, we looked into a number of indicators which captured specific characteristics of the particular economies at the start of the transition. The adverse conditions reflected the impact of common factors, such as the level of development and the geographical location of the region, as well as factors that differed across the countries of the region. In particular, with respect to latter factors, the countries of SEE can be separated into two groups. The first one would include Albania, Bulgaria and Romania, where the adverse initial conditions primarily stemmed from the strict implementation of the rules of central planning which, as a result, led to significant structural and macroeconomic distortions. In addition, the high degree of isolation of the particular countries from the world economy constituted another adverse characteristic as well. The second group would include Croatia and FYROM which, by being part of Yugoslavia, had experienced the functioning of at least some rudimentary form of market mechanism as well as the development of entrepreneurial activity which had arisen as a result. This favourable experience, however, was largely nullified by the very unfavourable political developments, such as armed conflicts, that these countries had to deal with initially.

Principal component analysis for initial conditions

In order to be able to summarize the overall impact of initial conditions while taking care of the fact that some of them may be correlated with each other, we shall rely on the method of principal components. More specifically, following the work of De Melo *et al.* (1997), we constructed an index of 'distortions' by considering all the elements of initial conditions. The particular procedure is called factor or principal component analysis, which is based on the correlations of all initial conditions with each other. It generates the so-called 'common factors', which can be interpreted as summary indicators for all the initial conditions used. As a result, each country is assigned a score for each common factor which can be used for cross-country comparisons.[2] The set variables that we used to compute the common factors of initial conditions are the same as the ones used by De Melo *et al.* (1997).

In particular, we include the following ten variables: GNP per capita in 1989, at PPP exchange rates; pre-transition growth; degree of urbanization; extent of industrialization; trade dependence on CMEA; repressed inflation; black market exchange rate premium; location; years under central planning; and a dummy capturing whether a particular country was an independent state prior to transition. Note that the difference between our analysis and that of De Melo *et al.* (1997) concerns the number of countries used: we used a smaller sample of countries which included the ten countries of SEE and CE as well as seven of the countries that resulted from the break-up of the former Soviet Union and belong to European continent.[3] Note also that the sample used by De Melo *et al.* (1997), in addition to the transition economies of Central and Eastern Europe, included China, Mongolia and Vietnam.

In our analysis, the first two principal components accounted for most of the variation. In particular, our first principal component explains 49 per cent of the total variance over all initial conditions. Our second one explains just above 26 per cent, so the two together explain 75 per cent of the variability of initial conditions. According to the information in Table 3.3, the first principal component has high positive correlations for the macroeconomic distortions (i.e., black market premium and repressed inflation) and with respect to the share of trade with CMEA. Furthermore, it has a high positive correlation with respect to the variable capturing the years under central planning as well. In contrast, there is significant negative correlation with respect to whether a country was an independent state prior to transition. Thus countries with lower scores with respect to the first principal component had more favourable initial conditions. In our case, as we can see from Figure 3.1, all ten countries under consideration have negative values for the first principal component (Prin. Comp. 1). Thus the more negative the score the more favourable the initial conditions. Turning to the second

Table 3.3 Results from the principal component analysis

Variable	**Eigenvectors**	
	Principal comp. 1	**Principal comp. 2**
Share of trade with CMEA	0.45	0.01
Black market premium	0.45	−0.10
Years under central planning	0.37	−0.17
GDP growth 1985–89	0.32	−0.20
Location	−0.01	0.57
Repressed inflation	0.38	−0.12
Urbanization	0.22	0.45
Industrialization	0.10	0.20
Independent state prior to transition	−0.37	−0.15
GNP per capita 1989	0.15	0.58

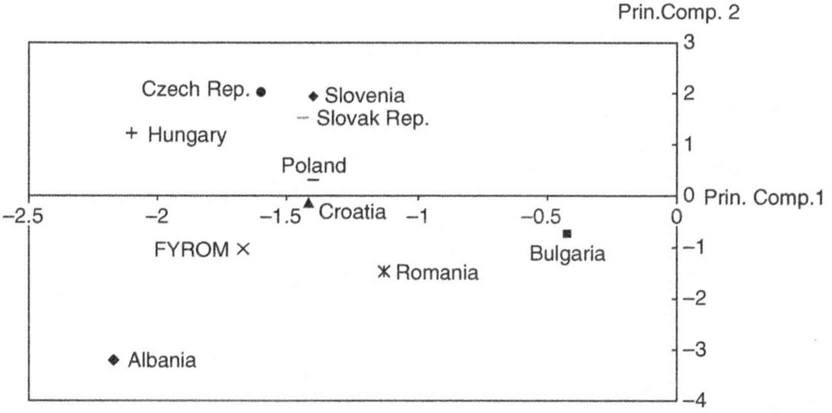

Figure 3.1 Ranking of the countries of SEE and CE by the first two principal components

principal component, we see that it has high positive correlations for location, urbanization and GNP per capita in 1989. Thus, countries with higher initial per capita income, higher urbanization and geographical proximity to the EU will have higher values for the second principal component which, in turn, corresponds to more favourable initial conditions. Note, as we look at Figure 3.1, that the countries of SEE have negative values for the second principal component (Prin. Comp. 2), while the ones in CE have positive values. This, in turn, implies more adverse initial conditions for the former countries.

In Figure 3.1 the ten countries of the two regions are grouped by the two principal components. The positioning of the five countries of SEE corresponds to worse initial conditions relative to their counterparts in CE: that is, with respect to the Prin. Comp. 1, they assume negative scores which, however, are lower in absolute terms compared to the corresponding scores of the countries of CE. Next, with respect to the Prin. Comp. 2, they assume negative scores again, whereas the countries of CE have positive scores. In both cases the scores of the countries of SEE correspond to worse initial conditions relative to the countries of CE. Looking at the performance of individual countries, we see that the two former Yugoslav republics had more favourable initial conditions than Bulgaria and Romania. Albania appears to be a rather peculiar case with particularly favourable positioning with respect to Prin. Comp. 1 but a very bad one with respect to Prin. Comp. 2. Finally, the scores of the countries in both regions with respect to the first principal component will be used further in Chapter 7 where we will, among other things, try to evaluate the importance of initial conditions on economic growth empirically.

4

Macroeconomic Stabilization and Performance I: The Period prior to the Kosovo War

Macroeconomic stabilization has been a vital part of the transition process since it constituted a key precondition for the objective of raising efficiency and promoting growth. In Chapter 2 we pointed out that the rise in inflation and the decline in output constituted the two major stylized facts of transition which were particularly profound in the case of the economies of SEE. Furthermore, we indicated that the slow recovery as well as the output reversals that some of the South East European economies experienced were closely connected to ineffective disinflation which was manifested through corresponding inflation reversals. This, except for cases of civil strife and war, constituted significant evidence for the strong linkage between consistent macroeconomic policies and sustainable growth.

Tables 4.1 and 4.2 present the inflation and output performance respectively of SEE during the period 1989–98. First, with respect to inflation, it is apparent from Table 4.1 that the disinflation process was not as successful for the majority of South East European economies. As a matter of fact, only two countries, namely Croatia and FYROM, were able to bring inflation down to single digits. The remaining three experienced very significant inflation reversals which constituted a serious setback to their stabilization efforts and largely reflected the consequences of weak financial policies and slow structural reform. Turning to Table 4.2, we see that the output performance of the individual countries of SEE has been particularly weak. More specifically, the output reversals experienced by Albania, Bulgaria and Romania were the direct consequence of the corresponding inflation setbacks and the inadequacy of the policies adopted. Croatia was the only country with strong output recovery while, as indicated in Chapter 2, FYROM's output growth was modest and occurred after six years of consecutive decline.

In this chapter we will look into different aspects of the macroeconomic policies and performance of the South East European economies from the beginning of the transition process until 1998. Our aim is to reveal the macroeconomic policies adopted by the countries of SEE and to examine the extent to which inconsistencies and lack of discipline in the stabilization

Table 4.1 Annual inflation rates (period average in retail/consumer price level)

	1990	1991	1992	1993	1994	1995	1996	1997	1998
Albania	0.0	36.0	226.0	85.0	22.6	7.8	12.7	33.2	20.6
Bulgaria	26.3	333.5	82.0	73.0	96.3	62.1	123.0	1,082.0	22.2
Croatia	500.0	122.2	625.0	1,500.0	107.3	2.0	3.5	3.6	5.7
FYROM	608.0	229.7	1,664.4	338.4	126.6	16.4	2.7	1.1	0.5
Romania	37.7	230.6	211.2	255.2	136.8	32.2	38.8	154.8	59.1
SEE mean[a]	*233.9*	*191.4*	*563.6*	*450.3*	*97.9*	*24.1*	*36.0*	*250.3*	*21.6*
CE mean[a]	*231.2*	*69.3*	*58.1*	*27.1*	*19.1*	*17.6*	*13.5*	*11.4*	*10.3*

[a] Unweighted average.
Source: EBRD (1999, 2004b).

Table 4.2 Growth in real GDP

	1990	1991	1992	1993	1994	1995	1996	1997	1998	GDP 1998/89 ratio
Albania	−10.0	−27.7	−7.2	9.6	9.4	8.9	9.1	−7.0	12.7	86.4
Bulgaria	−9.1	−11.7	−7.3	−1.5	1.8	2.1	−10.1	−7.0	4.0	65.9
Croatia	−7.1	−21.1	−11.7	−8.0	5.9	6.8	6.0	6.5	2.5	77.8
FYROM	−9.9	−7.0	−8.0	−9.1	−1.8	−1.2	1.2	1.4	3.4	71.6
Romania	−5.6	−12.9	−8.8	1.5	3.9	7.1	4.1	−6.9	−4.8	76.1
SEE[a]	*−7.1*	*−14.8*	*−8.3*	*−1.4*	*2.6*	*5.1*	*2.7*	*−3.0*	*−1.0*	*75.1*
CE[a]	*−6.0*	*−10.5*	*−0.9*	*1.7*	*4.5*	*5.5*	*5.1*	*5.7*	*4.0*	*107.5*

[a] Weighted average: the regions' growth was calculated by using current nominal GDP, expressed in terms of US dollars, as weights.
Source: EBRD (1999, 2004b).

effort contributed to their poor economic performance during the period under consideration. In particular, assessing the consistency between fiscal and monetary policies constitutes a vital task which is particularly important in explaining the limited success of some of these economies to disinflate and thus generate conditions that would favour sustainable economic growth. As indicated, our analysis does not include the two late starters of transition in the region (i.e., BH and SM).

Fiscal consolidation

While the initial spike in inflation reflected the impact of the monetary overhang and the need to liberalize prices, the biggest challenge for effective inflation reduction was the control over the fiscal deficits. Countries that faced high and persistent inflation rates were the ones that encountered significant difficulties in achieving fiscal consolidation. This was particularly true for most countries of SEE since their slow response to reducing the large fiscal deficits, at the beginning of the reform process, turned out to be an important obstacle to effective disinflation and to output recovery. This largely reflected the fact that, at least early in transition, fiscal and monetary policies were closely inter-related because monetary policy served to finance the large fiscal deficits contradicting, as a result, the monetary objectives.[1] This also reflected the lack of a developed banking system and the absence of markets for debt instruments such as government securities.

The legacies of central planning complicated the implementation of macroeconomic stabilization in the transition economies and posed crucial macroeconomic challenges. First of all, as we will see below, the rudimentary nature of the financial systems (at least initially) limited significantly the conduct of monetary policy which, in turn, made a strategy for monetary targeting rather unrealistic. The biggest challenge, however, was related to fiscal policy. This is because the transition process by itself generated fiscal pressures. The early phase of transition was accompanied by large fiscal imbalances in virtually all transition economies, as a result of relatively rigid public expenditure and declining revenues.[2] In particular, on the revenue side, the output declines as well as the tax system reform, together with the lack of a system for effective tax collection (due to the growth of the private sector), led to large revenue reductions. On the expenditure side, the already high level of government spending was cut but, at least initially, it remained high enough due to additional spending generated by the structural reform measures.

The general government revenue and expenditure of the countries of the region for the period until 1998 appear in Table 4.3. The drop in the revenues was substantial for Albania, Bulgaria and Romania. As a matter of fact, these three countries had the sharpest drop in the revenue to GDP ratio in both SEE and CE. More specifically, the fiscal revenue to GDP ratio fell below 20 per cent of GDP in Albania while it dropped close to 30 per cent in Bulgaria and below 30 per cent in Romania. It is apparent that the drop in revenue imposed major constraints on the these countries' efforts to implement much-needed fiscal reforms, including the establishment of efficient tax administration and tax collection systems. Croatia's and FYROM's revenue to GDP ratio showed remarkable stability. The early reform measures and the establishment of private firms when these two countries were still part of Yugoslavia constituted an important factor which contributed to this particular outcome. As Table 4.3 indicates, overall general government expenditures were reduced at a slower pace, mostly reflecting the persistence of practices inherited from central planning, such as budgetary policies that allowed former state enterprises to preserve soft budget constraints. Thus in the economies of the region the resulting fiscal imbalances were largely linked to the speed and effectiveness of structural reform: that is, slow structural and institutional reform for the majority of the countries of SEE meant

Table 4.3 General government expenditure and revenue (as % of GDP)

	1990	1991	1992	1993	1994	1995	1996	1997	1998
Expenditure									
Albania	62.1	61.9	44.0	34.9	36.4	33.4	30.3	29.4	30.7
Bulgaria	65.9	45.6	43.6	48.1	45.7	41.3	42.0	32.7	34.5
Croatia	n.a.	39.0	36.1	35.0	40.6	44.9	45.3	44.4	46.7
FYROM	n.a.	n.a.	48.2	55.3	45.8	39.0	37.1	35.1	35.0
Romania	39.3	40.4	42.0	34.2	33.9	34.7	33.8	34.0	34.9
SEE[a]	*55.8*	*46.7*	*42.8*	*41.5*	*40.5*	*38.7*	*37.7*	*35.1*	*36.4*
CE[a]	*52.6*	*50.1*	*50.9*	*49.0*	*48.0*	*46.3*	*45.6*	*45.8*	*44.3*
Revenue									
Albania	47.1	30.9	22.5	24.9	23.3	23.4	18.3	16.9	20.3
Bulgaria	n.a.	40.4	38.4	37.2	39.9	35.7	31.7	30.7	35.4
Croatia	n.a.	n.a.	32.2	34.2	42.2	43.5	44.3	42.5	45.6
FYROM	n.a.	n.a.	39.3	40.2	43.1	37.9	35.7	34.8	33.3
Romania	39.7	41.9	37.4	33.9	32.1	31.4	28.9	27.1	28.1
SEE[a]	*43.4*	*37.7*	*34.0*	*34.1*	*36.1*	*34.4*	*31.8*	*30.4*	*32.5*
CE[a]	*53.6*	*49.0*	*45.7*	*46.3*	*45.7*	*45.0*	*44.2*	*42.7*	*41.4*

n.a. = not available.
[a] Unweighted average.
Source: EBRD (1999, 2000).

that they continued to maintain large subsidies for enterprises as well as price and capital controls. In short, budget deficits were highly endogenous to the reform process and private sector responses. This, in turn (to the extent that the financing of the budget by the central bank became essential), led to rapid growth in the money supply, causing high inflation to persist.

In Table 4.4, the overall general government balance as a percentage of GDP for each of the South East European economies appears in the first row for each country. Albania, and to a lesser extent Bulgaria, have had the largest fiscal imbalances among the five countries of SEE during the period under consideration. Croatia and FYROM were the two countries of the region which succeeded in controlling fiscal imbalances most quickly. Finally, Romania appears to be an intermediate case with its fiscal deficit being at moderate levels. Looking at the inflation performance of these countries (Table 4.1), we see that for three of them (i.e., Bulgaria, Croatia and FYROM) it seems to be largely in line with the degree of fiscal discipline they demonstrated during the period under consideration.[3] This is particularly true for Croatia and Bulgaria, which represent two characteristic examples of a successful story and of an unsuccessful one respectively. In contrast, the cases of Albania and Romania are two examples where it is hard to reconcile the fiscal situation with the inflation performance; in the case of Albania the process of disinflation was quite effective in spite of the presence of large

Table 4.4 Overall general government balance, seigniorage, central bank financing to the government, quasi-fiscal operations (% of GDP)

	1990	1991	1992	1993	1994	1995	1996	1997	1998
Albania									
Government balance	−6.1	−20.7	−23.1	−15.5	−12.6	−10.1	−12.1	−12.6	−10.4
Seigniorage	n.a.	n.a.	n.a.	n.a.	n.a.	5.5	3.0	8.3	0.3
Central bank financing	n.a.	n.a.	20.0	9.1	6.6	2.0	2.9	9.0	−1.6
Quasi-fiscal operations[a]	n.a.	n.a.	n.a.	n.a.	n.a.	1.2	−1.6	−0.1	3.2
Bulgaria									
Government balance	−8.1	−4.5	−2.9	−8.7	−3.9	−5.7	−10.3	−2.0	0.9
Seigniorage	n.a.	n.a.	6.5	1.6	6.1	5.9	5.7	7.7	0.5
Central bank financing	n.a.	n.a.	4.3	3.3	−2.1	4.3	9.6	−1.0	−0.1
Quasi-fiscal operations[a]	n.a.	n.a.	1.3	2.4	5.2	1.2	2.2	4.9	0.2
Croatia									
Government balance	n.a.	n.a.	−3.9	−0.8	1.2	−1.4	−1.0	−1.9	−1.0
Seigniorage	n.a.	n.a.	6.8	5.2	4.3	0.8	1.1	0.9	0.2
Central bank financing	n.a.	n.a.	1.4	1.2	−0.7	0.3	−0.1	−0.1	−0.4
Quasi-fiscal operations[a]	n.a.	n.a.	n.a.	0.8	0.3	1.0	0.2	0.3	0.1
FYROM									
Government balance	n.a.	−4.5	−9.8	−13.4	−2.7	−1.0	−1.4	−0.4	−1.7
Seigniorage	n.a.	n.a.	n.a.	n.a.	2.0	0.9	−0.2	0.8	0.2
Central bank financing	n.a.	n.a.	n.a.	n.a.	1.3	0.1	0.1	0.4	−0.6
Quasi-fiscal operations[a]	n.a.	n.a.	n.a.	n.a.	0.3	−0.5	−0.4	0.1	−0.2
Romania									
Government balance	n.a.	3.3	−4.6	−0.4	−2.2	−2.5	−3.9	−4.6	−5.0
Seigniorage	n.a.	12.0	8.8	8.0	4.2	2.2	1.8	1.5	0.7
Central bank financing	n.a.	n.a.	1.7	−1.3	1.2	0.7	−0.6	0.5	1.7
Quasi-fiscal operations[a]	n.a.	n.a.	9.0	2.9	5.6	1.5	2.0	1.0	0.1

n.a. = not available.
[a] Central bank only.
Sources: EBRD (1999, 2000); International Monetary Fund (IMF) (International Financial Statistics, Yearbook 2000, and Country Reports); and author's own calculations.

fiscal imbalances, while in the case of Romania relatively moderate deficits were associated with a very disappointing inflation performance.

One issue that must be addressed, since it is directly related to the inflationary consequences of fiscal imbalances, refers to the method of financing such deficits. The strength of the link between fiscal deficits and inflation crucially depends on whether the former are financed through issuance of domestic and/or foreign debt or via the extension of direct central bank credit to the government. When fiscal deficits are financed through central bank credit they affect the monetary base directly which, depending on the size of the multiplier, then leads to higher money supply. Thus the higher the portion of the deficit financed through a direct increase of the money supply, the stronger the inflationary pressures. As a result, the lack of alternative financing methods, at least during the early stages of transition, made the need for fiscal consolidation a rather urgent condition for an effective stabilization strategy.

In order to examine whether the large budget deficits led to excessive monetary financing, we look into two relative measures: seigniorage and the net central bank credit to the government. The notion of seigniorage is related to the privilege of the authorities issuing fiat-money to derive net revenue from the holders of such monetary claims. Seigniorage refers to the expansion of the monetary base and thus to overall money creation, while the net central bank credit to government indicates the portion of the increase in the monetary base which is due to the financing needs of the government, and thus it is directly linked to the fiscal imbalance.

The next two rows (the second and third) for each country in Table 4.4 present these two measures of monetary financing as a percentage of GDP for the countries of SEE. The second row, labelled 'seigniorage', shows the sum of the two forms of such financing: the printing of additional money (cash) and the increase of commercial bank reserves with the central bank. The third row includes the central bank credit (net) to the government which reflects the extent of direct financing of a fiscal deficit by the central bank (irrespective of the manner of financing, i.e., through printing of money or the purchase of Treasury bills by the central bank). Seigniorage was particularly high in countries with large fiscal deficits such as Bulgaria (and, to a lesser extent, Albania). Furthermore, we see that most of the time central bank financing absorbs most of the increases in seigniorage in these two countries. Note, however, that there was a considerable decline in the two measures of monetary financing in both countries during 1998. This, as we will see below, primarily reflected their renewed efforts towards stabilization. Again, the two former Yugoslav republics were the two countries where seigniorage was low, largely explaining the successful disinflation strategy. Romania started with very high seigniorage, which has declined considerably since 1995. The same argument we made about the evolution of fiscal imbalances holds for the two monetary measures as well: that is, their trend cannot provide an adequate explanation for the persistence of inflation in the particular country. This, in turn, brings our attention to the role of quasi-fiscal deficits.

Quasi-fiscal deficits

In assessing the role of fiscal policy in stabilization and the extent of true fiscal disequilibrium, the operations of public agencies must also be included. This particularly refers to the role of central bank operations or state commercial banks, especially during the early stages of transition. In many transition economies the central bank was used as a key fiscal agent in performing quasi-fiscal operations. These operations can affect the overall public sector balance without affecting the budget deficit as conventionally defined. More specifically, the fact that in most transition economies the fiscal accounting standards did not exactly meet the international ones enabled the governments to shift outlays and receipts from the conventionally measured government budget, where they should have normally been, to the central bank (Buiter 1997).[4]

The quasi-fiscal operations may take various forms. As Mackenzie and Stella (1996) and Buiter (1997) have stated, some of these activities may be associated with: purchases and sales of foreign currencies under the use of multiple exchange rates; the offer of subsidies as exchange risk insurance; lending by the central bank at subsidized rates of interest; guaranteeing the liabilities of commercial banks or enterprises; and tolerating enterprises' tax arrears. These operations are the result of restrictions on financial markets or reflect preferential treatment of particular sectors or enterprises by the government. Although these operations constitute forms of taxation or subsidization, they are not included in the conventionally measured government budget.

Among other things, the existence of quasi-fiscal operations constitutes a matter of concern with respect to policy implications. For one thing, they hide the government's true financial balance and give misleading information about the macroeconomic impact of fiscal activity. In particular, the losses accruing to the central bank because of these operations are directly linked to base money leading, through the money multiplier, to rapid money supply growth and contributing, as a result, to persistent inflation. Note that even when they are conducted by commercial banks, the central bank has the ultimate responsibility and will eventually assume the accruing losses.

Although the notion of quasi-fiscal operations has been examined extensively enough by the literature and appears to be, at least conceptually, rather clear, the decision about a good operational definition which would facilitate the precise measurement of the phenomenon is not such an easy task.[5] Buiter (1997) uses a simple operational definition for transition economies according to which any central bank credit to any sector of the economy other than the government sector can be considered as a de facto quasi-fiscal operation. Following the above definition, we can derive from the balance sheet of a central bank the following equation for quasi-fiscal deficits:

$$QFD = \Delta NDC_p - \Delta NOI = \Delta RM - NFA - \Delta NDC_g \qquad (4.1)$$

where QFD = quasi-fiscal deficit, $NDCp$ = net domestic credit to non-government sectors, NOI = net other items, $NDCg$ = net domestic credit to the government, RM = reserve money, and NFA = net foreign assets. Also, note that 'Δ' stands for 'change'. We use the above equation to calculate the magnitude of the quasi-fiscal deficits for the countries of the region.[6] The fourth row in Table 4.4 shows the results of our estimation with respect to the size of the quasi-fiscal deficits for the countries of SEE.

Quasi-fiscal operations appeared to have played a very significant role, primarily in Romania and to a lesser extent in Bulgaria, during the period under consideration. The reasons for these operations were common in the two countries. More specifically, the slow progress in structural reform and the resulting soft budget constraints of the state-owned enterprises generated the need for large quasi-fiscal support in the two countries.[7] In fact, although the budgetary subsidies extended to enterprises were reduced considerably, in practice they were largely replaced by quasi-fiscal support in both countries. Note that the budgetary financing of the loss-making enterprises was largely facilitated though tax arrears.

In the case of Bulgaria the widespread soft budget constraints of financial and non-financial enterprises led to large quasi-fiscal losses: there have been large quasi-fiscal deficits through central bank credit related to bank rescues and clearing of inter-enterprise arrears. The dramatic increase in non-performing loans that were extended to loss-making enterprises, which led to continuous bailing-out of the troubled banks by the central bank, became the primary factor behind the financial crisis of 1996. In the absence of structural reforms, state-owned enterprises were unable to service debts and commercial banks kept rolling over the outstanding credits while capitalizing interest payments, a process that eventually led to the decapitalization of the banking system.[8] In Romania large quasi-fiscal deficits existed because of the channelling of large subsidies to agriculture and energy sectors through cheap central bank credit. Furthermore, the National Bank of Romania extended loans to troubled commercial banks on very favourable terms. As in the case of Bulgaria, the large quasi-fiscal deficits were forced by the continuation of subsidies to the state-owned enterprises, a situation that largely reflected the delays in their restructuring and privatization.[9]

Overall, quasi-fiscal operations resulted from delays in structural reforms. As earlier studies indicated, they were concentrated in slow reforming countries, while the successful implementation of stabilization programmes and other institutional reforms led to a diminishing tendency of such operations which, as a result, were either reduced or transferred to budget accounts.

Debt-financing fiscal deficits

The absence of well developed debt markets, particularly at the start of the reform process, made the case of money-financed deficits the predominant source of deficit financing. In the region of SEE, Bulgaria was the first country to introduce a domestic Treasury bill market in 1993; Albania followed in 1994, and Croatia in 1996. Romania introduced domestic Treasury bills in 1997, while FYROM had not done so by the end of 1998. The development of domestic debt markets led to the gradual increase in the share of fiscal deficits financed by issuing domestic government securities. Furthermore, external borrowing from official as well as private sources was becoming of increasing importance. This increase in domestic as well as external borrowing led to significant debt accumulation across the transition economies. The extent of indebtedness, however, of each country depended on both the persistence of fiscal imbalances as well as on the initial debt burden.

The transition economies of SEE started the transition with very different levels of public (external) debts. Bulgaria and (to a lesser extent) Albania were heavily indebted, while the two former Yugoslav republics and Romania recorded a low level of public debt. This, in turn, meant that the individual countries had not the same potential for further debt expansion. Table 4.5 shows the developments in general government debt, as well as in external debt of the particular countries during the 1991–98 period. Bulgaria represents the most heavily indebted country. The debt of the general government exceeded the level of 100 per cent until 1997. Note that it remained high despite the substantial reduction in external debt of Bulgaria in 1995, which was the result of debt reduction agreements with its commercial creditors (see UN/ECE 1997). Albania's external debt ratio has been reduced, partially reflecting a gradual shift to domestic debt. As in the case of Bulgaria, part of Albania's external debt was written off in 1995 as well (UN/ECE 1997). Romania started the transition process with no debt, but afterwards there was substantial debt accumulation (mostly foreign) which, however, remained at relatively low levels by the end of 1998. Croatia and FYROM started with low external indebtedness which gradually increased during the 1991–98 period. By the end of 1998, in both countries the external debt was more than 40 per cent of GDP.

While massive external and domestic borrowing could solve fiscal problems and support macroeconomic stability, at least in the short run, it could, however, raise problems of fiscal sustainability over the medium and long run. More specifically, continuous debt accumulation, particularly when

Table 4.5 General government and external debt (% of GDP)

	1991	**1992**	**1993**	**1994**	**1995**	**1996**	**1997**	**1998**
Albania								
General government debt	n.a.	n.a.	n.a.	n.a.	57.5	55.2	75.6	75.9
External debt	55.7	123.9	78.9	55.6	31.9	31.5	39.4	36.9
Bulgaria								
General government debt	n.a.	n.a.	n.a.	183.2	114.9	319.8	122.2	95.6
External debt	157.4	145.6	128.3	116.8	77.4	97.0	93.7	80.6
Croatia								
General government debt	n.a.	n.a.	n.a.	22.2	19.3	29.2	31.9	38.8
External debt	16.4	26.7	22.8	20.7	20.2	26.7	37.1	44.3
FYROM								
General government debt	n.a.	n.a.	n.a.	n.a.	n.a.	41.5	48.1	45.7
External debt	15.9	32.7	32.6	24.9	23.8	25.4	31.3	40.1
Romania								
General government debt	n.a.	n.a.	n.a.	n.a.	17.6	28.1	27.7	27.8
External debt	7.4	16.6	16.1	18.3	18.3	23.6	26.9	23.7

n.a. = not available.
Source: EBRD (1999).

combined with falling output, could lead to a dramatic increase in interest payments, making the fiscal position unsustainable. This, in turn, means that countries with large debt service payments are prime candidates for falling into a 'debt trap' whereby the enormous growth of debt service payments make the financing either by taxes or by borrowing implausible; as a result, money creation becomes the only feasible method of financing. Thus, under such circumstances, debt financing becomes clearly inflationary over the long run (Sargent and Wallace 1981). Consequently, the long-term effectiveness of a disinflation policy crucially depends on the issue of fiscal sustainability.

In the transition economies, the narrow capacity of the domestic debt markets, together with the limited access to foreign financial markets, make fiscal sustainability a vital issue. Buiter (1996), and then Budina and van Wijnbergen (1997), examined the question of public sector solvency for all the transition economies of central and eastern Europe, as well as for the former Soviet Union.[10] In particular, in the latter study the two authors attempted to assess empirically whether the fiscal stance of particular countries during the period 1991–96 was sustainable using two measures of sustainability: a long-run measure and a short-run one. The former looks into the question of long-run sustainability by adopting two alternative scenarios about the difference between the real interest rate and the growth rate in the long run: an optimistic one where the difference stands at 1 per cent and a pessimistic one with the difference at 5 per cent. According to the latter, which is called 'myopic', the calculation of the sustainable primary deficit is based on the difference between the actual (current) real rate of interest and output growth.

We use the approach of Budina and van Wijnbergen (1997) in order to extend their results on long-run sustainability until 1998. In their analysis the inter-temporal budget constraint which is used as a measure for fiscal sustainability is expressed as

$$\Delta b = (r - n)b + pd - \sigma \tag{4.2}$$

where, Δb stands for change in public debt to GDP ratio; r is the real interest rate; n is the real growth rate; pd is the primary fiscal deficit as a proportion of GDP; and σ is seigniorage revenue, which is expressed as a share of GDP as well. The aim is the derivation of the sustainable primary surplus or deficit that would maintain the debt output ratio at a chosen target level: it is assumed that $\Delta b = 0$, while the target level for the debt to GDP ratio for each year is taken to be its current level. Another issue is the estimation of the long-run seigniorage revenue for given inflation targets for each country. The long-run seigniorage revenues assumed are 2.65 per cent of GDP for Bulgaria, 1.3 per cent of GDP for Romania and 2 per cent for the remaining countries (for more details, see Budina and van Wijnbergen, 1997).

Table 4.6 reports the results of the exercise for the economies of the SEE for the entire 1991–98 period. The information for each country is summarized in three rows. The first row reports the actual primary fiscal balance, while the second and third rows present the estimations for the sustainable primary balances in the optimistic case ($r - n = 1\%$) and in the pessimistic case ($r - n = 5\%$) respectively. For the current fiscal stance to be sustainable the current level of primary fiscal deficit (surplus) must fall short of (exceed) the sustainable primary deficit (surplus). According to the results, fiscal policy has been clearly unsustainable in the case of Albania throughout the entire period, reflecting the large primary fiscal deficits that this country ran at least until 1997. In contrast, two clearly sustainable cases are represented by the two former Yugoslav republics, Croatia and FYROM. In the case of Croatia, fiscal policy has been sustainable throughout, chiefly reflecting the fact that the particular country has been running primary surpluses since 1992. The year 1995 constituted the only exception where a primary deficit of about 1 per cent of GDP appeared to be marginally unsustainable under the pessimistic scenario. The increased military spending, as a result of the armed conflict that took place, was the main reason for the particular development.[11] FYROM has been running primary budget surpluses since 1994 and fiscal policy has been sustainable from that year until 1998. The cases of Bulgaria and Romania are not as straightforward and must be examined in more detail.

Bulgaria has been running rather large primary surpluses since 1994 and this was the main reason for the long-run sustainability of fiscal policy. In particular, 1993 was the last year during which fiscal policy was unsustainable under both scenarios. After that, it was sustainable apart from 1996, and then it was only not sustainable under the pessimistic scenario. There are, however, two factors which should make us cautious when analysing the situation in Bulgaria, particularly until 1996. The first refers to the fact that the high primary surpluses may be misleading because of the existence of large quasi-deficits, an estimation of which we presented in Table 4.3. As pointed out, the quasi-deficits primarily included central bank credit to rescue loss-making enterprises and banks. The second has to do with the fact that Bulgaria was already highly indebted from the beginning of transition. It is the combination of these two factors which, as the massive bailing-out of loss-making enterprises led to a substantial increase in the debt burden of the government, brought the economy to a real debt trap contributing to the 1996–97 crisis (Dabrowski 1999). The situation after 1996 improved considerably, largely reflecting the outcome of the new stabilization strategy and the external debt restructuring which further improved the long-term fiscal position.

Turning to Romania and looking at Table 4.6, we observe that for most of the period fiscal policy has been unsustainable under both scenarios. In particular it has been sustainable in 1991 and 1993, and also marginally

Table 4.6 Assessing fiscal sustainability for the economies of SEE (% GDP)

	1991	1992	1993	1994	1995	1996	1997	1998
Albania								
Actual primary balance	−30.7	−20.6	−13.0	−10.6	−8.2	−9.0	−7.1	−2.6
Sustainable primary balance for $r-n=1\%$	−1.6	−1.0	−1.3	−1.5	−1.5	−1.7	−1.3	−1.4
Sustainable primary balance for $r-n=5\%$	0.2	0.3	1.6	0.8	0.7	0.2	1.5	1.0
Bulgaria								
Actual primary deficit	−14.1	1.2	−1.6	7.7	8.5	9.3	5.9	5.4
Sustainable primary balance for $r-n=1\%$	−0.7	−1.1	−1.3	−1.3	−1.6	0.6	−1.4	−1.7
Sustainable primary balance for $r-n=5\%$	7.3	5.0	4.0	4.0	3.2	13.3	3.5	2.1
Croatia								
Actual primary deficit	−4.9	−4.6	2.1	1.9	−1.1	0.8	0.3	1.5
Sustainable primary balance for $r-n=1\%$	−1.8	−1.7	−1.8	−1.7	−1.8	−1.7	−1.7	−1.7
Sustainable primary balance for $r-n=5\%$	−0.8	−0.7	−0.8	−0.7	−0.8	−0.5	−0.5	−0.3
FYROM								
Actual primary deficit	n.a.	n.a.	−9.7	−0.2	0.5	1.8	1.0	0.8
Sustainable primary balance for $r-n=1\%$	−1.8	−1.6	−1.6	−1.6	−1.7	−1.6	−1.5	−1.5
Sustainable primary balance for $r-n=5\%$	−1.1	−0.16	0.1	−0.1	−0.5	0.1	0.4	0.3
Romania								
Actual primary deficit	3.3	−4.4	0.5	−0.8	−2.0	−3.1	−1.4	−0.8
Sustainable primary balance for $r-n=1\%$	−1.3	−1.1	−1.1	−1.1	−1.1	−1.0	−1.0	−1.0
Sustainable primary balance for $r-n=5\%$	−1.3	−0.4	−0.2	−0.5	−0.4	0.1	0.1	0.1

n.a. = not available.

in 1994 and 1998 with respect to the optimistic scenario only. Thus fiscal policy was more expansionary than was strictly necessary for fiscal sustainability. However, the situation in Romania was even more fragile than the particular figures show: the huge quasi-fiscal deficits in the Romanian economy (Table 4.3) dramatically augmented the conventional government imbalances, making the true fiscal situation drastically worse and clearly unsustainable. Unlike Bulgaria, Romania started the transition process with almost zero indebtedness, which in turn meant that long-run fiscal sustainability did not require very high primary surpluses. This was clearly verified by the estimated sustainable fiscal deficits, which stood at 1 per cent of GDP in the case of the optimistic scenario and around 0 per cent in the case of the pessimistic scenario for most years. This, in turn, manifested the extent of inconsistency in the policies followed, particularly with respect to fiscal policy. The foreign debt to GDP ratio has been growing fast due to high fiscal deficits and quasi-fiscal imbalances, particularly after 1995. This, in conjunction with the high market interest rate that it yielded (due to large risk premia), and the negative rates of output growth, constituted the main threat to fiscal sustainability.

Monetary policy

The experience of transition, particularly during the initial stabilization phase, suggested that the extent of monetization of a transition economy was largely affected by the consistency of fiscal policy. From the preceding analysis it must have become clear that for tight money to be a feasible objective it would require fiscal consolidation as a vital precondition. Table 4.7 reports broad money growth during the 1991–98 period for the transition economies of SEE. As we see, money growth gradually was stabilized, reflecting inflation stabilization. Notable exceptions are the cases of Bulgaria and Romania in which the re-emergence of inflation was accompanied by a substantial increase in the rate of growth in broad money during 1996–97 for the former and in 1997 for the latter.

Table 4.7 Broad money growth (end-year)

	1991	**1992**	**1993**	**1994**	**1995**	**1996**	**1997**	**1998**
Albania (M3)	104.4	152.7	75.0	40.6	51.4	40.0	28.5	20.6
Bulgaria (M3)	110.0	53.6	47.6	78.6	39.6	124.5	359.3	9.6
Croatia (M4)	n.a.	n.a.	n.a.	75.7	39.3	49.1	38.3	13.0
FYROM (M4)	n.a.	n.a.	n.a.	8.9	−59.3	0.5	19.6	14.0
Romania (M3)	101.2	79.6	141.0	138.1	71.6	66.0	104.9	48.9

n.a. = not available.
Source: EBRD (1999, 2000).

Although changes in inflation were closely followed by changes in monetary aggregates, the relation of money supply and inflation was far from being a straightforward matter in the transition economies. Figures 4.1 and 4.2 will help us look into the matter more closely. Figure 4.1 displays the rates of growth in broad money and prices in the five economies of SEE during the period 1994–98. It can be seen that it is hard to find any consistency between the rates of change in broad money and inflation in all countries under consideration.[12] This, in turn, reveals the weakness of the former when attempting to use it as a reliable indicator for future inflation. Figure 4.2 shows the values of correlation coefficients for inflation and lagged changes in broad money. We used quarterly data for the two variables for the period 1994–98 for Bulgaria and Romania and 1995–98 for the remaining three countries. In most of the countries, broad money appeared to exert some impact on inflation but this was not consistent. Overall, no systematic positive relationship for money-prices can be traced since in most instances the correlation values are either not as strong or negative.[13] In the cases of

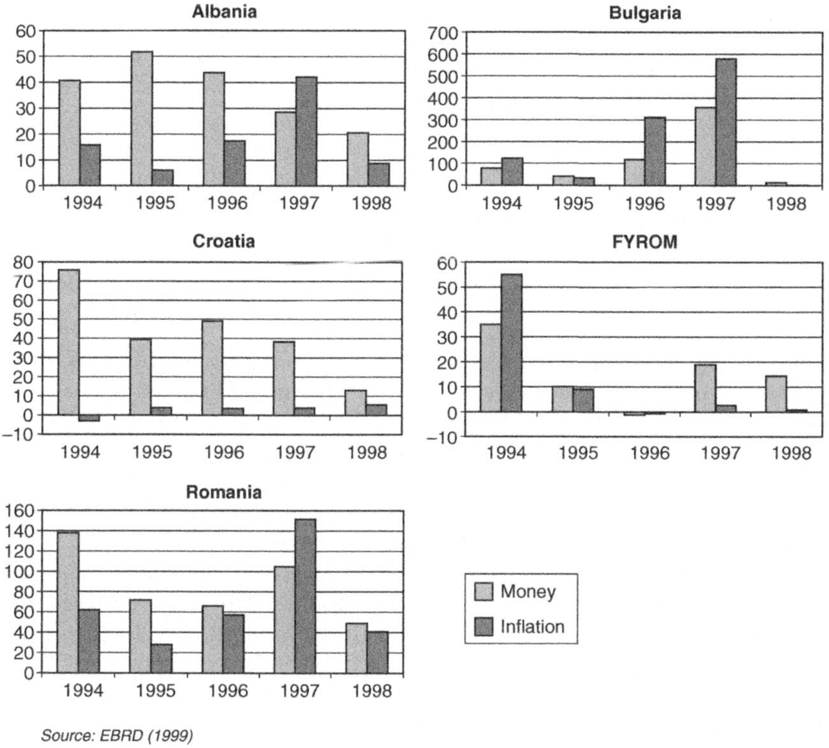

Figure 4.1 Broad money (percentage change) and inflation (end-year)

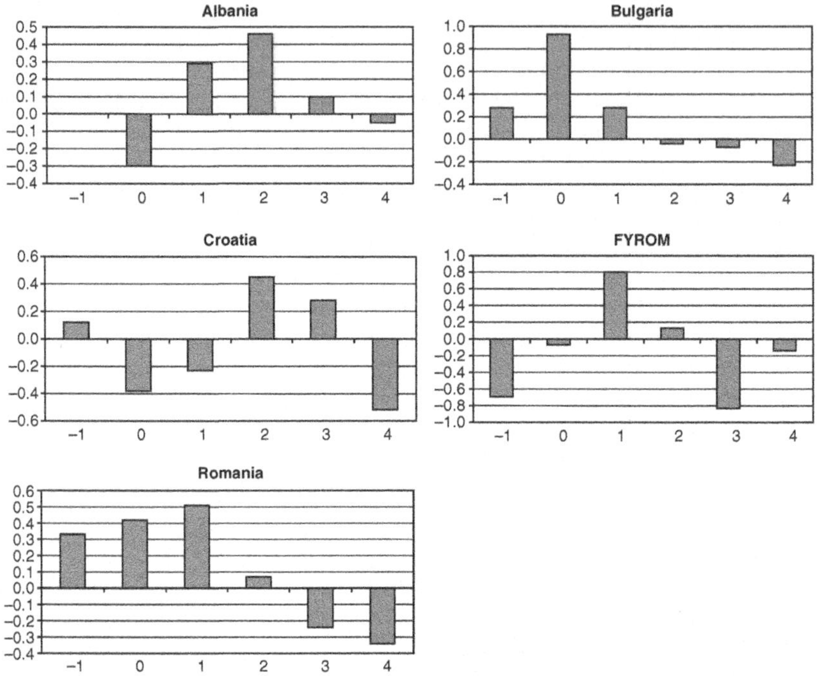

Note: The graphs show the values of correlation coefficients calculated for the percentage changes in quarterly money supply and the lagged changes in the consumer price index (CPI) with lags in quarters measured on the horizontal axis. A negative value of the lag corresponds to correlation between a change in the CPI and a lagged change in the money supply (see also UN/ECE 1995).

Figure 4.2 Correlation of broad money (percentage change) and inflation (end-year)

FYROM and Romania, inflation appeared to have followed growth in broad money with a lag of about one quarter. In Albania and Croatia it seems to be a lag of two quarters, while there was no lag in the case of Bulgaria. In the cases of Bulgaria and Romania, given the re-emergence of inflation during the particular period it is possible to have an inverse relationship, suggesting that increases in the money supply were rather accommodating in nature.

From the above observations it becomes apparent that changes in broad money, while important, cannot by themselves explain the inflationary pressures experienced by the particular economies. The observed weak and inconsistent relation means that changes in the monetization level (money velocity) had a significant role in determining inflation in most of these countries. Table 4.8 reports the degree of monetization in the economies of SEE during the period 1992–98. In particular it reports narrow, total broad money and broad money in domestic currency as shares of GDP, as well as foreign currency deposits as a percentage of total broad money. In these

Table 4.8 Monetization in the economies of SEE (% of GDP)

	1992	1993	1994	1995	1996	1997	1998
Albania							
Narrow money (M1)	n.a.	n.a.	21.0	25.8	32.2	26.8	18.2
Total broad money (BM)	56.8	40.2	38.4	46.8	55.0	58.1	52.0
BM in domestic currency	42.0	32.0	31.2	38.0	42.9	47.5	43.3
Foreign currency deposits[a]	23.6	20.2	18.8	18.7	21.9	18.2	16.8
Bulgaria							
Narrow money (M1)	18.8	16.2	14.3	12.3	13.5	13.4	12.8
Total broad money (BM)	74.6	77.6	78.0	65.4	71.0	32.8	28.5
BM in domestic currency	56.4	51.7	52.1	47.4	33.2	17.7	16.5
Foreign currency deposits[a]	23.4	20.3	32.6	27.2	50.5	43.6	39.2
Croatia							
Narrow money (M1)	n.a.	8.0	7.6	8.4	10.6	11.2	9.8
Total broad money (BM)	38.0	25.8	20.2	25.0	34.0	41.0	38.0
BM in domestic currency	25.0	10.0	10.0	11.0	14.0	16.0	10.4
Foreign currency deposits[a]	n.a.	54.1	50.3	57.5	59.6	61.7	66.3
FYROM							
Narrow money (M1)	14.1	9.4	6.8	7.4	6.9	7.6	7.9
Total broad money (BM)	17.4	22.9	12.6	12.2	11.6	13.6	14.9
BM in domestic currency	17.4	15.5	10.2	10.4	9.4	10.4	11.5
Foreign currency deposits[a]	0.0	32.4	19.3	20.5	18.8	23.5	23.2
Romania							
Narrow money (M1)	17.6	10.3	8.6	9.4	9.9	7.2	5.7
Total broad money (BM)	30.8	22.3	21.4	25.3	27.9	24.6	24.9
BM in domestic currency	25.8	15.9	16.7	19.6	21.3	17.6	16.8
Foreign currency deposits[a]	15.3	29.0	22.1	21.8	23.4	28.5	32.6

n.a. = not available.
[a] In percentage of total broad money.
Source: IMF (International Financial Statistics, 2000 Yearbook).

economies the broad money to GDP ratio more or less followed the same trend as in the majority of transition economies: that is, the degree of monetization initially fell as the existing monetary overhang was eliminated through price and interest rate increases, and then it increased to the extent that due to stabilization efforts the demand for money recovered and confidence in domestic currency was restored. On the other hand, the narrow money to GDP ratio in most countries followed a declining trend. Notable exceptions are Croatia and FYROM, where the particular ratio appeared rather stable. This, as we will see below, was not unrelated to the fact that both countries relied on exchange rate targeting.

There are two basic observations with respect to Table 4.8. The first is in a static context since it refers to the level of monetization at a given moment of time across the countries. A clear-cut observation for most South East European countries is the rather low degree of monetization by international standards.[14] Except for Albania in which the degree of monetization was surprisingly high relative to its per capita income, the other countries had both the M1 and broad money to GDP ratios rather low.[15] This, in turn, primarily reflected the fact that the financial systems of the particular countries largely remained underdeveloped, which meant that the depth of the particular markets lagged considerably behind the ones in the developed market economies. As a result this relatively low level of monetization in SEE did not necessarily mean that there was room for less restrictive but still non-inflationary monetary policy. More specifically, while inflation appeared to be the crucial determinant of monetization during transition (see De Broeck, Krajnyak and Lorie 1997), their relation was not always a clear-cut one. There were countries with high inflation, such as Romania and Bulgaria, which were associated with a low degree of monetization in the former case and a high one in the latter (until 1996). On the other hand, in Albania and FYROM, two low-income countries where disinflation was quite effective, the degree of monetization was high in the former and very low in the latter. Thus, at least for the economies of SEE, the absolute level of monetization appeared to be compatible with different inflation rates which, in turn, significantly reduced the usefulness of monetary policy as a nominal anchor since it generated a great deal of uncertainty as to what extent there was scope for non-inflationary monetary expansion.

The second observation refers to monetization in a dynamic context: it concerns the behaviour of monetization through time which, in conjunction with changes in the price level, reflects the extent of stability in the demand for money function. In particular, no systematic correlation appeared to exist between the degree of monetization and the rates of inflation since decelerating inflation was compatible both with increasing and decreasing levels of monetization in different countries. This, in turn, is directly related to the stability of the demand for money and has important implications for the use of monetary targeting for inflation stabilization. There are a number of factors that contribute to the instability of money demand given the circumstances facing a transition economy. For one thing, the almost complete lack of capital markets and of other investment opportunities meant that broad money, which primarily included interest-bearing deposits in domestic and foreign currency deposits in the banking system, performed both the function of savings as well as that of a store of wealth. This, in turn, made the broad stock of money quite heterogeneous, meaning different demand for money functions for different subcomponents (see UN/ECE 1996).

Table 4.8 reports important information with respect to the broad money in domestic currency to GDP ratio and to the foreign currency deposits to total broad money ratio as well. The latter ratio captures the extent of currency substitution in SEE and, as such, largely reflects the inflationary expectations of the public, meaning that its evolution could be the result of changes in the overall level of confidence in the national currency. It is not by accident that the two countries, FYROM and Croatia, which followed exchange rate targeting exhibited a more stable foreign currency deposits to broad money ratio. In the case of Croatia the high ratio partly reflects historic tradition (UN/ECE 1997) rather than policy choices. In the other countries the trend in currency substitution largely followed the course of economic stabilization. Most notably it increased considerably in Bulgaria in 1996 and 1997 and in Romania in 1997 and 1998, due to financial crisis and the resurgence of inflation in both countries.

Looking into the experience of the individual countries, first of all we can say for Albania that even a low-income country can have a relatively high money demand when combined with effective disinflation and output growth. Note that the surprisingly strong and rather fast output recovery diminished the initial fall in money demand while the subsequent growth contributed to its quick recovery. The high money demand, largely explains the Albanian puzzle of persistent budget deficits and falling inflation. Finally, it is interesting to note that the fall of the pyramid schemes and the political instability that followed during 1997 did not affect significantly the high monetization in Albania.

In Bulgaria, monetization was high until 1996 and this was in spite of the high inflation and the disappointing growth performance. At the same time, however, domestic money monetization declined by more than 40 per cent between 1992 and 1996, and this was mirrored by the corresponding increase in the share of foreign money deposits in total broad money. This increase in currency substitution was the result of declining confidence and thus it constituted a strong indication that the high money demand could not be sustained. The banking crisis that followed led to a large decline in deposits which, together with the sharp increase in inflation, led to a drastic fall in the broad money to GDP ratio. Money demand recovered later as confidence was restored following the introduction of the currency board and successful stabilization.

The relatively low level of monetization in Romania is largely explained by the high and unstable inflation as well as by the persistent output decline. As expected, the resurgence of inflation in 1997 was accompanied by a further fall in monetization levels, primarily domestic.

In Croatia, in spite of the war, the sharp drop in inflation, together with the strong output recovery, led to a considerable increase in the demand for money which rose to about the average level that corresponds to countries with comparable per capita GDP. It is interesting to note in the case of Croatia the high proportion of foreign deposits in total broad money in spite of its very low inflation which, as pointed out, rather reflected tradition.

Finally, the level of monetization in FYROM was the lowest in the region, particularly with respect to broad money, and thus it clearly constituted the most 'undermonetized' country of the region in spite of its low per capita income and the effective disinflation. This to a large extent was a reflection of the highly underdeveloped financial sector and the resulting very low level of intermediation by the banking system. The money multiplier, calculated as the ratio of broad money to base money, was only 1.7 in 1996 and about 2 in 1998.

Besides the fact that monetization (velocity) was not as stable in the transition economies of SEE, there were other factors as well that made the use of a monetary target as a nominal anchor a rather difficult task. This was primarily associated with the uncertainty in predicting the changes in output and prices which, among other things, were closely linked to the progress in the reform measures (see Begg 1998). The extend of reform in the financial sector, for instance, would not only affect price and output developments but would also add to the lack of knowledge regarding the demand for money function (see Cottarelli and Doyle 1999). This uncertainty to a large extent justifies the fact that the countries of the SEE, or other transition economies as well, which primarily relied on monetary targeting for the curtailing of inflation, did not announce such explicit targets publicly.

The above analysis revealed significant problems that were associated with money targeting, particularly during the early stages of transition. This, however, did not prevent the majority of the SEE economies relying on money-based stabilization strategies, primarily at the beginning of transition. This, in most cases (as we will explain below), was not a matter of choice but rather reflected the fact that alternative targeting strategies were not always feasible. Nevertheless, the apparent success of Albania, as an example of quick disinflation that relied on monetary targeting, demonstrated that money-based stabilization could be effective as well. This, in turn, emphasized the role of other policy measures and the importance of being in line with the objectives of monetary targeting.[16]

Interest rates and instruments of monetary control

During the disinflation process, monetary policy primarily relied on interest rates in order to attain the intermediate target. This was the case with respect to the economies of SEE regardless of whether the intermediate target was the money supply or the exchange rate. In the case of a fixed exchange rate regime the interest rate is the main policy tool of the central bank for maintaining exchange rate stability, while monetary policy is more or less treated as endogenous. In the case of a flexible regime, the interest rate is again the main policy tool for attaining the money supply target. The use of the interest rate as the main policy tool can be achieved either through direct controls or through indirect controls, which operate through the market by affecting the supply and demand for credit.

In the economies of SEE, as in all transition economies, monetary control initially had to rely on direct instruments reflecting both the legacies of central planning but also the fact that a shift to indirect instruments was not such a simple procedure. Indirect controls are used extensively by the developed economies since they promote competition and contribute to efficient allocation of credit. However, effective use of indirect controls requires the existence of: (a) adequate market infrastructure for money, interbank deposits and securities; (b) sound financial institutions so that the transmission mechanism works effectively; and (c) macroeconomic stability which is necessary for the development and growth of a government securities market (see Begg 1996).

In the transition economies, and even more so in the countries of SEE, these three preconditions were far from being in place. As a matter of fact, in most economies of SEE the steps towards financial reform and stabilization were rather slow, and as a result the reliance on direct monetary control was extensive. For instance, an important prerequisite for financial deepening that would allow the shift to indirect instruments refers to positive real interest rates on deposits. This, however, did not appear to be an easy matter, as governments were forced to pressure central banks for low real interest rates because of the need to finance large fiscal deficits. This, in turn, explains the extensive reliance on direct monetary instruments, particularly for most countries of SEE, since the introduction of indirect monetary instruments, among other things, presupposes significant progress in macroeconomic stabilization and fiscal consolidation (Begg 1996). Furthermore, governments encouraged reliance on direct controls since this allowed political interference in credit allocation, by enabling them to direct credit to certain sectors or to specific public enterprises. This reason was particularly profound in the countries of SEE and contributed to prolonged structural weaknesses in the banking sector, by protecting state banks from price competition and from the entry of new (private) banks, as well as in enterprises, by prolonging their reliance on soft budget constraints. Thus, in most SEE countries, restrictions on money and credit were the main instruments and the shift towards indirect monetary instruments such as open market operations in primary and secondary markets were developed gradually. This, in turn, seriously constrained the effectiveness of an active interest rate policy.

Turning to specific practices by the particular economies, the central bank of Albania largely relied on direct instruments of control such as bank-by-bank credit ceilings and floors on interest rates on deposits with state banks. Monetary policy was constrained by the rudimentary financial framework and the need to finance large fiscal deficits. The Treasury bill market was quite thin with the savings bank being very often the sole bidder in the auction for primary Treasury bills.[17] In the case of Bulgaria, monetary policy relied on several instruments prior to the introduction of the currency board. The use of credit ceilings was an important monetary instrument at the very beginning of the transition period. Refinancing of commercial banks was another important instrument used during the period until the adoption of the currency board as well. Later on, reserve requirements and open market operations came into practice. The latter by 1995 had become the major instrument of monetary policy (see Mihov 2001).

Croatia may be the only country of the region that shifted rather early to indirect instruments of monetary control. Note, however, that the segmented nature of the money market reduced the effectiveness of interest rate policy since there was no single interest rate exactly reflecting the prevailing monetary conditions. The central bank of FYROM heavily relied on bank-by-bank credit ceilings to control the expansion of domestic credit. In addition, credit auctions were used as the main short-term instrument to provide liquidity to the financial system. Until 1998 the use of indirect monetary instruments was very limited and the interest rate policy of the central bank was constrained by the low level of financial market development (IMF 1998a). In Romania, the central bank initially relied on two credit facilities, auction credit and the discount window, which were the main instruments until 1997 for the injection of liquidity. The discount window was the main facility through which directed credit was provided to certain sectors at heavily subsidized rates. Open market operations, particularly deposit-reducing ones, began in 1997 and became the main instrument for absorbing the increased liquidity that resulted from the central bank's purchases of foreign exchange.

Figure 4.3 highlights interest rate developments for the countries of SEE during the period under consideration. In particular there are two figures for each country. The first one reports nominal and real central bank interest rates. The nominal rates were set by the central bank and were indicative of the monetary policy stance. The other one exhibits nominal deposit and lending rates in each country. As pointed out, a restrictive interest rate policy was the primary instrument for reducing inflation and, as a result, most of the economies of SEE relied on high interest rates as well, regardless of the intermediate nominal target used. However, as Figure 4.3 indicates, interest rates did not follow the same pattern in the particular economies. More specifically, Croatia and FYROM, which adopted the exchange rate as a nominal anchor, pursued a more consistent interest rate policy. The reference rates of their central banks were consistently kept positive and high in real terms in order to maintain the exchange rate at the targeted level. Furthermore, lending rates in both countries were higher than the central bank rates, reflecting the restrictive stance of monetary policy even after price stability had been achieved.

In the other three countries real interest rates were not always positive. Albania appears to have relied heavily on high interest rates. In particular, real interest rates were positive and high during the entire period except for 1997, the year of the financial crisis. In the cases of Bulgaria and Romania interest rate policy was not always restrictive, reflecting periods of lax monetary policy stance in both countries. In the case of Bulgaria the real base rate was negative throughout until 1997. The lending rate was negative in 1992,

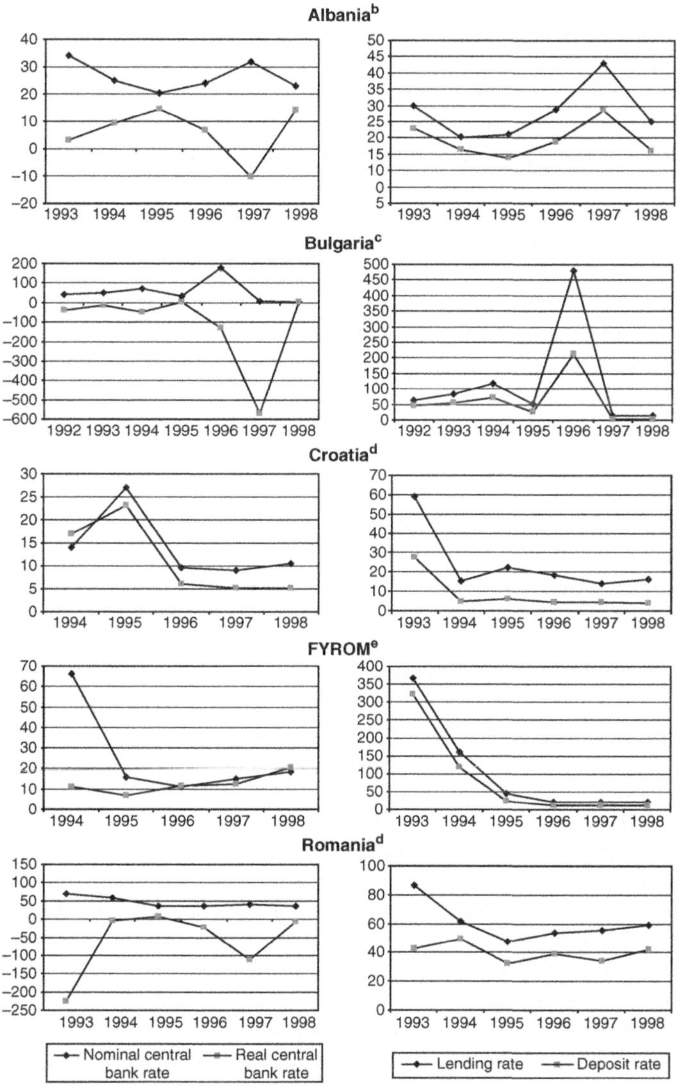

[a] Central bank rate: Refinancing rate for Albania and Croatia, base interest rate for Bulgaria, basic rate for FYROM and discount rate for Romania.

[b] Deposit and lending rates until 1995 refer to the floor and the guideline rate respectively set by the central bank. Thereafter refer to weighted average interest rate on new 1-year deposits in and for 1-year loans by commercial banks.

[c] One month deposit rate and less than a year lending rate.

[d] Weighted average of deposits and loans of all maturities.

[e] Household deposit rate (3–6 months) and lending rate to small enterprises. Minimum rates offered.

Source: EBRD (1999).

Figure 4.3 Interest rates: central bank rate[a], lending and deposit rates (% p.a., end-year)

as well as in 1996 and 1997. The situation did not differ much in Romania. The real discount rate was negative during the whole period, except for 1995. The lending rate was also negative in real terms in 1993 and 1997. Note that in the case of Bulgaria the introduction of currency board in 1998 led to a rapid drop in inflation and nominal interest rates, while real interest rates became positive and remained high. Note that in the case of a currency board regime interest rates are market-determined and the monetary authorities cannot influence interest rates directly. Finally, another point regarding interest rates in most economies of SEE, and common in other transition economies as well, referred to the large spread between lending and deposit rates. This, on the one hand, was the result of inefficient financial intermediation and low competition, while, on the other hand, it was largely a reflection of the significant proportions of bad loans in the balance sheets of commercial banks.

Exchange rate regimes

While, as discussed earlier, monetary targeting was not such an easy matter, at least during the early stages of transition, all the countries of SEE started the transition process by relying on money-based stabilization. This, however, was not always a matter of choice. According to Begg (1996), for countries to adopt an exchange rate target two conditions were necessary: a tolerably sound fiscal policy and an adequate level of foreign exchange reserves.[18] First, fiscal fundamentals, which refer to the size of the budget deficit and to the manner in which it was financed, constituted the crucial requirement for stabilization. Large fiscal imbalances could lead to rapid money growth, making the policy of a fixed nominal exchange rate not sustainable. Lack of adequate reserves would also undermine the feasibility of a fixed regime since the capacity of the central bank to intervene on the foreign exchange market in order to stabilize the currency is restricted. Note, however, that as Begg (1996) pointed out, the first condition is the fundamental one while the need for international reserves could be satisfied through the help of international organizations, such as the IMF.

Looking at the information on Table 4.9, we first see that all the countries of SEE, at the start of the transition process and prior to the launching of the official stabilization strategies, initially adopted flexible exchange rate regimes implying reliance on monetary targeting. In the cases of Albania and Bulgaria this classification is of limited practical importance since stabilization started soon after the beginning of transition. However, in the cases of the other three counties the period until the launching of the stabilization programmes was not as short. Croatia and FYROM, the two states of the former Yugoslav Republic, gained their independence in June and September 1991 respectively. They could not, however, adopt independent monetary policies until December 1991 and April 1992 respectively, when their

Table 4.9 Exchange rate regimes, stabilization programmes and inflation

Country	Exchange rate regime prior to stabilization[a]	Stock of international reserves in the year before the start of stabilization[b,c]	Fiscal balance in the year before the start of stabilization (% of GDP)[c]	Inflation rate prior to stabilization[d]	Stabilization programme date	Exchange rate regime adopted	Year in which inflation fell below 50%[e]	Exchange rate regime in 1998	Inflation rate in 1998
Albania	Flexible	0.0	−31.0	293	August 1992	Flexible	1994(22,6)	Flexible	20.6
Bulgaria	Flexible	0.8	−8.1	245	February 1991[h]	Flexible	1998(18,7)	Fixed[j]	18.7
Croatia	Flexible[f]	0.4	−3.9	1,903	October 1993	Fixed[i]	1995(4,0)	Fixed	6.4
FYROM	Flexible[g]	1.2	−13.4	248	January 1994	Fixed[i]	1995(16,4)	Fixed	0.5
Romania	Flexible	1.5	−4.6	314	October 1993[h]	Flexible	1995(32,2)	Flexible	59.1

[a] This refers to period between the start of the transition and the launching of the stabilization programmes. It is more relevant in the cases of Croatia, FYROM and Romania.

[b] In months of current account expenditures, excluding transfers.

[c] This refers to following years: 1991 for Albania; 1990 for Bulgaria; 1992 for Croatia; 1993 for FYROM; 1992 for Romania.

[d] This is the inflation rate in the month prior to the one that the stabilization programme was launched, on a yearly basis. All other inflations are from December to December (period average).

[e] The numbers in parentheses correspond to particular inflation rates (period average).

[f] Croatia gained its independence from Yugoslavia in June 1991. Independent monetary policy since December 1991, when the Croatian dinar was introduced.

[g] FYROM gained its independence from Yugoslavia in September 1991. Independent monetary policy since April 1992, when its new currency, the Denar, was introduced.

[h] The date of the first stabilization attempt.

[i] Croatia and FYROM de facto adopted fixed but adjustable exchange rates.

[j] Bulgaria adopted a currency board in July 1997.

Sources: Fischer and Sahay (2000); IMF (International Financial Statistics, 2000 yearbook and Country Reports); and EBRD (1999).

new currencies were introduced. Even so, their stabilization programmes were not launched until October 1993 in the case of Croatia and January 1994 in the case of FYROM (see Table 4.9). Finally, Romania started its official stabilization in October 1993, although transition had been under way since 1991.

The pattern of sharp initial devaluations that was initiated by all the transition countries, preceding the start of the stabilization programme, was followed by the economies of SEE as well. This either took the form of an up-front devaluation, as in Bulgaria, or a series of consecutive devaluations, as in the cases of Romania, Albania, Croatia and FYROM.[19] Furthermore, in all cases the initial devaluations were combined with the introduction of at least some degree of convertibility of the domestic currency.[20] This particularly referred to trade transactions, while capital account transactions remained under strict control. After the initial devaluations, further adjustments generally lagged behind domestic inflation. This, in turn, was reflected in the strong appreciation of all domestic currencies in real terms early in transition, except for the case of Romania.

This initial reliance on exchange rate flexibility by all countries was not unrelated to the large financial imbalances faced by their respective general governments and the fact that international reserves were too low. Thus, as shown in Table 4.9, international reserves were too low and fiscal policies too lax to contemplate exchange rate pegging. Recall that, particularly in the case of Romania, the smaller fiscal deficit was largely misleading due to large quasi-fiscal deficits (Table 4.4). The launching of the stabilization programmes did not alter the initial choice considerably: that is, at the beginning of their stabilization programmes the countries of SEE adopted exchange rate regimes that to a larger or lesser degree preserved flexibility. Thus, according to Table 4.9, no country adopted a hard peg and that continued to be the case until 1997 when Bulgaria made a shift to a currency board regime.[21]

More specifically, in Albania, Bulgaria and Romania the initial choice of a flexible regime was adopted in the stabilization programme as well, and thus monetary policy primarily continued relying on monetary targeting (Table 4.9). In Bulgaria and Romania delayed structural reforms and the resulting soft budget constraints constituted an enormous obstacle to restrictive monetary and fiscal policies which, in turn, made the sustainability of a fixed regime an extremely difficult task. In the case of Albania, while the currency was left to float freely, the strategy was to target a fairly stable nominal exchange rate against the US dollar. This strategy had been quite successful until 1996 largely due to rapid disinflation and to surprisingly strong output recovery, and in spite of the large budget deficits. A further similarity in the stabilization experience of these three countries was associated with the fact that they went through a major financial crisis that led to the resurgence of inflation in 1997, when inconsistent policies and structural weaknesses in public enterprises and the banking sector constituted the common causes that led to the stabilization setback.[22]

Croatia and FYROM chose exchange rate stability to be the centrepiece of their stabilization strategy since they relied on the de facto adoption of a fixed but adjustable exchange rate. Thus the exchange rate was used as a nominal anchor to curb inflationary expectations while, at the same time, the option of exchange rate adjustment was preserved in order to deal with cases of persistent external imbalances or destabilizing capital inflows. In particular, the exchange rate initially was de facto pegged to the Deutsche Mark (DM): in the case of Croatia, a fluctuation band was targeted, while in the case of FYROM the targeting was aimed at a specific level.[23]

As we shall see below, a common characteristic of these two countries is the quick disinflation, which primarily reflected the fact that the sustainability of the exchange rate as the nominal anchor largely necessitated the implementation of tight monetary and fiscal policies. In the case of Croatia, an exchange rate floor was announced at the beginning of the stabilization programme and this aimed at a quick breaking of inflationary expectations. The central bank promised to satisfy all demand for foreign exchange at the rate of the announced floor, if the market level was higher (see Sonje and Skreb 1997). This was quite successful in curbing expectation and was soon abandoned as a new law passed according to which the exchange rate was determined in the interbank foreign exchange market. The central bank preserved exchange rate stability through interventions allowing, at the same time, some movement within a fluctuation band, which had a width of plus or minus 6 per cent (see Sonje and Vujcic 2001).

Exchange rate regimes and disinflation

Figure 4.4 shows disinflation effectiveness in the five countries of SEE. Starting with Croatia and FYROM, it is apparent that, after the initial depreciations, the two countries of the former Yugoslav republic were able to preserve exchange rate stability. In addition, Figure 4.4 verifies the fact that the choice of policy towards exchange rate stability seemed to have had a stronger anti-inflationary impact. In Croatia and FYROM, the successful implementation of the exchange rate targeting stabilization strategy gave the necessary credibility to monetary policy and led to rapid disinflation. The particular stabilization policy imposed discipline in all macroeconomic policies and this primarily referred to the consistency of fiscal policy. In particular, both countries managed to reduce their fiscal deficits considerably since the beginning of their stabilization programme (see Table 4.4). This, in turn, as shown in Figure 4.4, allowed the establishment of tight control over the money supply growth, a vital precondition in safeguarding the exchange rate objective. The common course of successful stabilization in both countries, however, did not generate the same results with respect to the strength of output recovery: while Croatia experienced a particularly strong output

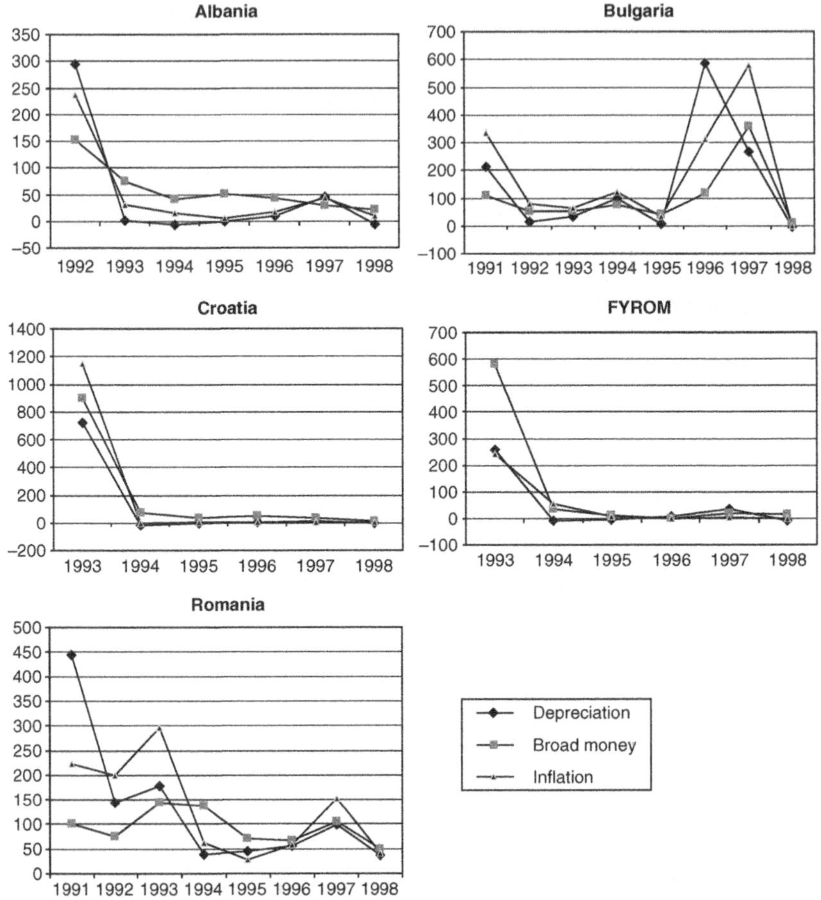

Sources: IMF (International Financial Statistics, 2000 yearbook and Country Reports) and EBRD (1999, 2000).

Figure 4.4 Broad money growth, exchange rate depreciation and inflation (end of period, in %)

growth for five consecutive years from 1994 until 1998, FYROM moved to modest rates of growth in 1996 after six years of stagnation (Table 4.2). As we will see in Chapter 6, the slow pace of structural change, particularly with respect to enterprise restructuring and financial sector reform, provides an important explanation for the poor economic performance of FYROM.

Next, with respect to the three countries that chose exchange rate flexibility and thus relied on monetary targeting, the stabilization process was not as successful. This particularly refers to Romania and Bulgaria which, as

Figure 4.4 illustrates, failed to reduce inflation below double digits during the period until the end of 1998, while Albania constituted the exception of the group since it was much more successful in its disinflation effort. Bulgaria (until 1997) and Romania, despite their repeated stabilization attempts, were not able to achieve price stability and this largely reflected the fact that the monetary targeting strategy was accompanied by inconsistent macroeconomic policies, particularly fiscal policy, which in turn led to a loose monetary stand as well. Note, as pointed out earlier, that the slow progress in structural reform in both countries was to a large extent responsible for the lack of restrictive macroeconomic policies. As a result of the growing macroeconomic imbalances, both countries went through a major financial crisis in 1996–97 that led to rapid depreciation of the domestic currencies and almost caused a hyperinflation situation. This, in the case of Bulgaria, led to the change of the exchange rate regime and the adoption of a currency board. The effectiveness of the new regime in breaking inflationary expectation was spectacular. The re-establishment of tight control over money supply led to rapid disinflation which fell below 1 per cent by the end of 1998 (Table 4.1). Romania, on the other hand, put forward a renewed stabilization strategy without, however, altering the exchange rate regime. By the end of 1998, Romania's inflation rate was still above 50 per cent (Table 4.1).

Furthermore, the limited effectiveness of the disinflation process in the two countries had serious implications for the sustainability of output growth. As a matter of fact, the initial output growth was not sustained in either country. In the case of Bulgaria, the moderate output growth during 1994 and 1995 was interrupted by the financial crisis and output fell sharply in 1996 and 1997 (Table 4.2). Output growth recovered in 1998, largely reflecting the effectiveness of the new stabilization strategy. Romania, on the other hand, although it experienced stronger economic growth between 1993 and 1996, suffered persistent macroeconomic imbalances and the resurgence of inflation which undermined growth sustainability as well, causing a significant drop in economic activity during the period 1997–99.

Albania was much more effective in bringing down inflation. More specifically, inflation was brought down to single figures in 1995, while output recovery was strong and occurred as early as in 1993. The early disinflation, together with the output growth, enabled the Albanian central bank to maintain exchange rate stability while running large fiscal imbalances. As seen in Figure 4.4, the rate of growth of broad money was clearly above the inflation rate, reflecting the impact of persisting fiscal deficits. This, however, did not accelerate depreciation and thus did not undermine the disinflation process until 1995. As a matter of fact the domestic currency appreciated *vis-à-vis* the US dollar in 1994 and 1995. The resulting sharp increase in money demand for domestic money, primarily reflecting the quick disinflation and the early output recovery, constituted the main force behind the nominal appreciation. The situation, however, was not sustainable. The deteriorating fiscal imbalances and the emergence of the pyramid schemes in 1996 eventually led to the financial crisis of early 1997 and to a resurgence of inflation. These developments, together with the public unrest that resulted as a consequence, caused a large drop in output during the same year. Note, however, that restrictive macroeconomic policies were introduced once more in 1998, causing a sharp decline in inflation while output growth returned to strong positive rates.

The external sector

Persistent current account deficits have been a common characteristic in the external sectors of most countries in the region. Table 4.10 reports the current account and trade balances of the particular economies, expressed as a percentage of GDP, during the period 1990–98. The initial increase in current account deficits, a rather common experience by all transition economies, reflected, on the one hand, the loss of the exporting markets as the CMEA was dismantled and, on the other hand, the fact that imports became more widely available. The increase in the latter was mostly the result of a considerable recovery in consumption and to a lesser extent in investment for the purpose of replacing part of existing capital stock that was obsolete. Thus the emergence of significant trade deficits was primarily responsible for initial imbalances in the current account. The subsequent trend in current account deficits was largely affected by the degree of consistency in the stabilization effort, the extent of output recovery and the effectiveness of export reorientation, as well as the extent of increase in capital flows into the region. According to Table 4.10, current accounts have largely followed developments in external trade, such that growing trade deficits in most South East European countries appeared to be the main reason behind the trend for high current account imbalances. This was true to a lesser extent for Croatia due to the large tourist sector, while Bulgaria was a notable exception since small imbalances in trade helped maintain current account stability during the period 1994–98.

The pattern of growing trade deficits, being the result of a faster increase in imports relative to exports, reflected a combination of rising domestic demand and a relatively poor export performance. In some countries, lax macroeconomic policies, primarily with respect to fiscal consolidation, and increased spending stimulated imports. Romania constituted a prime example of fast rising imports during 1994–97 due to macroeconomic policies. Albania, Croatia and FYROM experienced a significant rise in imports as well during the same period which, however, was primarily the result of output recovery. Note that imports were not affected significantly in Bulgaria during 1995–98 despite the decline in economic activity. Overall, although high domestic demand appeared to be the common reason for the region's high current account deficits, the causes for the increased spending differed from country to country.

Table 4.10 Current account and trade balances (% of GDP)

	1990	1991	1992	1993	1994	1995	1996	1997	1998
Albania									
Current account balance	n.a.	−22.2	−16.7	−30.1	−14.4	−7.2	−9.1	−12.4	−6.6
Trade balance	n.a.	−18.5	−72.8	−41.3	−23.8	−19.2	−25.3	−23.4	−19.8
Bulgaria									
Current account balance	−8.2	−1.0	−4.2	−10.1	−0.3	−0.2	0.2	4.1	−0.5
Trade balance	−2.1	9.0	−6.3	−9.6	−2.1	−2.3	−1.8	0.1	−6.0
Croatia									
Current account balance	n.a.	−3.4	3.2	5.7	5.9	−7.7	−5.5	−11.6	−6.7
Trade balance	n.a.	−2.9	1.3	−7.0	−6.6	−15.3	−15.6	−24.5	−17.7
FYROM									
Current account balance	−9.1	−5.5	−0.8	0.6	−5.3	−5.0	−6.5	−7.8	−7.5
Trade balance	−9.0	−3.8	−0.3	−5.2	−11.7	−11.6	−1.9	−14.6	15.0
Romania									
Current account balance	−9.6	−3.5	−8.0	−4.5	−1.4	−5.0	−7.3	−6.1	−6.9
Trade balance	−6.8	−5.3	−9.7	−6.2	−3.2	−6.7	−9.5	−8.1	−8.5
SEE[a]									
Current account balance	−9.0	−7.1	−5.3	−7.7	−3.1	−5.0	−5.6	−6.8	−5.6
CE[a]									
Current account balance	n.a.	0.1	1.8	−2.3	−0.4	−0.4	−4.4	−4.3	−4.3

n.a. = not available.
[a] Unweighted average.
Sources: EBRD (2000) and WIIW (The Vienna Institute for International Economic Studies).

The export performance of region was particularly weak. Indeed, according to Table 4.11, export values appeared to grow at a very slow pace and this was true for all the countries of the region. The significant recovery of exports in Bulgaria and Romania during 1995 and 1994–95 respectively, causing a temporary output recovery as well, did not last largely due to inadequate stabilization and reform measures. The overall poor export performance was primarily the result of the region's slow pace of structural reform. In particular, the relatively slow enterprise restructuring limited the ability of the particular countries, although there was still unused capacity, to supply higher-quality goods. Furthermore, armed conflicts as well as the relative larger geographic distance from major Western European centres also had an adverse impact on the region's exports. A more detailed analysis concerning international trade will be presented in Chapter 8.

Price competitiveness appeared to have played a rather limited role in affecting export performance. Owing to data limitations, the only readily available measure of the real exchange rate for all South East European economies is the Consumer Price Index (CPI)-based real effective exchange rate. The course of this real exchange rate measure for the economies of SEE during the period 1993–98 is shown in Figure 4.5. The data clearly show that the real exchange rate appreciation, which has been a characteristic particularly common for the Central European economies, was not as profound in the case of the South East European economies. Following the appreciation at the early stages of transition, after the initial depreciation the real exchange rate remained stable for most countries. As a matter of fact, the real exchange rate was remarkably stable in the case of Croatia; it depreciated after 1994 in FYROM; while it did not start appreciating strongly until after 1996 in Albania, Bulgaria and Romania. This stability for most of the period suggests that external competitiveness as measured by the CPI-based real effective exchange rate could not account for the weak export performance of the countries of the region.

Furthermore, to the extent that there was some real appreciation it did not necessarily mean that it affected adversely the export performance of the particular countries. As Halpern and Wyploz (1997) and Krajnyak and Zettelmeyer (1998) pointed out, real exchange rate appreciation in many transition economies primarily reflected the impact of structural reform which led to significant productivity and efficiency gains and thus, as such, it constituted appreciation in the equilibrium rate, not affecting external competitiveness.[24] This can be simply verified by the observation that several of these economies experienced significant exchange rate appreciations while registering substantial export growth. This, in turn, meant that given the specific conditions of the transition economies in general and of the South East European ones in particular, the notion of competitiveness was more closely related to structural reform as the most effective way for sustaining the particular countries' penetration of exports into external markets.

Table 4.11 Exports, imports and trade balance (in US$ mil.)

	1990	**1991**	**1992**	**1993**	**1994**	**1995**	**1996**	**1997**	**1998**
Albania									
Exports	322	73	70	112	141	205	244	159	208
Imports	456	281	524	604	601	680	909	694	812
Trade balance	*–134*	*–208*	*–454*	*–492*	*–460*	*–475*	*–665*	*–535*	*–604*
Bulgaria									
Exports	5,232	3,434	2,444	2,282	3,359	5,220	4,781	4,314	4,150
Imports	5,584	2,715	4,345	4,462	4,670	5,469	4,891	3,880	5,044
Trade balance	*–352*	*719*	*–1,901*	*–2,180*	*–1,311*	*–249*	*–110*	*434*	*–894*
Croatia									
Exports	4,020	3,310	4,353	3,904	4,260	4,632	4,512	4,332	4,557
Imports	5,133	3,811	4,346	4,666	5,229	7,510	7,787	9,100	8,327
Trade balance	*–1,113*	*–501*	*7*	*–762*	*–969*	*–2,878*	*–3,275*	*–4,768*	*–3,770*
FYROM									
Exports	1,113	1,095	1,199	1,056	1,086	1,202	1,148	1,237	1,311
Imports	1,531	1,274	1,206	1,199	1,484	1,708	1,625	1,774	1,915
Trade balance	*–418*	*–179*	*–7*	*–143*	*–398*	*–506*	*–477*	*–537*	*–604*
Romania									
Exports	5,867	4,269	4,367	4,892	6,160	8,061	7,645	8,387	8,315
Imports	9,200	5,203	5,582	5,929	6,466	9,443	9,058	10,129	10,802
Trade balance	*–3,333*	*–934*	*–1,215*	*–1,037*	*–306*	*–1,382*	*–1,413*	*–1,742*	*–2,487*

n.a. = not available.
Source: WIIW database.

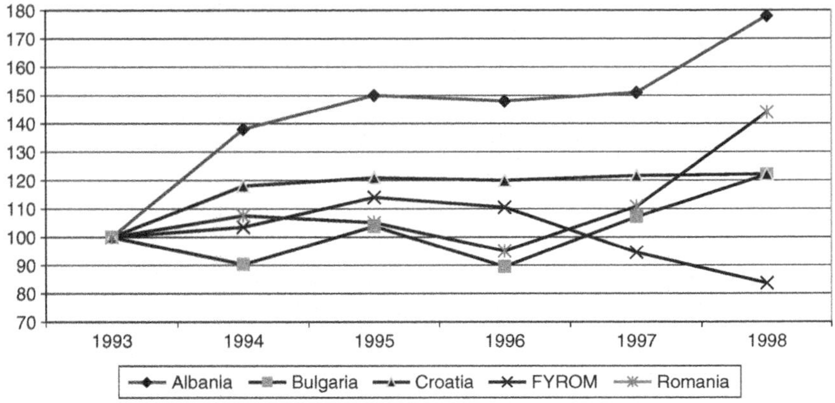

Source: IMF (International Financial Statistics, 2000 Yearbook and Country Reports)

Figure 4.5 Real effective exchange rate (CPI based 1993 = 100)

Thus, for the economies of SEE the poor external trade performance was largely linked to the delays in economic restructuring and thus to lower than expected productivity gains.

Capital inflows

Soon after the transformation process started and the macroeconomic stabilization was getting under way, most transition economies began gaining access to international capital markets. Capital inflows have played an essential role which significantly affected the transition process. In particular, on the one hand, they may have contributed to rising current account deficits by stimulating domestic demand but, on the other hand, they constituted a major source of financing these imbalances and thus reducing the need for official funds, while contributing to higher economic performance.

The net capital inflows into the region are presented in Figure 4.6 and in Table 4.12. In particular, Figure 4.6 presents the total inflows, net, to each country and to the region during 1993–98. It can be seen that these increased from about US$2 billion in 1993 to more than US$6.8 billion in 1997, but fell to around US$4 billion in 1998. Table 4.12 reports the composition of net capital inflows to each country and to the entire region consisting of three categories: FDI, portfolio investment and other investment. The data clearly indicate that the particular countries were not as successful in attracting significant amounts of capital inflows. As a matter of fact, inflows into two countries (i.e., Croatia and Romania) represented the largest share of the total inflows into the region. In particular, most FDI flows were directed to Romania and to a lesser extent Bulgaria, particularly during 1997–98, while

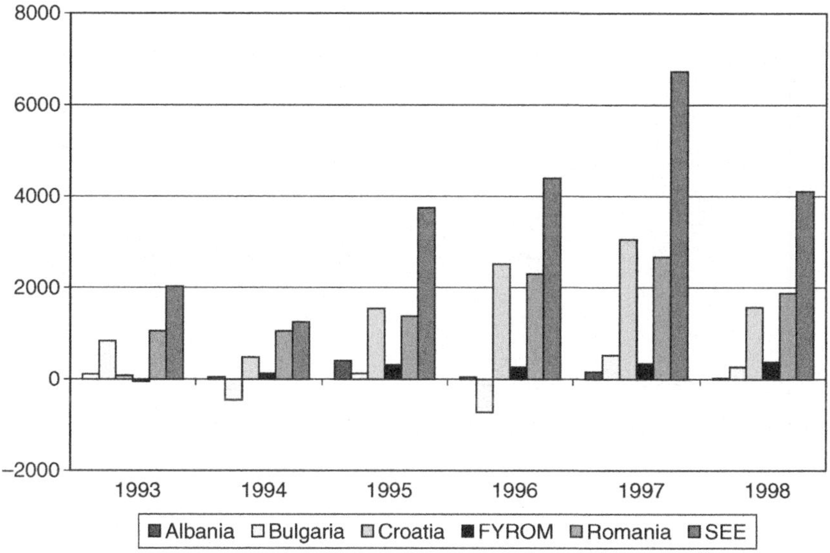

Source: WIIW and IMF Country Reports

Figure 4.6 Net capital inflows (in US$ mil.)

in Croatia there was a surge in other investment primarily as the result of an increase in foreign currency deposits. Furthermore, Bulgaria was the only country that experienced negative net inflows in 1994 and 1996, as a result of the net outflows in portfolio investment during 1994–96, which reflected the weak financial policies and the loss of confidence during the same period. Note, however, that portfolio investment was relatively low, largely reflecting the low level of financial development of the countries of SEE. Figure 4.7 also shows each country's contribution to the overall size and composition of the region's total inflows during the period under consideration.

The poor performance of SEE becomes particularly evident when compared to the corresponding performance of the economies of CE. Figure 4.7 presents the net cumulative capital inflows, together with their composition, to each country as well as to both the SEE and CE regions over the period 1993–98. The performance of the region was particularly disappointing when compared to that of CE. In particular, by the end of 1998 the net cumulative capital inflows into the SEE were less than 30 per cent of the corresponding ones into the CE. The comparison with respect to FDI was much less favourable for the economies of SEE. In particular, the cumulative FDI flows to SEE were just above US$8 billion while, in the case of

Table 4.12 Net capital inflows (in US$ mil.)

	1993	1994	1995	1996	1997	1998
Albania	**110.2**	**47.8**	**403.3**	**49.6**	**152.9**	**23.9**
FDI	58.0	52.9	70.0	90.1	47.5	45.0
Portfolio investment	0.0	0.0	0.0	0.0	0.0	0.0
Other investment	52.2	−5.1	333.3	−40.5	105.4	−21.1
Bulgaria	**834.0**	**−460.2**	**109.9**	**−755.8**	**518.9**	**266.8**
FDI	40.0	105.4	88.4	107.5	504.6	537.2
Portfolio investment	0.0	−231.8	−65.8	−129.3	132.9	−241.4
Other investment	794.0	−333.8	87.3	−734.0	−118.6	−29.0
Croatia	**78.0**	**481.4**	**1,539.7**	**2,507.6**	**3,155.1**	**1,567.1**
FDI	101.7	110.2	109.7	481.7	443.7	800.5
Portfolio investment	0.0	10.9	4.9	628.3	577.0	14.9
Other investment	−23.7	360.3	1,425.1	1,397.6	2,134.4	751.7
FYROM	**−53.0**	**125.5**	**313.3**	**261.7**	**339.7**	**374.9**
FDI	n.a.	19.0	9.5	11.2	15.8	117.7
Portfolio investment	0.0	0.0	2.7	0.3	2.1	7.8
Other investment	−53.0	106.5	301.1	250.2	321.8	249.4
Romania	**1,050.0**	**1,052.0**	**1,373.0**	**2,295.0**	**2,654.0**	**1,872.0**
FDI	87.0	341.0	417.0	263.0	1,214.0	2,040.0
Portfolio investment	−73.0	75.0	32.0	1,222.0	883.0	130.0
Other investment	1,036.0	636.0	924.0	810.0	557.0	−298.0
SEE	**2,019.2**	**1,246.5**	**3,739.2**	**4,358.1**	**6,820.6**	**4,104.7**
FDI	286.7	628.5	694.6	953.5	2,225.6	3,540.4
Portfolio investment	−73.0	−145.9	−26.2	1,721.3	1,595.0	−88.7
Other investment	1,805.5	763.9	3,070.8	1,683.3	3,000.0	653.0
CE	**9,282.0**	**8,362.5**	**18,801.5**	**12,146.0**	**10,403.0**	**18,717.0**
FDI	3,706.0	2,689.0	8,375.0	6,493.0	6,359.0	10,676.0
Portfolio investment	1,034.0	198.5	2,765.5	1,701.0	3,445.0	5,265.0
Other investment	4,542.0	5,475.0	7,661.0	3,952.0	599.0	2,776.0

n.a. = not available.
Sources: WIIW and IMF (Country Reports).

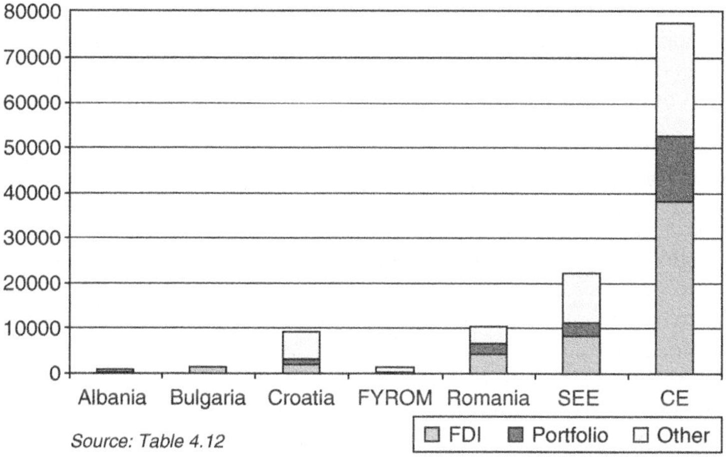

Source: Table 4.12

Figure 4.7 Net cumulative capital inflows 1993–98 (in US$ mil.)

CE, it was by far the dominant form of capital inflow, reaching more than US$38 billion.

The inability of the economies of SEE to obtain access to foreign capital primarily reflected the limited success of the stabilization effort and the slow progress of structural reform. In particular, significant access to capital markets cannot occur without the introduction of credible stabilization programmes that would enhance foreign investors' confidence, while FDI is more likely to be directed to countries with a strong reform commitment which is combined with attractive investment opportunities. This limited access to foreign capital, in turn, diminished the growth prospects of these countries, and this was one of the reasons for the rather disappointing economic performance of the region. This is particularly true of FDI since it has been found that it enhances economic growth more than the other forms of capital inflows. Note that a more detailed analysis of the FDI inflows into the region will be presented in Chapter 9.

Another important issue, which was closely related to the low level of private capital inflows into the region, had to do with the question of sustainability of the current account deficits of the particular countries. That is to say, lack of FDI, the basic non-debt creating source of finance, together with limited access to external borrowing, meant that official financing as well as foreign assistance had to carry the bulk of the current account financing needs. Thus, for most South East European economies, in contrast to the experience of the ones in CE, net private capital flows made little contribution to financing current account imbalances, leaving most of the financing to official funds. This, in turn, raises the issue of external vulnerability for the countries of the region, particularly as foreign official assistance has recently been declining. This is an issue that we are going to examine in some detail for the more recent period in the next chapter where two more countries of the region with serious external sustainability problems will be added to our analysis: Bosnia and Herzegovina, and Serbia and Montenegro.

Concluding remarks

The first decade of transition was not as successful for the economies of SEE with respect to macroeconomic stabilization and performance. In particular, none of these economies, with the possible exception of Croatia, was able to overcome the initial output decline and move to a path of sustained economic growth. Macroeconomic stabilization was particularly problematic for most of them and this was clearly manifested by the financial crises that emerged. Overall, the poor economic performance of most South East European economies was not only due to inconsistent stop–go polices but also to the lack of coherent reform measures. As a matter of fact, slow reform measures severely restricted the effectiveness of macroeconomic stabilization. The slow reform in enterprise restructuring, for instance, which led to excessive reliance on soft budget constraints and delays in banking reform as well, significantly contributed to the emergence of the financial crises and to the considerable undermining of the urgently needed macroeconomic adjustment. A detailed analysis concerning progress with respect to structural reform measures will be presented in Chapter 6.

Generally speaking, the policy approach of rapid liberalization accompanied by austerity measures for the achievement of quick macroeconomic stabilization and sustained economic recovery did not have the expected results in the region of SEE. Most of the countries of SEE were not prepared to deal effectively with the consequences of the rather fast opening of their economies. Moreover, the requirement for relatively quick restructuring and, thus, increasing reliance on the market mechanism was far from being fulfilled. As indicated earlier in the book, other factors that contributed to the disappointing performance of the economies of SEE, particularly in relation to the economies of CE, included the more adverse inherited economic distortions, the lack of adequate institutional development and the relative geographic isolation.[25]

Finally, the emergence of political instability and major armed conflicts in the region during the period under consideration constituted an additional and particularly important destabilizing factor. More specifically, the break-up of the SFR of Yugoslavia and the subsequent conflicts in Croatia and BH considerably affected the region's economic performance. The impact of the Kosovo War will be examined in the next chapter.

5
Macroeconomic Stabilization and Performance II: The Period after the Kosovo War

The first decade of transition (i.e., the last decade of the twentieth century) had been exceptionally difficult for the people and the countries of SEE. Hostilities, particularly as a result of ethnic conflicts, the considerable lack of political consensus, poor democratic traditions and absence of strong institutions have all largely constrained the degree of economic and political progress in most South East European countries. Thus, as pointed out in the previous chapter, the region experienced a disappointing economic performance, which also reflected ineffective implementation of stabilization and reform programmes, causing, as a result, rising unemployment and declining living standards.

The prospects for the future of the countries of SEE appeared to be much more favourable at the turn of the new century. For one thing, the end of the Kosovo War seemed to have brought lasting peace in the area, a vital precondition for the development of the region. Furthermore, the countries made a much stronger commitment towards reform and consistent macroeconomic stabilization. Finally, the international community in general and the EU in particular have been determined to assist the formulation and implementation of such policies and encourage the region's integration into the world economy.

In this chapter the analysis of macroeconomic stabilization and performance covers to the period from the Kosovo War until the present day. Furthermore, we include two more South East European states that were left out in the previous chapter: Bosnia and Herzegovina (BH) and Serbia and Montenegro (SM). As explained, the war and political instability that prevailed in the particular countries during most of the 1990s in effect prevented the transition process from effectively getting started. Thus, our analysis in this chapter extends to all seven countries of the region.

The economic impact of the Kosovo conflict

The economic implications of the Kosovo War were not as severe as initially expected. This was primarily due to the relatively short duration of the conflict as well as to the substantial relief provided through foreign assistance. Nevertheless, the economic impact was particularly devastating for SM, while it constituted an especially strong negative external shock for the economies of the neighbouring countries. The fact that the economies of most surrounding countries were still particularly fragile when the war occurred, constituted a significant enough reason for the rather considerable worsening of their economic conditions.

The most direct and destructive impact was inflicted on the economy of SM. The entire infrastructure of the particular country almost collapsed. According to Group-17, the total economic damage caused to the economy of SM was estimated at US$30 billion.[1] More specifically, industrial production and total GDP for 1999 were estimated to have declined by about 45 and 40 per cent relative to their 1998 levels. Per capita GDP dropped to one-third of its 1989 level in 1999, and from about half of what it had been in 1998. Furthermore, export receipts were estimated to have been cut in half in 1999 when compared to their 1998 level.

The impact of the crisis on the neighbouring countries, although considerably less damaging, was significant enough to adversely affect output growth in 1999. The refugee problem, created by the large outflow of people from Kosovo into the surrounding countries, constituted an almost instant consequence of the war which generated an immediate strain on the economies of the neighbouring countries, particularly Albania and FYROM,[2] so that although a large part of the support to refugees came from foreign agencies, the already fragile fiscal position of the host countries deteriorated further due to the rise in spending.

Besides the refugee problem, the impact of the war on the trade flows and infrastructure links constituted the main channels through which the crisis affected the region. The neighbouring countries lost markets in SM and this reflected, on the one hand, the enormous damage to the economy and, on the other, the almost complete destruction of the transport links. FYROM was hit hardest since SM was the destination of about 20 per cent of its total exports.[3] SM was also significant export market for BH, Bulgaria and Romania. The disruption of transport routes was particularly damaging as well and resulted in considerable losses for FYROM, Albania and Bulgaria. Croatia was primarily hit through the decline in tourist receipts. Furthermore, the war affected the confidence of investors and this constrained access to international financial markets, raising the cost of borrowing for the particular countries, but these conditions eased rather quickly. Finally, the impact of the war on the inflow of FDI into the region was temporary and rather weak.

The combined effects of all these negative factors generated a serious macroeconomic impact comprising a severe balance of payments shock, a decline in real output, deterioration in the fiscal position and increased unemployment. Estimates regarding the cost of the war for the individual countries could not be made easily due to lack of accurate information and to methodological difficulties as well. In a study by Gligorov and Sundstrom (1999), the impact of the Kosovo conflict was treated as an external shock that adversely affected the aggregate demand curve. According to them, the likely costs of the war to the surrounding countries possibly ranged from 1 to 5 percentage points of their GDP growth rates in 1999. Similar results for the individual countries are also found by EBRD (1999). Furthermore, according to EBRD (1999), the weighted average growth for the region for 1999 fell from 0.3 per cent just before the beginning of the war to −1.1 per cent in August of the same year.

A positive side effect, which occurred as a result of the Kosovo War, resulted from the fact that the international community decided to play a more active role in alleviating the region's economic problems as well as in responding to the urgent need for reconstruction. As a result, a new initiative took place according to which the international community as well as the countries of the region committed themselves to a renewed effort in order to create conditions of peace, stability and prosperity in SEE. This initiative led to the launching of the 'Stability Pact for South-Eastern Europe' which provided a framework that would lead to the long-term security and stability in the region. The strategic perspective of the Pact was to bring together the countries of the region, Western donor countries and international organizations for the achievement of these objectives. More specifically, the Stability Pact included all EU member states and G-8 countries, Albania, BH, Bulgaria, Croatia, Hungary, Romania, Slovenia, FYROM, Turkey and almost all major international organizations and regional initiatives which were active in the region.[4] The Pact also declared that SM would become a full and equal participant in the Stability Pact following the political settlement of Kosovo (Article 11, paragraph 2).

The economic integration of the region, within itself and into the European and global structures, particularly the European Union, was the prime objective of the Pact. In fact, the role of the EU was essential to draw the countries of the region closer to the prospect of European integration as a way of promoting reform and intra-regional integration. In the context of the Pact, the key element of the EU's strategy was the signing of Stability and Association Process whose main instrument was the Stability and Association Agreements with five countries of the region: Albania, BH, Croatia, FYROM and SM.[5] The Stability and Association Process, however, imposed certain demanding conditions on the particular countries in order to open negotiations on the new association agreements. These conditions referred to progress in democratization and economic reform, while emphasizing the need for intra-regional cooperation.[6] Furthermore, the major donors assigned the European Commission and the World Bank the task of coordinating economic assistance to the region. To support this coordination the donor community put together a High-Level Steering Group (HLSG) which was chaired by the European Commission and the World Bank.

Macroeconomic performance

The analysis in Chapter 4 clearly indicated that the economic performance of the countries of SEE during the period 1989–98 was disappointing. This was reflected in the overall slow progress in establishing a functional market economy, achieving macroeconomic stability and thus fostering economic growth. Specifically, among other things, the poor economic performance has been the result of the adverse initial conditions, the hesitant and, in some cases, inconsistent implementation of economic policies and reform programmes. In addition, hostilities, political instability, and the lack of a strong tradition in democratic institutions had a considerably adverse impact as well. In this respect, the Kosovo War constituted a major event which had a destabilizing impact on the economies of the region and led to further setbacks for structural reform and macroeconomic stabilization. Note, however, that, although at the end of the war most of the countries were facing particularly challenging economic problems, their determination to take the necessary policy measures that would allow them to improve overall economic performance was strengthened. This, as indicated, was further encouraged by the prompt response of the international community which came to assist this renewed effort.

Thus, the post-war period has been characterized by a consistent effort by all countries of the region to try to generate conditions for long-term growth. This, in turn, meant that domestic policies were directed towards achieving and safeguarding macroeconomic stability as well as generating a structural reform momentum. For the two largest economies of the region (i.e., Bulgaria and Romania), the challenge of joining the EU as full members by 2007 constituted the major driving force for macroeconomic stabilization and further reform. For the countries of the former Yugoslav Republic and Albania, with the exception of Croatia, stabilization and reform were essential policy priorities in order to generate the necessary conditions for sustainable growth that would eventually make their economies less fragile and thus less dependent on international aid.

Output and inflation developments

Economic growth in the countries of SEE recovered in 2000 and continued strongly until 2003, despite the slowdown of the world economy. Table 5.1 reports the growth rates of the particular countries during the 1998–2003

Table 5.1 Growth in real GDP

	1998	1999	2000	2001	2002	2003	Estimated level of real GDP in 2003 (1989=100)
Albania	12.7	8.9	7.7	6.9	4.7	6.0	129.0
BH	15.6	9.6	5.6	4.5	5.5	3.5	57.0
Bulgaria	4.0	2.3	5.4	4.0	4.8	4.3	84.0
Croatia	2.5	−0.9	2.9	3.8	5.2	4.3	91.0
FYROM	3.4	4.3	4.5	−4.5	0.7	3.1	78.0
Romania	−4.8	−1.2	1.8	5.3	4.9	5.0	92.0
SM	1.9	−18.0	5.0	5.5	4.0	3.0	52.0
SEE[a]	*0.3*	*−2.2*	*3.4*	*4.4*	*4.8*	*4.3*	*86.0*
CE[a]	*4.0*	*3.8*	*4.2*	*2.0*	*2.1*	*3.3*	*130.0*

[a] Weighted average: the region's growth was calculated by using current nominal GDP, expressed in terms of US dollars, as weights.
Source: EBRD (2004b).

period. As a matter of fact, the average rate of growth in SEE has been greater that that of the five Central European countries (Table 5.1). The only exception is FYROM, where the ethnic conflict led to a fall in output in 2001 and to moderate growth in 2002. The stable environment that emerged after the war, particularly in the states of the former Yugoslav republic, permitted the continuation of the stabilization and reform process in the region, which considerably improved the economic environment. Furthermore, it directly contributed to economic growth by helping domestic demand and industrial production to recover while, at the same time, allowing intra-regional trade to grow as well. In addition, the increased ties between the countries of SEE and the EU, and the donors' support to the five former Yugoslav republics and Albania, have also played a significant role in meeting financing needs and thus sustaining the momentum of growth.

The average yearly growth for the region has been well above 4 per cent since 2000. Albania continued to achieve high rates of growth and it is the only country of the region whose level of GDP was above the 1989 level at the end of 2003. Romania eventually came out of the three-year consecutive output decline and reported positive output growth in 2000, which accelerated considerably during the following three years. Bulgaria's growth has been particularly strong during the entire period, largely reflecting the firm steps that have been taken with respect to stabilization and the reform process. FYROM experienced a significant drop in output in 2001 as a result of the domestic civil crisis. The crisis, however, proved to be temporary and as a result monetary stability was maintained while positive output growth resumed in 2002. The output recovery in Bosnia and Herzegovina as well as in Serbia and Montenegro has been significant. Agricultural output recovery, the high level of reconstruction and foreign aid have all helped the two countries to achieve positive rates of output growth. Finally, Croatia, the richest country in the region, has been quite successful in achieving a relatively high level of integration into the world economy. Increased tourist receipts as well as strong domestic demand significantly contributed to Croatia's positive growth rates after the year 2000. Croatia's economic progress was manifested by the fact that it was given EU candidate status by the European Council in June 2004 (EBRD 2004b).

Inflationary trends in the region have clearly been on a downward trend. Table 5.2 reports the inflation rates of the countries of the region for the period 1998–2003. Since 1999, the majority of these countries have reduced their average inflation rate to single figures. Romania and SM constituted the two notable exceptions. In the case of Romania, inflation has proved to be rather stubborn, declining gradually, largely reflecting adjustments in administrative prices as well as slow implementation of tighter policy measures. In the case of SM, the price liberalization that took place in 2000 was the primary reason for the jump in inflation. Another point that comes out of Table 5.2 refers to the fact that the Federation and Republika Srpska, the two entities of BH, appeared to have quite divergent inflation rates, particularly during the years 1999 and 2000. Afterwards, however, the two inflation rates converged significantly on a downward trend, reflecting a deceleration of inflation in the Republika Srpska, clearly manifesting the increased economic integration between the two entities.

The effective disinflation policy of the countries of the region has been largely due to monetary and exchange rate policies that were firmly oriented towards price stability. In particular, with respect to the exchange rate, all the countries of the region (either formally or informally) continued to rely on exchange rate stability. More specifically, the currencies of Bulgaria and

Table 5.2 Annual inflation rates (Period average in consumer price level, %)

	1998	**1999**	**2000**	**2001**	**2002**	**2003**
Albania	20.6	0.4	0.1	3.1	5.2	2.4
BH						
Federation	5.1	−0.9	1.9	1.9	−0.2	−0.5
Republika Srpska	−14.0	14.1	14.0	7.0	1.7	1.9
Bulgaria	22.2	0.7	9.9	7.4	5.9	2.3
Croatia	5.7	4.2	6.2	4.9	2.4	1.8
FYROM	0.5	−1.3	6.5	5.3	2.4	1.1
Romania	59.1	45.8	45.7	34.5	22.5	15.4
SM	29.5	37.1	60.4	91.3	21.4	11.2
SEE[a]	*22.9*	*14.5*	*21.5*	*24.4*	*9.9*	*5.7*
CE[a]	*10.3*	*7.2*	*8.9*	*7.0*	*3.8*	*3.9*

[a] Unweighted average. BH is not included.
Source: EBRD (2004b).

more recently BH have been formally linked to the euro through a currency board regime. The remaining countries, although the exchange rate regimes in most of them are officially described as managed float, in practice are aiming at exchange rate stability. In Romania, the central bank aims at an annual exchange rate target consistent with the inflation target and modest real appreciation. In Albania, although the exchange rate regime is classified as an independent floating, its currency has been informally pegged to the US dollar. The use of the exchange rate as a nominal anchor has been a vital part of the stabilization policies in Croatia and FYROM. In particular, in the case of FYROM, the National Bank was quite successful in defending the anchor of the denar to the euro during the domestic crisis of 2001. In SM, the need for macroeconomic stability relied on tight monetary policies and exchange rate stability. Note that in Montenegro and Kosovo the euro has been circulating as legal tender. In the former it is the sole legal tender, while in the later the dinar, the currency of SM, remains the legal tender as well. The role of the euro with respect to the exchange rate regimes of the countries of SEE will be examined in Chapter 10.

Fiscal policy

Fiscal as well as external imbalances have been the two most serious macroeconomic policy challenges for the economies of SEE. First, with respect to fiscal policy, Table 5.3 reports general government balances before grants, as well as the corresponding government revenues and expenditures for each country of SEE for the period 1999–2003. The overall average deficit for the region initially was quite high, but then there was considerable improvement in fiscal discipline. Gradual fiscal consolidation has clearly been a very significant development, which allowed the implementation of appropriate monetary policies leading, as a result, to an effective disinflation process. Bulgaria and Romania, the two candidate countries for EU accession in 2007, have been more successful in controlling fiscal imbalances. This has been particularly true for Bulgaria where, due to the currency board regime, fiscal policy has been vital to macroeconomic stability. BH, the other country of the region with a currency board regime, has improved its fiscal position considerably; however, it remains fragile particularly due to large public debt stock. As we will see below, BH's large fiscal deficits were mostly financed by external grants. FYROM experienced a considerable worsening of its fiscal position due to the increase in military spending caused by the internal ethnic conflict, but the situation improved considerably in 2003. Fiscal deficits in SM were low in 2001 and 2002, primarily reflecting a lower level of spending due to delays in receiving revenues from privatization and foreign financial assistance, but also due to large quasi-fiscal activities and arrears accumulation.[7] Finally, there has been a gradual but steady improvement in Albania's fiscal position.

The improved fiscal positions, despite the more efficient revenue performance and higher collection rates, mostly reflected the gradual convergence

Table 5.3 General government balance (before grants, % of GDP)

	1999	2000	2001	2002	2003[a]
Albania					
Revenues	22.7	22.8	22.2	22.1	23.0
Expenditures	34.8	31.9	30.4	29.0	28.5
Fiscal balance	−12.1	−9.1	−8.2	−6.9	−5.5
BH					
Revenues	48.0	46.3	44.4	46.5	46.4
Expenditures	70.4	66.0	57.6	56.2	52.8
Fiscal balance	−22.4	−19.7	−13.2	−9.7	−6.4
Bulgaria					
Revenues	37.6	37.9	36.4	35.6	36.0
Expenditures	39.5	39.7	38.4	37.2	36.8
Fiscal balance	−1.9	−1.8	−2.0	−1.6	−0.8
Croatia					
Revenues	48.4	46.1	44.7	45.2	44.9
Expenditures	56.6	52.7	51.5	50.0	49.5
Fiscal balance	−8.2	−6.6	−6.8	−4.8	−4.6
FYROM					
Revenues	34.2	35.4	34.2	35.8	34.0
Expenditures	35.4	34.9	41.6	41.5	36.5
Fiscal balance	−1.2	0.5	−7.4	−5.7	−2.5
Romania					
Revenues	31.9	31.2	30.1	29.7	30.4
Expenditures	35.5	35.3	33.4	32.3	33.1
Fiscal balance	−3.6	−4.1	−3.3	−2.6	−2.7
SM					
Revenues	n.a.	36.0	38.2	41.7	39.8
Expenditures	n.a.	37.6	40.3	47.3	45.1
Fiscal balance	n.a.	−1.6	−2.1	−5.6	−5.3

[a] Estimates.
n.a. = not available.
Sources: EBRD (2004b) and WIIW database.

of expenditure towards more sustainable levels (see Table 5.3). This was more profound in the cases of BH and Croatia, where the ratio of government spending to GDP was in excess of 50 per cent. Note, however, that for countries with a lower ratio of public expenditure to GDP, such as Albania, FYROM and Romania, further improvement in the fiscal position would require a further strengthening of the tax system and broadening of the tax bases.

Figure 5.1 illustrates the way that each of the countries of SEE financed their fiscal deficits during the 1999–2003 period. One general remark concerns the fact that, in contrast to the initial transition period, the monetization of fiscal deficits has been virtually eliminated. The main sources of financing for the fiscal deficits involve external grants, internal borrowing from banks or

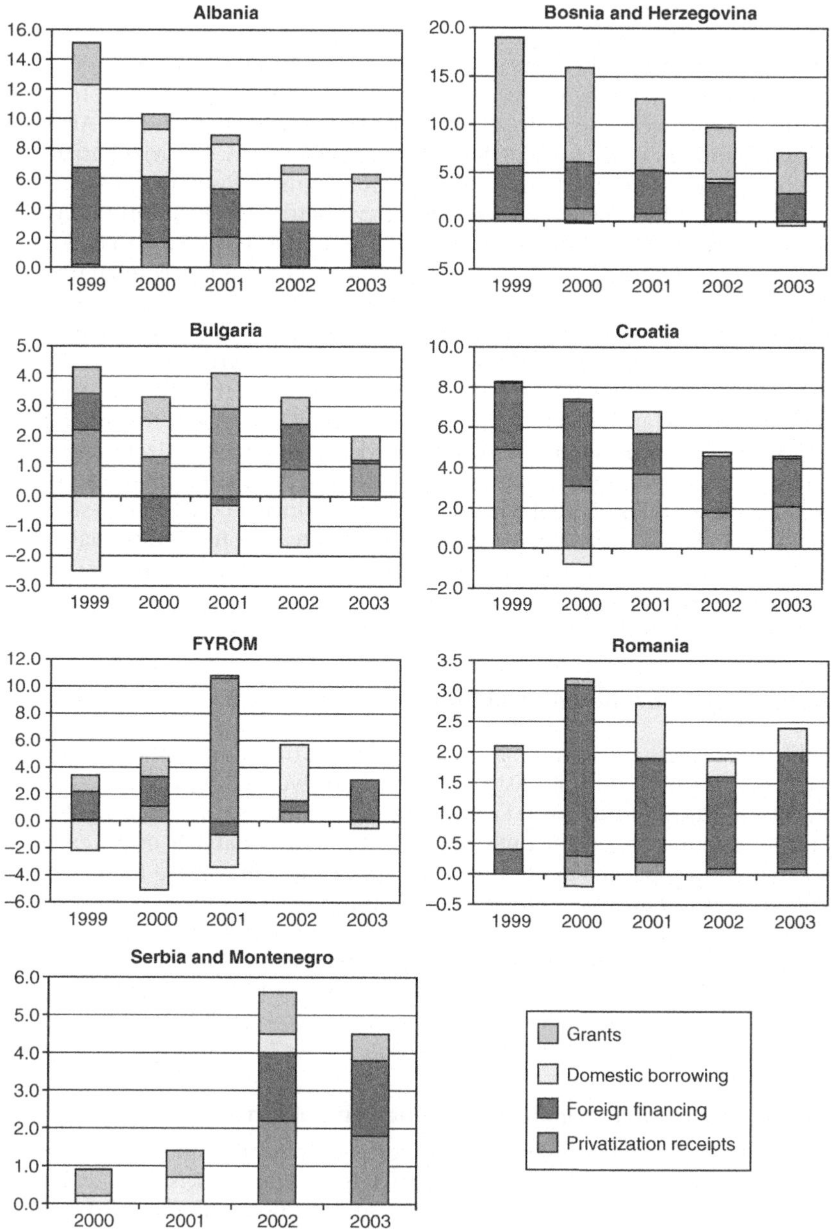

Source: WIIW database and IMF Country Reports

Figure 5.1 The financing of fiscal deficits

households, foreign borrowing and privatization receipts. The international community has played a significant role in assisting some of the countries of SEE to maintain fiscal sustainability although, to differing extents, all the countries have received considerable budgetary support in the form of grants. Grants were the main source of finance for BH and also for Albania, Bulgaria and SM during the period under consideration. Internal borrowing has been important to Albania and to a minor degree to Romania. Note for the two countries that operate under a currency board regime, BH and Bulgaria, borrowing from the central bank is not allowed. Furthermore, in FYROM and SM Treasury bills and bonds have not been introduced as yet. Foreign finance has been important in most of the countries of the region, given the limited availability of domestic resources. In countries such as Albania, BH and SM, which have limited borrowing capacity, at least part of the external borrowing has been provided at favourable terms.[8] On the other hand, for countries such as Croatia (and, to a lesser degree, Romania), external borrowing reflected better access to international capital markets. Finally, privatization receipts have gained importance in some countries of the region as public enterprises were being sold. This is a vital source of finance since it constitutes a significant part of FDI inflows which provide non-debt creating funds essential to the growth prospects of particular countries. It is, however, a rather irregular source of funding and, among the countries of the region, only Croatia has managed to have a steady inflow of privatization receipts.

Assessing external vulnerability

Table 5.4 reports the current account deficits of the countries of SEE during the period 1999–2003. Persistently high and even rising current account deficits for most of the South East European economies constitute a very serious policy concern, raising questions about the sustainability of the external position of the particular countries which, in turn, may have increased the vulnerability of at least some of these economies to external crises. In this section we shall attempt to address this very important issue by trying to assess the external vulnerability of the particular economies to balance of payments crises. More specifically, we will look into key variables, the so-called external vulnerability indicators, which convey information on the external vulnerability of the particular economies.[9]

External vulnerability indicators: some general remarks

According to several studies, the problem of external vulnerability for the transition economies has been primarily reflecting weak solvency fundamentals as well as lack of liquidity.[10] Our analysis will follow the same methodology and will rely on a narrow set of external vulnerability indicators, which can be divided into two categories: solvency indicators and liquidity indicators.

Table 5.4 Current account balance (before grants, % of GDP)

	1999	2000	2001	2002	2003[a]
Albania	−7.9	−7.4	−6.2	−9.0	−8.4
BH	−26.3	−13.3	−16.1	−20.4	−15.7
Bulgaria	−5.3	−5.6	−6.2	−4.4	−8.3
Croatia	−7.0	−2.5	−3.7	−7.2	−6.8
FYROM	−2.9	−5.8	−8.2	−11.3	−5.4
Romania	−3.6	−3.9	−5.5	−3.4	−6.1
SM	−7.5	−7.1	−9.7	−12.8	−11.6

[a] Estimates.
Sources: WIIW database and IMF staff Country Reports.

First, with respect to solvency, a country is solvent when the net present value of its future stream of current account surpluses is at least equal to its outstanding stock of net external debt. Thus the first variable, which is vital to external vulnerability, refers to the stock of net external debt, which is normally scaled by two different variables: GDP and exports of goods and non-factor services (GNFS). Next, the existence of solid fundamentals is necessary in order to generate favourable conditions in the external sector and thus preserve solvency by reducing the vulnerability of a country. Since the fundamentals (otherwise known as solvency indicators) are used to evaluate whether the trends developed in the external sector help a country to remain solvent, this means that evolution of variables such as the current account balance, the export growth and the real exchange rate is of vital importance. More specifically, reduced current account deficits lead to lower external borrowing and thus slow down the accumulation of foreign liabilities. High export growth means smaller debt service, when the latter is expressed as a percentage of external receipts, for a given current account deficit, while changes in the real exchange rate affect the future path of the current account deficit. Note that the trend of these fundamentals, given the size of the external debt, largely reflects the extent of sustainability of the balance of payments: that is, solvency primarily means external debt sustainability which is enhanced when the external debt stock to GDP ratio follows a declining trend. Thus current account deficits that can be financed through non-debt creating financial flows, such as FDI, allow a country to preserve or even improve (in the case of positive output growth) external sustainability. In our analysis we will use two more solvency indicators in order to address the sustainability question as well. In particular, we will use the external debt service to exports (goods and services) ratio, in order to evaluate the burden imposed by the external debt obligations and the current account position after official transfers and FDI. The latter is particularly important since, as pointed out, it constitutes the biggest source of non-debt creating flows.

Liquidity indicators are important since high liquidity may counterbalance the increased vulnerability of a country due to weak fundamentals: higher liquidity can, for instance, limit the adverse impact of high current account deficits and of an appreciating real exchange rate.[11] Thus liquidity indicators could be either reinforcing or offsetting the impact of the solvency indicators. International reserves constitute a vital indicator of liquidity, and in particular the reserves to short-term debt ratio. Adequate reserve coverage of short-term debt reduces external vulnerability, enabling a country to effectively service its immediate debt obligations, particularly in periods of contagion. A rule of thumb of reserves to short-term ratio being equal to one, for countries with modest current account deficits and slightly appreciated exchange rates, has been suggested by Greenspan (1999) and supported empirically by Brussiere and Mulder (1999). Two other important scale measures of reserves, which are commonly used for the purpose of accessing liquidity, refer to reserves to imports and reserves to broad money ratios. The latter is particularly important for countries with fixed exchange rate regimes since it captures the potential for capital flight by the residents.

The external vulnerability of the South Eastern Europe economies

Table 5.5 reports the vulnerability indicators for each of the seven economies of SEE. The indicators included are the ones we analysed in the previous section and refer to period 1999–2003. Note that the figures for 2003 are preliminary. In this section we analyse the trend in the particular vulnerability indicators for each country in the region. Our aim is to assess short-term external vulnerability of the particular economies and examine whether it has improved during the period under consideration.

Albania's external vulnerability indicators suggest that Albania's short-term external vulnerability remains low despite the high current account deficits. In particular the current account deficit before official transfers has been running at a high level over the entire period, reaching 9 per cent of GDP in 2002 and about 8.5 per cent in 2003. Note, however that official grants and FDI inflows reduced the deficit to 3.7 per cent in 2002 and to around 3 per cent in 2003. Albania's external debt has been low, falling well below 25 per cent of GDP by the end of 2003. Thus, despite the widening current account deficits, the external debt to GDP ratio has been declining. This, on the one hand, reflects the high rates of output growth of the economy (Table 5.1) and, on the other, the significant role of official transfers and FDI in reducing the need for external financing. As a result, there is no significant concern with respect to short-term sustainability of the external debt as well. This is also reflected by the relatively low external debt service to exports ratio. Furthermore, export growth has been satisfactory, contributing to the steady decline in the external debt to exports ratio. The indicators of liquidity position are rather favourable. More specifically,

Table 5.5 External vulnerability indicators for the countries of SEE

	1999	2000	2001	2002	2003[a]
Albania					
External debt (% of GDP)	32.3	31.8	28.2	24.4	23.3
Exernal debt (% of exports)	203.6	166.2	142.8	128.7	129.5
Exernal debt service (% of exports of GNFS)	3.8	4.0	4.2	6.4	5.1
Current account balance (% of GDP)	−7.9	−7.4	−6.2	−9.0	−8.4
Current account balance after official grants (% of GDP)	−3.9	−4.4	−3.2	−6.5	−6.3
Current account balance after official grants and FDI (% of GDP)	−2.4	−0.5	1.6	−3.7	−3.1
Exports of GNFS (% change, in terms of US dollars)	47.0	5.8	14.1	7.0	n.a.
Real effective exchange rate appreciation (CPI-based)	12.3	7.0	4.3	−0.5	−3.8
Gross International Reserves (GIR) in months of imports	3.8	4.2	4.3	4.3	4.4
GIR in per cent of broad money	20.0	30.0	30.0	30.0	20.0
Short-term external debt in per cent of GIR	4.4	3.4	2.8	5.2	4.7
Bosnia and Herzegovina					
External debt (% of GDP)	66.2	62.8	50.0	41.2	34.7
Exernal debt (% of exports of GNFS)	269.0	213.3	179.7	155.3	140.6
Exernal debt service (% of exports of GNFS)	13.8	11.2	5.8	8.4	9.3
Current account balance (% of GDP)	−26.3	−13.3	−16.1	−20.4	−15.7
Current account balance after official grants (% of GDP)	−12.8	−3.7	−8.3	−15.2	−13.7
Current account balance after official grants and FDI (% of GDP)	−9.0	−0.4	−5.6	−10.8	−9.2
Exports of GNFS (% change, in terms of US dollars)	2.1	−0.8	0.0	6.4	23.8
Real effective exchange rate appreciation (CPI-based)	4.0	3.0	−7.4	−3.9	n.a.
GIR in months of imports	1.9	2.1	5.0	4.7	4.5
GIR in per cent of broad money	40.3	41.6	59.0	49.3	45.1
Bulgaria					
External debt (% of GDP)	78.7	88.9	78.1	70.3	57.2
Exernal debt (% of exports of GNFS)	176.1	160.0	141.1	133.9	108.2
Exernal debt service (% of exports of GNFS)	19.2	16.4	17.3	14.7	12.2

Table 5.5 (Continued)

	1999	**2000**	**2001**	**2002**	**2003**[a]
Current account balance (% of GDP)	−5.3	−5.6	−6.2	−4.4	−8.3
Current account balance after FDI (% of GDP)	1.2	2.4	−1.2	−1.4	−1.6
Exports of GNFS (% change, in terms of US dollars)	−3.2	20.8	7.7	9.9	30.0
Real effective exchange rate appreciation (CPI-based)	2.0	2.7	4.7	4.4	5.7
GIR in months of imports	5.3	5.4	5.0	5.8	4.8
GIR in per cent of broad money	83.1	73.5	63.8	63.9	55.0
Short-term external debt in per cent of GIR	19.4	22.6	34.0	32.8	30.0
Croatia					
External debt (% of GDP)	49.6	60.0	58.0	68.2	83.5
Exernal debt (% of exports of GNFS)	123.0	127.5	117.5	145.6	201.3
Exernal debt service (% of exports of GNFS)	21.1	23.8	18.8	22.3	16.6
Current account balance (% of GDP)	−7.0	−2.5	−3.7	−7.2	−6.8
Current account balance after FDI (% of GDP)	0.1	3.4	3.5	−3.2	−1.0
Exports of GNFS (% change, in terms of US dollars)	−5.0	6.7	11.2	9.5	40.0
Real effective exchange rate appreciation (CPI-based)	−4.0	2.0	4.3	0.5	−1.5
GIR in months of imports of GNFS	3.7	4.4	5.2	5.6	5.6
GIR in per cent of broad money	41.0	39.0	37.0	36.0	36.0
Short-term external debt in per cent of GIR	60.0	64.4	50.0	38.5	36.0
FYROM					
External debt (% of GDP)	40.6	41.5	39.8	40.2	36.1
Exernal debt (% of exports of GNFS)	102.1	90.9	97.8	110.8	105.3
Exernal debt service (% of exports of GNFS)	13.7	13.0	19.3	16.6	12.8
Current account balance (% of GDP)	−2.9	−5.8	−8.2	−11.3	−5.4
Current account balance after official grants (% of GDP)	−0.9	−2.1	−6.8	−8.6	−4.3
Current account balance after official grants and FDI (% of GDP)	0.0	2.8	4.7	−6.5	−3.3
Exports of GNFS (% change, in terms of US dollars)	6.9	19.0	−12.5	−4.4	23.0
Real effective exchange rate appreciation (CPI-based)	2.9	−1.4	0.2	−1.0	0.3

GIR in months of imports of GNFS	2.9	3.7	4.6	4.1	4.1
GIR in per cent of broad money	67.1	89.9	65.6	59.1	56.7
Short-term external debt in per cent of GIR	39.2	27.2	33.3	31.8	28.6
Romania					
External debt (% of GDP)	25.9	27.7	31.0	33.6	35.7
Exernal debt (% of exports of GNFS)	93.4	84.7	93.5	94.0	94.1
Exernal debt service (% of exports of GNFS)	29.0	25.3	20.2	18.5	17.4
Current account balance (% of GDP)	−3.6	−3.9	−5.5	−3.4	−6.1
Current account balance after FDI (% of GDP)	−0.8	−0.9	−2.4	−0.9	−3.3
Exports of GNFS (% change, in terms of US dollars)	10.5	24.1	10.6	9.6	27.0
Real effective exchange rate appreciation (CPI-based)	−14.8	9.5	1.6	2.7	0.5
GIR in months of imports of GNFS	1.6	2.1	2.9	3.9	3.9
GIR in per cent of broad money	33.5	48.6	39.5	62.5	57.9
Short-term external debt in per cent of GIR	68.1	60.8	58.5	56.6	62.4
Serbia and Montenegro					
External debt (% of GDP)	105.2	132.5	103.2	76.1	68.5
Exernal debt (% of exports of GNFS)	500.0	448.0	435.5	365.0	360.0
Exernal debt service (% of exports of GNFS)	4.6	2.2	3.9	6.3	13.4
Current account balance (% of GDP)	−7.5	−7.1	−9.7	−12.8	−11.6
Current account balance after grants and FDI (% of GDP)	−6.4	−3.6	−3.1	−5.2	−4.5
Exports (% change, in terms of US dollars)	−44.7	14.7	10.4	19.5	20.7
Real effective exchange rate appreciation (CPI-based)	−27.0	−23.2	59.5	11.6	5.3
GIR in months of imports	0.9	1.5	2.7	4.4	5.3
GIR in per cent of broad money	30.0	50.0	73.0	72.0	79.0
Short-term external debt in per cent of GIR	341.7	229.8	91.4	53.7	45.0

[a] Estimates.
Sources: EBRD (2004b) and WIIW database.

the official reserves average more than 4 months of imports while the short-term debt to reserves ratio (in percentage terms) has been quite low. Note, however, that the ratio of official reserves to broad money is low as well.

The fragile economic situation in Bosnia and Herzegovina is reflected also in the external position of the country. The country has been running large current account deficits which would not have been sustainable if it were not for the external assistance which, in turn, contributed to high rates of output growth as well. More specifically, current account deficits remain above 15 per cent of GDP, adversely affecting external vulnerability. As pointed out, external assistance, by reducing the financing need of the deficit while, at the same time, boosting output growth, contributed to a falling external debt to output ratio which declined to about 35 per cent by the end of 2003. FDI inflows have also had a significant contribution in financing part of the current account deficit. Overall, the challenge for the economy of BH would be to lower external sector fragility by considerably reducing the current account deficit and, to this end, exports of goods and non-factor services need to excibit a lasting increase. This need is also reinforced by the fact that external assistance, particularly from the EU, has been declining considerably. The liquidity indicators are more favourable. Gross international reserves have increased to about $4\frac{1}{2}$ months of imports, while they were 45 per cent of broad money at the end of 2003. The short-term debt is a very small portion of the total debt and, as a result, its ratio to gross international reserves is not reported.

Bulgaria has been operating under a currency board and thus safeguarding external vulnerability is of vital importance to the sustainability of the particular exchange rate regime. Large current account deficits have been a serious policy concern since they averaged well above 5 per cent of GDP during the period under consideration, while exceeding the 8 per cent mark in 2003. Nevertheless, FDI inflows contributed significantly to the financing of the deficits, eliminating or sharply reducing the need for debt-creating funds. This, in conjunction with the strong output growth, led to a considerable reduction in the external debt to output ratio. As a matter of fact, the external debt dropped from almost 90 per cent of output in 2000 to below 60 per cent in 2003. The strong recovery in exports of goods and non-factor services after 1999, in spite of the weakening in price competitiveness, has further reduced vulnerability while strengthening the sustainability of external debt. In particular, with respect to sustainability, it led to a considerable decline in the external debt service which fell to about 12 per cent of exports of goods and non-factor services in 2003. Furthermore, the external debt as a portion of exports of GNFS decreased quite significantly as well, dropping to about 108 per cent in 2003 from 176 per cent in 1999. External liquidity is of vital importance to the Bulgarian economy since the increased volume of international capital flows could pose a significant threat to the currency board regime in the case of balance of payments crises. Short-term debt constitutes a relatively low portion of official reserves strengthening Bulgaria's liquidity. The only adverse development has been associated with the decline of the official reserves as a percentage of broad money, from 83 per cent in 1999 to 55 per cent in 2003.

Croatia's current account deficits have remained high on average during the period under consideration and this, in conjunction with the rising stock of external debt, has increased its external vulnerability. In particular, the current account deficit which stood at 7 per cent of GDP in 1999 fell over 2000 and 2001 but then widened again to 7.2 and 6.8 per cent of GDP in 2002 and 2003 respectively. External debt increased from about 50 per cent of GDP in 1999 to about 68 per cent in 2002 and to over 80 per cent in 2003. The increase of external debt to 60 per cent of GDP in 2000 primarily reflected the valuation effect due to a more than 15 per cent depreciation of the domestic currency *vis-à-vis* the US dollar. Note, however, that except for the period 2002–03, FDI inflows have been providing necessary funds which more than covered the financing of the current account deficits. In addition, exports have been growing rapidly since 1999, while the real exchange rate appreciation has been rather moderate. Overall, during the period under consideration, the solvency indicators suggest a modest increase of external vulnerability, primarily as a result of the increase in the external debt to GDP ratio. This is true with respect to the sustainability question as well. An improvement would require a lasting reduction in the current account deficit that would lead to lower external debt.

In contrast, external liquidity has increased over the period under consideration. International reserves increased to about six months of imports of goods and non-factor services. Short-term debt as a percentage of international reserves has fallen from 60 per cent in 1999 to about 36 per cent in 2003. Note, however, that the fall in this ratio also reflected the fact that Croatia's better access to capital markets made possible the replacement of short-term inflows with longer-term borrowing. Finally, international reserves declined modestly to 36 per cent of broad money in 2003. With respect to the increase in international reserves, we must point out the role of a new regulation according to which, since 1998, commercial banks are required to hold reserve deposits in foreign exchange with the central bank against their foreign currency deposits. Thus, part of the increase of the reserves reflected a rise in the stock of foreign currency liabilities of the monetary authorities to residents.

FYROM's growing current account deficits after 1999, which reached 11 per cent of GDP in 2002, constituted a serious concern to external vulnerability. Note, however, that during the period under consideration, with the exception of the year 2002, the inflows of official transfers and FDI have more than covered the current account deficits. This, in turn, explains the relative stability of external debt as a percentage of GDP. Overall, the impact of both the Kosovo War in 1999 and the internal ethnic conflict in 2001–2 have greatly contributed to the deterioration of most solvency indicators during the period 1999–2002. The effect of the particular conflicts, however, was temporary as there was a notable improvement in all indicators during 2003. Regarding the external liquidity position, the respective indicators remained rather favourable. International reserves averaged about four months of imports of goods and non-factor services. Short-term debt as a percentage of international reserves fell from about 39 per cent in 1999 to below 30 per cent in 2003. Finally, the international reserves as a percentage of broad money, although still high, have suffered a modest decline since 1999.

Romania has historically been running large current account deficits, which constituted the main threat to external vulnerability since its external indebtedness has been relatively low. Note, however, that the current account deficits have been lower during the period under consideration. As a matter of fact, they have been, on average, the lowest in the region. In addition, the need for external financing has been reduced even more when FDI receipts are included. Nevertheless, following the overall trend in the region, there was a marked deterioration of the current account deficit in 2003. The external debt stood at about 36 per cent of GDP and well below the 100 mark when expressed as a percentage of exports of goods and non-factor services at the end of 2003. Also, the rapid growth in exports during the period under consideration has further reduced external liquidity while it has enhanced the sustainability of external debt. External liquidity has been strengthened by the fact that international reserves increased to almost 4 months of imports in GNFS in 2003 from about 1.5 months in 1999. Furthermore, reserves have increased considerably as a percentage of broad money. On the other hand, external liquidity has weakened as the short-term external debt to reserves ratio increased in 2003. Overall, the liquidity indicators have not improved considerably during the period under consideration.

Serbia and Montenegro was the most indebted country of the region with an external debt reaching more than 130 per cent of GDP in 2000. The situation, however, improved considerably afterwards largely because of the role of foreign aid. External debt has been particularly high when expressed as a portion of exports in GNFS, also reflecting the very low level of exports, which started recovering after 1999. The large current account deficits have further contributed to the external fragility of SM, even though official grants and FDI inflows cover up a significant part of the financing needs. Turning to liquidity indicators, gross international reserves increased to more than 5 months of imports in 2003 from just 1 month in 1999. In addition, they increased from 30 per cent of broad money to almost 80 per cent in 2003, while short-term external debt declined from almost 350 per cent of official reserves in 1999 to 45 per cent in 2003. Overall, although the improvement in the external vulnerability indicators has been considerable, the external position of SM remains particularly fragile.

External vulnerability indicators in a regional perspective

Overall, the analysis indicated that external vulnerability indicators have improved for most of the countries of the region. With respect to external solvency indicators, the widening current account deficits constituted a serious concern while most of the remaining indicators followed an improving trend. The liquidity indicators appeared more favourable as well. An interesting exercise, however, will be to use comparative analysis and examine how the South East European region compares to the Central European region with respect to basic external vulnerability indicators. More specifically, in this section we will use each region's unweighted average in eight basic vulnerability indicators in order to access their relative vulnerability position. Furthermore, this will enable us to see how the particular vulnerability indicators in each country compare *vis-à-vis* the two regions' averages. In Figure 5.2, each of the eight charts corresponds to each of the eight indicators. We mostly rely on data for the year 2003 but for some variables the data for the particular year constitute preliminary estimates. Note that in each chart the horizontal line represents the average for the South East European region.

Starting our analysis with respect to solvency indicators, the external debt stock at the end of 2003, expressed as a percentage of GDP, appears in Chart 1. According to the particular Chart, the average external debt level of the region of SEE was at a comparable level with the corresponding level of CE (48.5 per cent compared to 46.5 per cent respectively). Three countries of the SEE region, Bulgaria, Croatia and SM, had an external debt to GDP ratio above the region's average, while Albania, BH, FYROM and Romania were the less indebted countries. Note that the external indebtedness of these four countries was below the CE average as well. In contrast, with respect to the current account deficit, the comparison is considerably less favourable for the South East European economies. Indeed, the unweighted average current account deficit over the period 2001–03, expressed as a percentage of GDP, was more than twice as large for the South East European countries relative to CE (8.9 per cent versus 3.7 per cent respectively). Note, however, that the large current account deficits of BH, and to a lesser extent for SM, have been the primary reason for the significant divergence between the two regions. On the other hand, there are countries in SEE, namely Bulgaria, Croatia and Romania, whose current account deficits have been of a size comparable to the Central European average.

An important variable, which was particularly unfavourable for the countries of the SEE during the first decade of transition, refers to FDI inflows (see the detailed analysis in Chapter 9 below). Chart 3 shows the average net FDI inflows as a percentage of GDP over the period 2001–03. The FDI inflows were higher in SEE relative to CE (4.5 per cent of GDP as compared to 4.2 per cent in CE). This primarily reflected the fact that the speeding-up of the privatization process led to the significant recovery of FDI into SEE, especially in 2003. This was particularly true for three countries, Bulgaria,

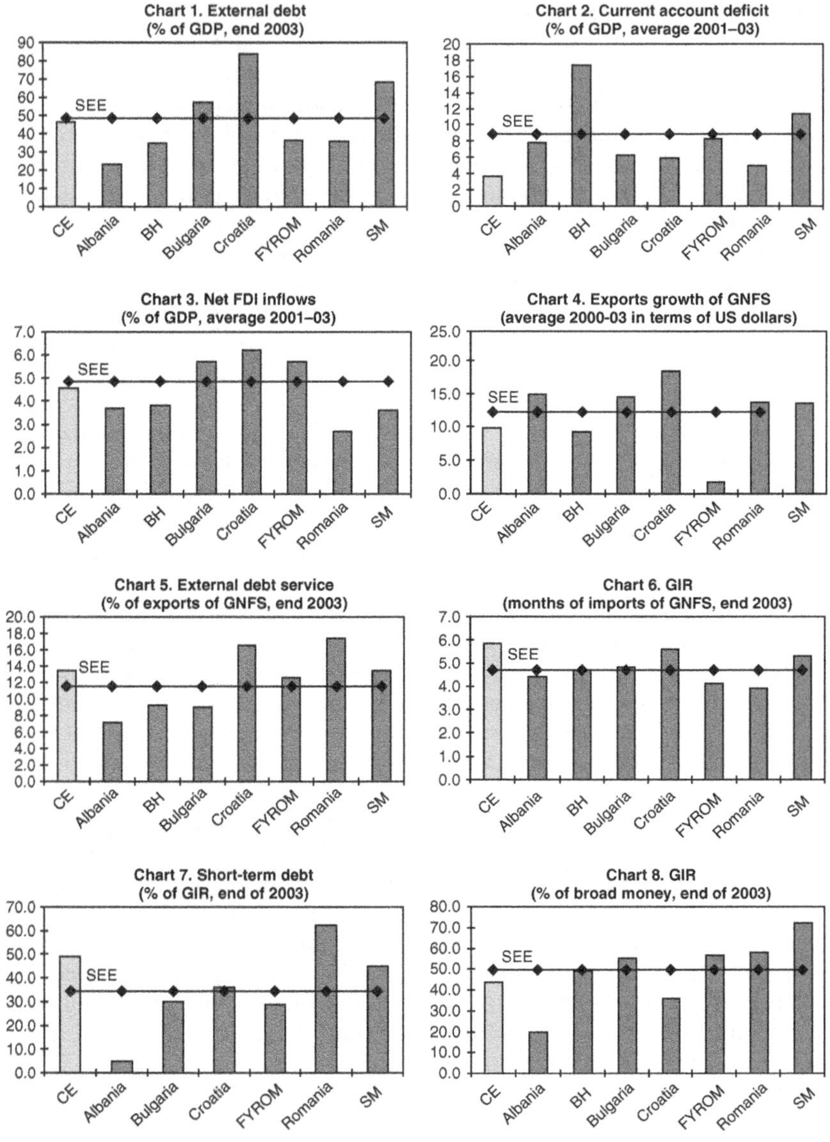

Sources: Table 5.5; EBRD (2004b); and WIIW database

Figure 5.2 External vulnerability indicators in regional perspective

Croatia and FYROM, which had inflows higher than the region's average. In Chart 4, the average export growth of goods and non-factor services over the period 2001–03 in SEE has been higher than the corresponding average of CE (13.5 per cent versus 10.7 per cent respectively). Note that the depreciation of the dollar in 2003 contributed to higher rates of growth in exports of GNFS since they are expressed in terms of US dollars. Finally, turning to Chart 5, the external debt service in percentage of exports of goods and non-factor services at the end of 2003 was marginally lower for SEE (12.2 per cent as compared to 13.4 per cent for CE). Overall, except maybe for the current account, the situation in SEE has improved and as a result the other solvency indicators do not differ significantly between the two regions. As a matter of fact, there are countries in SEE which perform better than the Central European average on most solvency indicators.

The last three charts refer to liquidity indicators. In particular, Chart 6 shows Gross International Reserves (GIR) in months of imports of goods and non-factor services at the end of 2003. The average for SEE was around 4.7 months of imports of goods and non-factor services, while the corresponding one for CE was just below 6 months. Chart 7 refers to short-term debt as a percentage of GIR at the end of 2003. This liquidity indicator was considerably more favourable for SEE since the average of the particular ratio stood at 35 per cent against about 50 per cent for CE. Finally, the last indicator was also more favourable. In particular, according to Chart 8, the GIR as a percentage of broad money averaged about 50 per cent for SEE (as compared to less than 45 per cent for CE) at the end of 2003.

Concluding this section, we should point out that the preceding analysis clearly indicated that the external vulnerability of the South East European economies has improved. Except for the current account deficits, most of the remaining indicators turned out to be more favourable, largely reflecting the better economic performance of the countries of the region during recent years. One, however, must be very cautious about interpreting some results, particularly when drawing comparisons with respect to the countries of CE. The economies of CE are more developed and more stable than their counterparts in SEE with a much easier access to international capital markets. Furthermore, the countries of CE have already become full members of the EU, which by itself considerably reduces the importance of external vulnerability for these countries. Thus, comparability or even better performance in some indicators for the South East European economies *vis-à-vis* the Central European ones does not necessarily mean similar or even lower external vulnerability.

Some concluding remarks

The macroeconomic performance of the region of SEE has improved considerably since the end of the Kosovo War. Output growth has been strong since the year 2000 while inflation rates, although continuing to vary across the region, have clearly been on a downward trend. As indicated, the fall in inflation was achieved mostly though continued reliance on exchange rate stability. In addition, all the countries of the region improved their fiscal positions since they were able to limit their fiscal deficits. The widening current account deficits constituted the only major concern since they were in excess of 5 per cent of GDP for all the countries of the region in 2003. Large trade imbalances have been primarily responsible for the current account deficits. As we will see in Chapter 7 below, high imports of goods, coupled with low competitiveness of the export sector together with the particularly low level of intra-regional trade, have all contributed to the region's high trade imbalances.

External vulnerability of the particular countries constituted another important issue, which we examined in some detail in this chapter. The widening of current account deficits and thus their sustainability constitutes a major challenge for most of the economies of the region. Our assessment was that, except for the marked deterioration of the external positions in 2003, the external vulnerability indicators have improved over the period under consideration. For one thing, the surge in FDI inflows, particularly in 2003, provided considerable resources for the financing of the current account deficits. In addition, external debt has been declining while exports in most counties appeared to follow a recovering trend. Furthermore, the liquidity indicators followed a favourable trend in most countries of the region as well. Political stability, particularly for the successor states of former Yugoslavia, constitutes an especially vital factor as well for external vulnerability. Finally, it must be remembered that the preceding analysis referred to the short-run external vulnerability. In the long run, current account deficits of the size that most South East European economies exhibited are clearly not sustainable unless decisive policy initiatives are taken.

As explained, the comparison with respect to vulnerability indicators between SEE and CE was an attempt to ascertain how the countries of the former region compare relative to more advanced economies of the latter, which have already become full members of the EU. The size of the current account deficits appeared to be the most significant difference between the two regions, while the other indicators were of comparable magnitude. As pointed out, however, the results must be interpreted with caution given the overall outlook of the economies of SEE relative to that of the ones in CE.

6
Structural Reform

Structural reform constitutes the essence of transition. It encompasses all the necessary adjustments for a successful transformation of the transition economies towards the market system. Its basic objective is directed at reallocating the resources of the particular economies so as to better reflect the influence of market forces correcting, as a result, for the distortions inherited from the previous regime. This reallocation, in spite of the output decline that it caused across all transition economies initially, brought about significant efficiency gains, a necessary precondition for the resumption of output growth. As we will see in the next chapter, a wide body of research suggests that the countries which attempted to correct more rapidly the distortions inherited from central planning were the ones that experienced a substantial and sustained improvement in economic performance as well as a faster reduction in inflation.

Reform progress has been uneven across transition economies. Especially for the countries of SEE, progress towards structural reform has been slow, particularly when compared to the advances made by the economies of CE. This was especially true during the first decade of transition, since reforms were characterized by the lack of commitment and slow implementation. This, as pointed out in previous chapters, contributed significantly to the poor economic performance of the region during the same period. After the Kosovo War the progress towards reform has accelerated, but for most of the countries there is still considerable distance to be covered.

Structural reform encompasses different dimensions of transition. In this chapter we will look into some different areas of structural reform and reveal the slow progress of the South East European economies. In particular we will examine the progress of the particular economies, mostly by relying on the transition indicators provided by the *Transition Reports* published by the European Bank for Reconstruction and Development (EBRD). More specifically, we will provide assessments with respect to the progress made in three key areas of structural reform: (a) privatization and restructuring; (b) market liberalization and competition; and (c) financial market reform.

In line with the EBRD's indicators, each of these areas of reform will include different indicators capturing the progress made in distinct aspects of each reform area. The EBRD's indicators range from 1, being the lowest score, to 4+, the highest score.[1] In the analysis that follows the transition indicators are linearized by assigning a value of +1/3 to a '+' sign and a value of −1/3 to a '−' sign.[2] Thus, for instance, a score of 3+ is expressed as 3.3, while a score of 3− is designated as 2.7.

Privatization and restructuring

Privatization and restructuring is of primary importance to transition economies since its key objective was the removal of state from enterprise ownership. It is in this respect that it was claimed that privatization 'is' transition (Brada 1996). In addition, it aims at improving the performance of enterprises by hardening budget constraints and contributing to the creation of a competitive environment. As a result, privatization and restructuring constitutes a vital institutional change necessary for the efficient allocation of resources and for enhancing the prospects for long-term economic growth. As a matter of fact, there is a considerable literature which analyses the impact of privatization on transition economies and confirms, particularly with respect to advanced transition countries, improvements in financial performance and productivity.[3] In assessing the extent of progress in privatization and restructuring in the countries of SEE we rely on three quantitative indicators developed by EBRD. These particular indicators capture three different aspects of privatization and restructuring, which correspond to small-scale privatization, large-scale privatization and governance and enterprise restructuring.

The progress in privatization and restructuring is largely reflected in the extent of the increase in the size of the private sector. After all, if the countries of SEE are to catch up with the more advanced ones in CE this would be feasible only though a further expansion in the size and role of the private sector. In this section, therefore, we shall start our analysis by examining the evolution of the size of the private sector in the countries of SEE. Table 6.1 gives information regarding both the size of the private sector of the particular economies as well as the progress made in the three aspects of privatization and restructuring. More specifically, for each country as well as for the region as a whole (unweighted average) there are four rows which correspond to the size of the private sector, expressed as a share of GDP, and to EBRD's indices for small-scale privatization, large-scale privatization and enterprise restructuring. Note that in calculating the average scores for SEE, the scores of BH and SM have been taken into account since the years 1996 and 2001 respectively because, as indicated in Chapter 1, we consider the years 1996 and 2001 for BH and SM respectively to denote the beginning of the transition process in these two countries.

Table 6.1 Privatization and enterprise restructuring

	1991	1992	1993	1994	1995	1996	1997	1998	1999	2000	2001	2002	2003
Albania													
Size of private sector (% of GDP)	5.0	10.0	40.0	50.0	60.0	75.0	75.0	75.0	75.0	75.0	75.0	75.0	75.0
Small-scale privatization	2.0	2.0	3.0	3.0	4.0	4.0	4.0	4.0	4.0	4.0	4.0	4.0	4.0
Large-scale privatization	1.0	1.0	1.0	1.0	2.0	2.0	2.0	2.0	2.0	2.0	2.3	2.3	2.3
Enterprise restucturing	1.0	1.0	1.0	2.0	2.0	2.0	2.0	2.0	2.0	2.0	2.0	2.0	2.0
BH													
Size of private sector (% of GDP)	n.a.	n.a.	n.a.	n.a.	n.a.	n.a.	n.a.	35.0	35.0	35.0	40.0	45.0	50.0
Small-scale privatization	n.a.	n.a.	n.a.	n.a.	2.0	2.0	2.0	2.0	2.0	2.3	2.7	3.0	3.0
Large-scale privatization	n.a.	n.a.	n.a.	n.a.	1.0	1.0	1.0	2.0	2.0	2.0	2.3	2.3	2.3
Enterprise restucturing	n.a.	n.a.	n.a.	n.a.	1.0	1.0	1.0	1.7	1.7	1.7	1.7	1.7	2.0
Bulgaria													
Size of private sector (% of GDP)	20.0	25.0	35.0	40.0	50.0	55.0	60.0	65.0	70.0	70.0	70.0	75.0	75.0
Small-scale privatization	1.0	1.0	1.7	2.0	3.0	3.0	3.0	3.0	3.3	3.7	3.7	3.7	3.7
Large-scale privatization	1.0	1.7	2.0	2.0	2.0	2.0	3.0	3.0	3.0	3.7	3.7	3.7	3.7
Enterprise restucturing	1.0	1.0	1.0	2.0	2.0	2.0	2.3	2.3	2.3	2.3	2.3	2.3	2.7
Croatia													
Size of private sector (% of GDP)	20.0	25.0	30.0	35.0	40.0	50.0	55.0	55.0	60.0	60.0	60.0	60.0	60.0
Small-scale privatization	3.0	3.0	4.0	4.0	4.0	4.3	4.3	4.3	4.3	4.3	4.3	4.3	4.3
Large-scale privatization	1.0	2.0	2.0	2.0	3.0	3.0	3.0	3.0	3.0	3.0	3.0	3.0	3.3
Enterprise restucturing	1.0	1.0	1.0	2.0	2.0	2.7	2.7	2.7	2.7	2.7	2.7	2.7	2.7

Table 6.1 (Continued)

	1991	1992	1993	1994	1995	1996	1997	1998	1999	2000	2001	2002	2003
FYROM													
Size of private sector (% of GDP)	15.0	15.0	35.0	35.0	40.0	50.0	50.0	55.0	55.0	55.0	60.0	60.0	60.0
Small-scale privatization	3.0	3.0	3.0	4.0	4.0	4.0	4.0	4.0	4.0	4.0	4.0	4.0	4.0
Large-scale privatization	1.0	1.0	2.0	2.0	2.0	3.0	3.0	3.0	3.0	3.0	3.0	3.0	3.0
Enterprise restucturing	1.0	1.0	1.0	2.0	2.0	2.0	2.0	2.0	2.0	2.3	2.3	2.3	2.3
Romania													
Size of private sector (% of GDP)	25.0	25.0	35.0	40.0	45.0	55.0	60.0	60.0	60.0	60.0	65.0	65.0	65.0
Small-scale privatization	1.0	2.0	2.0	2.3	2.7	3.0	3.3	3.3	3.7	3.7	3.7	3.7	3.7
Large-scale privatization	1.7	1.7	2.0	2.0	2.0	2.7	2.7	2.7	2.7	3.0	3.3	3.3	3.3
Enterprise restucturing	1.0	1.0	2.0	2.0	2.0	2.0	2.0	2.0	2.0	2.0	2.0	2.0	2.0
SM													
Size of private sector (% of GDP)	n.a.	n.a.	n.a.	n.a.	n.a.	n.a.	n.a.	n.a.	n.a.	40.0	40.0	45.0	45.0
Small-scale privatization	n.a.	n.a.	n.a.	n.a.	3.0	3.0	3.0	3.0	3.0	3.0	3.0	3.0	3.0
Large-scale privatization	n.a.	n.a.	n.a.	n.a.	1.0	1.0	1.0	1.0	1.0	1.0	1.0	2.0	2.3
Enterprise restucturing	n.a.	n.a.	n.a.	n.a.	1.0	1.0	1.0	1.0	1.0	1.0	1.0	2.0	2.0
SEE													
Size of private sector (% of GDP)	17.0	20.0	35.0	40.0	47.0	57.0	60.0	57.5	59.2	59.2	58.6	60.7	61.4
Small-scale privatization	2.0	2.2	2.7	3.1	3.5	3.4	3.4	3.4	3.6	3.7	3.6	3.7	3.7
Large-scale privatization	1.1	1.5	1.8	1.8	2.2	2.3	2.5	2.6	2.6	2.8	2.7	2.8	2.9
Enterprise restucturing	1.0	1.0	1.2	2.0	2.0	2.0	2.0	2.1	2.1	2.2	2.0	2.1	2.2

n.a. = not available.
Source: EBRD (1999, 2003).

Starting with the size of the private sector, captured by the first row, we see that Albania's private sector experienced the most rapid increase in the region. Bulgaria's progress was considerable as well, while the other countries followed at a slower pace. Note that progress in BH and SM, for which transition started later, has lagged far behind the other South East European countries. In these two countries the private sector accounted for only 50 and 45 per cent of GDP respectively in 2003. Overall, however, the average share of the region has been low relative to the progress achieved by the Central European region. Figure 6.1 shows the expansion of private sector in the two regions (unweighted average) every four years starting in 1991 and continuing until 2003. The increase of the private sector share of GDP was much faster in the region of CE since it had reached more than 70 per cent of GDP by 1999, while the corresponding share for SEE was still below 60 per cent during the same year and only marginally above that in 2003. Note that the inclusion of BH and SM since 1998 and 2001 respectively has been largely responsible for the marginal increase in the average size of the private sector in SEE between 1999 and 2003. In particular, the average size of the private sector of the SEE-5 (i.e., excluding BH and SM) stood at 67 per cent of GDP in 2003. The lagging of SEE relative to CE can be interpreted as a summary statistic which, as we will see below, constitutes a clear reflection of the overall slow progress of the region with respect to privatization and restructuring. This was mostly true during the first decade of transition, since the private sector gained dominance in overall output after the end of the Kosovo War, primarily reflecting a marked increase in sales for large state-owned firms.

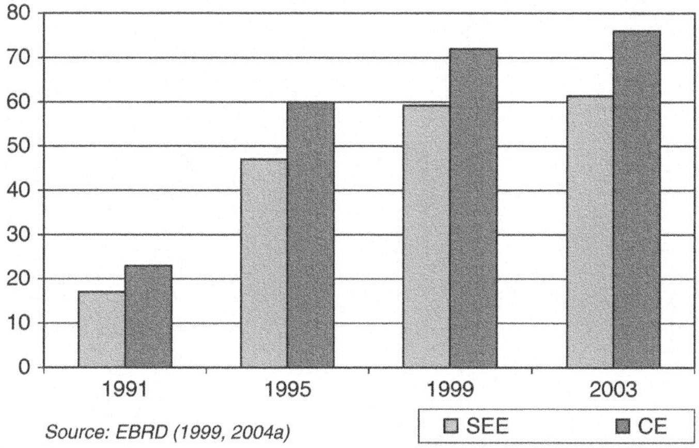

Source: EBRD (1999, 2004a)

Figure 6.1 Private sector share of GDP (%)

Privatization

The second and third rows for each country in Table 6.1 refer to small- and large-scale privatization respectively. First, with respect to small-scale privatization, it is apparent that it proceeded at a satisfactory pace and, for the majority of the South East European economies, it has been largely completed. Particularly in the case of former Yugoslav republics, an extensive small-scale private sector already existed under the previous regime. This, in turn, explains the fact that the particular countries, with the exception of BH, started the transition process with a score of 3.0 with respect to small-scale privatization. However, Bulgaria and Romania, the two countries that followed the legacies of central planning faithfully until the end, started with a score of 1.0. Note that despite the favourable start for some of the countries, the pace of small-scale privatization has been lagging behind that of CE. Figure 6.2 shows the progress of small-scale privatization in SEE relative to CE. The countries of CE had reached the highest score of 4.3, implying the completion of the process, by 1999, while the corresponding average score for SEE was still below 4 by the end of 2003. Note, however, that transition had started earlier for most countries of CE, and much later for BH and SM, which to a certain extent has distorted the outcome of the comparison between the two regions. Nevertheless the fact that, except for Croatia, no other country of the region of SEE reached the highest score on small-scale privatization by the end of 2003, constitutes clear evidence of its lagging behind CE.

The progress in privatization of large-scale enterprises has been particularly slow in the region of SEE. Table 6.1 reports information with respect to EBRD's index for the progress on large-scale privatization for each country of the region (third row). More specifically, it appears that large-scale privatization had started up at a very slow pace with limited progress for most

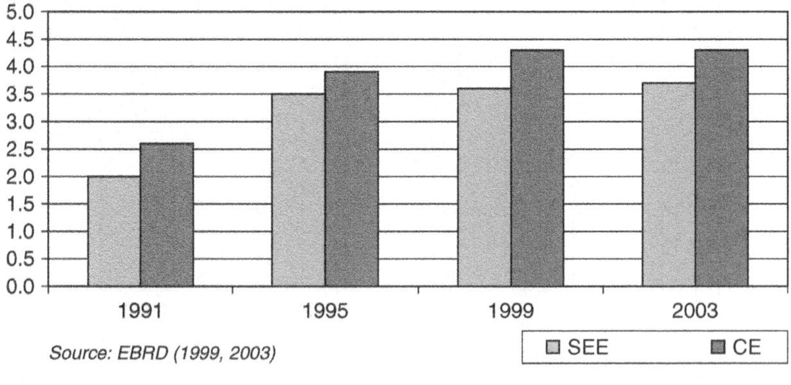

Source: EBRD (1999, 2003)

Figure 6.2 Small-scale privatization

countries and still, by the end of 2003, appears to be far from complete. Nevertheless, there was considerable progress after the Kosovo War, since significant proportions of large state-owned enterprises were privatized in all countries. Bulgaria and Romania, the two accession countries, in addition to Croatia have made the most progress, achieving scores higher than 3.0 at the end of 2003. FYROM follows with a score of 3.0, while Albania, BH and SM have made less progress. Furthermore, according to Figure 6.3 there has been considerable lagging of the region relative to the progress in CE. The progress of the latter countries during the first decade was vigorous enough since the average score of the region stood at 3.7 in 1999, while the corresponding average scores for SEE were 2.6 in 1999 and 2.9 in 2003. Again, the relatively slow progress of the region between the years 1999 and 2003 to a certain extent reflected the inclusion of BH and SM.

The analysis has clearly shown that the pace of privatization in SEE, particularly during the first decade of transition, has lagged behind that of CE. Thus an interesting issue refers to the basic reasons behind the slow progress of the privatization process in the region, particularly with respect to large-scale enterprises. First of all, lack of commitment, inconsistent policy measures, complicated legislation and administrative deficiencies constituted common characteristics that caused enormous difficulties and repeated delays in the process. Overall, the necessary political, legal and institutional conditions were not in place for the shifting towards a market system in general and for the launching of an effective privatization process in particular. The privatization process in most countries took the form of a power game involving the promotion of the objectives of special interest groups. This, in turn, led to widespread corruption practices, which became one of the striking features of transition in SEE.[4] These practices, together with the overall political instability and the emergence of armed conflicts, generated an environment

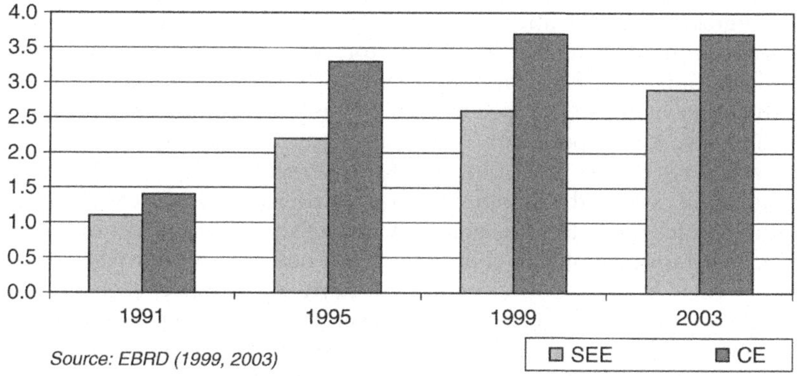

Source: EBRD (1999, 2003)

Figure 6.3 Large-scale privatization

of particularly high risk for investors, primarily foreign, to consider buying state-owned companies. The low level of FDI inflows into the region, relative to CE, has been indicative of the limited interest of foreigners in investing (details on FDI in Chapter 9 below).

Another issue had to do with the administrative capacities of the privatizing agencies, which were weak, since they remained under strong political influence despite their nominal independence. The emergence of potential conflicts of interest, insider favouring and corrupt behaviour played a significant role not only in affecting the pace of the process but also in the preferential use of some privatization techniques. This is not unrelated to the fact that in most countries privatization has benefited insiders, either through voucher privatization with significant concessions to insiders or through Management – Employee Buy-Outs (MEBOs), adding little to governance practices (see Table 6.2 below for the primary privatization methods followed by the South East European countries).[5] Finally, ineffective macroeconomic stabilization during the first decade of transition also affected the privatization process adversely. Nevertheless, the macroeconomic environment has improved considerably after the Kosovo conflict, although it is still fragile, and output growth has been solid enough. Overall, the beginning of the new century witnessed a significant acceleration in the process across the region and a considerable improvement in the procedures and their implementation. Many problems, however, still remain, particularly with respect to the transparency of the transactions, the application of selection criteria and post-privatization control.

Country experience

Let us now turn to a brief elaboration on the privatization experience of the individual countries in SEE. The experience of the individual countries of the region has been strikingly similar: the two basic conclusions of the preceding analysis with regard to the entire region describe quite accurately the progress of the privatization process in each country separately.[6] This, on the one hand, refers to the satisfactory progress of small-scale privatization as opposed to the modest progress of large-scale privatization and, on the other hand, to the speeding-up of the process during the latter part of transition. More specifically, political constraints and controversies and low incentives on the part of insiders led to significant delays in large-scale privatization, while the progress in transferring ownership of small- and medium-scale enterprises was relatively quick. Also, during most of the first decade of transition all the countries of SEE had been rather hesitant and slow in their privatization efforts, particularly with respect to large state-owned enterprises. As pointed out, however, there was afterwards a notable acceleration in large-scale privatization across the region. This speeding-up of the process primarily reflected important policy changes and a general diversification of the employed privatization schemes and methods.

In Albania, small-scale privatization was initiated in 1991 with the introduction of a law that regulated the privatization of small-scale entities which progressed rapidly through employee buy-outs. With respect to large-scale privatization, a voucher-based programme was introduced in 1995 which, however, has been proceeding with considerable delays. Inter-enterprise arrears represent a major obstacle to most remaining public enterprises. In BH, due to the civil war, transition basically started in 1996. Privatization laws were enacted during 1997 and 1998 in the Federation and in the Republika Srpska (RS) respectively. Small-scale privatization began in 1999, and by 2003 more than half of small enterprises in the Federation and more than three-quarters in RS had been privatized. In contrast, the privatization of large enterprises has been proceeding at a very slow pace As a result, many of the larger companies are still state-owned. The fact remains that BH is still rather unattractive to investors despite the efforts of the domestic authorities to privatize. Lack of sufficient information on enterprise debts discourages potential buyers as well.

Bulgaria has made significant progress in privatizing state assets. Small-scale privatization has been largely completed. Large-scale privatization, on the other hand, has proceeded at a slow pace, although it accelerated after the latter half of the 1990s. The basic law on privatization was passed in April 1992. A major amendment allowed a first round of voucher privatization to begin in 1996 while further improvements were made in 1997 and 1998. A new law was adopted in 2002 which aimed at increasing transparency and had as a major goal the completion of the deals for the remaining large-scale enterprises. Although large-scale privatization has made considerable advances recently, more progress is needed given the country's bid for full EU membership in 2007. In Romania, the first law on privatization was enacted in 1991 and mass voucher privatization began during the same year. Despite the early start, however, the process has been advancing slowly. In particular, while most medium and small-scale enterprises have been privatized, the privatization of large state-owned enterprises has been progressing more slowly. A new law was passed in 2002 to address some of the existing problems and in particular to speed up the process by simplifying the procedures employed. As in the case of Bulgaria, Romania's candidacy for full EU membership in 2007 makes more urgent the need for faster progress.

In Croatia, as pointed out, there was already a large enough small-scale private sector prior to transition. In spite of the favourable start, however, the small-scale privatization process progressed rather gradually. Turning to large-scale privatization, a voucher-based programme was introduced in 1998. Its pace remained slow and was characterized by insider favouring and lack of transparency, as well as increased concerns for alleged corruption. In FYROM there was a large small-scale private sector prior to transition as well. Overall, small-scale privatization has been close to completion. In contrast, the progress with respect to large-scale privatization has been slow, although a corresponding law was passed as early as 1993. More specifically, there have been considerable delays in implementing large-scale privatization, particularly with respect to loss-making enterprises. The initial intention of restructuring them was undermined by the companies' continuing accumulation of losses, making matters rather difficult and thus leaving the process of liquidation as the only feasible alternative. Finally, in SM the transition process basically started after the end of the Kosovo War. In Serbia, there were attempts at privatization under the former regime with limited success. Since the political change in October 2000 the process of privatization has accelerated. A new privatization law was enacted in 2001, which relied on selling as the primary method. In Montenegro a privatization council was established in 1998. Overall, by the end of 2003, small-scale privatization had made satisfactory progress but the sale of large enterprises through tenders and auctions has so far been less successful.

Enterprise restructuring

The issue of enterprise restructuring refers to the effective detaching of enterprises from their dependence on state support while, at the same time, ensuring their viability under market conditions. Privatization alone, although it constitutes a fundamental step towards enterprise restructuring, does not necessarily secure improved enterprise performance under market conditions. Successful enterprise restructuring depends not only on privatization but also on the structure of control and the financial constraints imposed on the enterprises. Thus effective restructuring requires increased competition through market liberalization, a reduction in access to 'soft' finance and changes in the structure of enterprise ownership. Effective enterprise restructuring aims at enhancing efficiency so that enterprises rely on their own performance.

The progress of the economies of SEE towards enterprise restructuring has been particularly modest. This is apparent from Table 6.1, which reports information with respect to the EBRD index on enterprise restructuring for each country of the region (fourth row). As we can see, progress has been particularly slow, with Croatia being the only exception. By the end of 2003, Croatia and Bulgaria had a score of 2.7, FYROM followed with a score of 2.3, while all the other countries stood at a score of 2.0. The slow progress of the region becomes more profound when compared to CE. Figure 6.4 shows the (unweighted) average progress in enterprise restructuring in the two regions every four years since 1991. The countries of CE had a better start, partly due to the earlier transition in most of them, and they succeeded in reaching a score of 3 by 1999. The overall progress of the region of SEE has been modest, reaching an average score of 2.2 by the end of 2003.

The slow progress of privatization, particularly the large-scale variety, has been a major reason that has contributed to the region's lagging in enterprise restructuring. In addition, however, significant delays in other important

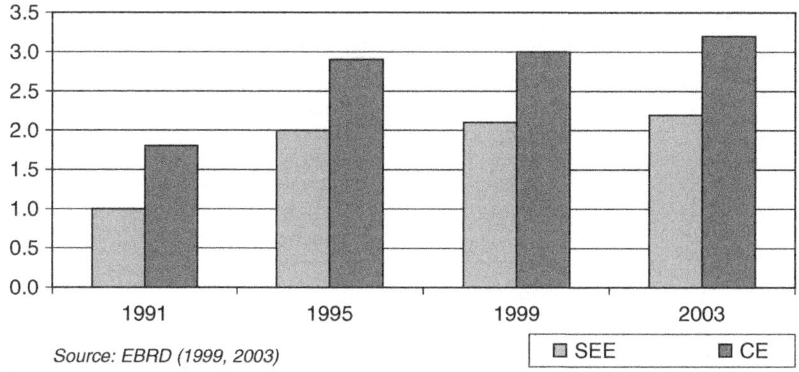

Figure 6.4 Enterprise restructuring

aspects of enterprise restructuring have been responsible as well for the region's poor performance. First, one important aspect of effective enterprise restructuring requires that enterprises must operate in a competitive environment. This refers to domestic price liberalization, opening the economy to international trade and the adoption of effective competition policy. This market liberalization aspect will be analysed in detail below. Another decisive factor for successful enterprise performance requires imposing hard budget constraints by detaching enterprises from soft banking loans and passive finance (features inherited from central planning). This, in turn, requires the imposition of discipline on outside sources of finance as well as the implementation of effective bankruptcy legislation. In this respect the building of market-oriented and stable financial sectors has been of vital importance. This issue was dealt with to a certain extent in Chapter 4, while issues concerning banking reform will be examined in some detail below. In particular, as already indicated and as analysed further in more detail below, soft budget constraints and the continuing accumulation of bad loans in the countries of SEE constituted resistance to structural change and restructuring, contributing to the poor economic performance as well as to slow financial market reform and giving rise to serious financial crises.

Finally, improving corporate governance practices is vital to enterprise performance as well. Privatization may play an important role in corporate governance to the extent that the new owners are able to pressurize management to improve the performance of the enterprises. The choice of privatization method for a particular enterprise largely determines whether it is considered to be viable or potentially viable under market conditions. Thus the privatization methods used have a significant impact on corporate governance practices. It has been shown that, on average, privatization to outsiders has been associated with 50 per cent more restructuring than privatization to insiders (Djankov and Murrell 2002).[7] In particular, MEBOs

Table 6.2 Primary privatization methods

Albania	MEBOs
BH	Vouchers
Bulgaria	Direct sales
Croatia	MEBOs
FYROM	MEBOs
Romania	MEBOs
SM	Vouchers

Source: EBRD (2003).

and voucher privatizations are usually considered to be less effective in facilitating the emergence of active private owners who aim at improving efficiency than direct sales to private investors. Table 6.2 reports the primary privatization methods followed by the economies of SEE. The majority of the countries of SEE relied on vouchers and MEBOs, in contrast to the CE where direct sales appeared to be the method adopted by most countries. As a matter of fact, Bulgaria is the only country in the South East European region where the primary privatization method has been in the form of direct sales. This, in turn, meant the impact of privatization on corporate governance practices was of limited significance in most of the countries of the region. Overall, common characteristics of ownership structures in most South East European countries still include significant control by insiders and state ownership and control over large firms and utilities.

Market liberalization and competition

Progress in market liberalization and competition is essential to a successful transition towards a market system. Only market-determined prices send out the scarcity signals, which lead to efficient allocation of resources and enable a market economy to work properly.[8] Thus price signals must be clear and free to move in response to market forces. Furthermore, external liberalization is as important as the domestic one. This primarily means trade liberalization and prevalence of world market prices as well as free access to foreign exchange. Competition policy is another area where effective implementation is essential to secure and promote a competitive environment.

Thus, in order to examine the progress of the countries of SEE with respect to market liberalization and competition we look into these three different aspects which correspond to price liberalization, trade and foreign exchange system liberalization, and competition policy. In particular, we rely on the corresponding EBRD indicators to analyse the progress made by the particular economies. These indicators are reported in Table 6.3, where for each country as well as for the region's unweighted average there are three

Table 6.3 Market liberalization

	1991	1992	1993	1994	1995	1996	1997	1998	1999	2000	2001	2002	2003
Albania													
Price liberalization	2.0	3.0	3.7	3.7	3.7	3.7	3.7	3.7	3.7	3.7	3.7	3.7	3.7
Trade and forex liberalization	1.0	4.0	4.0	4.0	4.0	4.0	4.0	4.0	4.0	4.3	4.3	4.3	4.3
Competition policy	1.0	1.0	1.0	1.0	1.0	1.7	1.7	1.7	1.7	1.7	1.7	1.7	1.7
BH													
Price liberalization	n.a.	n.a.	n.a.	n.a.	1.0	3.0	3.0	4.0	4.0	4.0	4.0	4.0	4.0
Trade and forex liberalization	n.a.	n.a.	n.a.	n.a.	1.0	1.0	3.0	3.0	3.0	3.0	3.0	3.0	3.7
Competition policy	n.a.	n.a.	n.a.	n.a.	1.0	1.0	1.0	1.0	1.0	1.0	1.0	1.0	1.0
Bulgaria													
Price liberalization	3.0	3.0	3.0	3.0	2.7	2.7	4.0	4.0	4.0	4.0	4.3	4.3	4.3
Trade and forex liberalization	3.0	3.0	3.0	4.0	4.0	4.0	4.0	4.0	4.3	4.3	4.3	4.3	4.3
Competition policy	2.0	2.0	2.0	2.0	2.0	2.0	2.3	2.3	2.3	2.3	2.3	2.3	2.3
Croatia													
Price liberalization	3.0	3.0	3.0	4.0	4.0	4.0	4.0	4.0	4.0	4.0	4.0	4.0	4.0
Trade and forex liberalization	3.0	3.0	3.0	4.0	4.0	4.0	4.0	4.0	4.0	4.3	4.3	4.3	4.3
Competition policy	1.0	1.0	1.0	1.0	1.0	2.0	2.3	2.3	2.3	2.3	2.3	2.3	2.3

Table 6.3 (Continued)

	1991	1992	1993	1994	1995	1996	1997	1998	1999	2000	2001	2002	2003
FYROM													
Price liberalization	3.0	3.0	3.0	4.0	4.0	4.0	4.0	4.0	4.0	4.0	4.0	4.0	4.0
Trade and forex liberalization	3.0	3.0	3.0	4.0	4.0	4.0	4.0	4.0	4.0	4.0	4.0	4.0	4.3
Competition policy	1.0	1.0	1.0	1.0	1.0	1.0	1.0	1.0	1.0	2.0	2.0	2.0	2.0
Romania													
Price liberalization	3.0	3.0	4.0	4.0	4.0	4.0	4.0	4.3	4.3	4.3	4.3	4.3	4.3
Trade and forex liberalization	1.0	3.0	3.0	4.0	4.0	3.0	4.0	4.0	4.0	4.0	4.0	4.0	4.0
Competition policy	1.0	1.0	1.0	1.0	1.0	1.0	2.3	2.3	2.3	2.3	2.3	2.3	2.3
SM													
Price liberalization	n.a.	n.a.	n.a.	n.a.	2.7	2.7	2.7	2.3	2.3	2.3	4.0	4.0	4.0
Trade and forex liberalization	n.a.	n.a.	n.a.	n.a.	1.0	1.0	1.0	1.0	1.0	1.0	3.0	3.3	3.3
Competition policy	n.a.	n.a.	n.a.	n.a.	1.0	1.0	1.0	1.0	1.0	1.0	1.0	1.0	1.0
SEE													
Price liberalization	2.8	3.0	3.3	3.7	3.7	3.6	3.8	4.0	4.0	4.0	4.0	4.0	4.0
Trade and forex liberalization	2.2	3.2	3.2	4.0	4.0	3.3	3.8	3.8	3.9	4.0	3.8	3.9	4.0
Competition policy	1.2	1.2	1.2	1.2	1.2	1.5	1.8	1.8	1.8	1.9	1.8	1.8	1.8

n.a. = not available.
Source: EBRD (1999, 2003).

rows, which correspond to EBRD's indices for price liberalization, trade and foreign exchange system liberalization and competition policy. Note that, as in the case of the privatization indices, in calculating the average scores for SEE the scores of BH and SM have been taken into account since the years 1996 and 2001 respectively.

The first row for each country in Table 6.3 refers to price liberalization. Progress in price liberalization by the countries of SEE has been substantial and was implemented very early in transition. According to Table 6.3, the process has been largely completed even for the late starters such as BH and SM. All the countries have made substantial progress in price liberalization, and state procurement at non-market prices has been largely phased out. In particular, the only price controls, if any, remain on very few goods, primarily utilities. The considerable progress of the region is verified by the fact that it has been lagging only marginally behind CE. Figure 6.5 shows the (unweighted) average progress in price liberalization in the two regions for every four years since 1991. The evolution of price liberalization has been quite similar in the two regions and this is manifested by the fact that the countries of SEE had an average score of 4.0 as compared to 4.2 for the ones in CE in 2003. In evaluating their relative progress one must take into consideration the fact that transition began earlier for most countries of CE, as well as the impact of the late start by BH and SM on SEE's average.

The liberalization of trade and foreign exchange has been quite rapid by the countries of the region as well (Table 6.3). The countries of the region either removed or considerably reduced all restrictions on imports and exports early in transition. Furthermore, the exchange system was freed

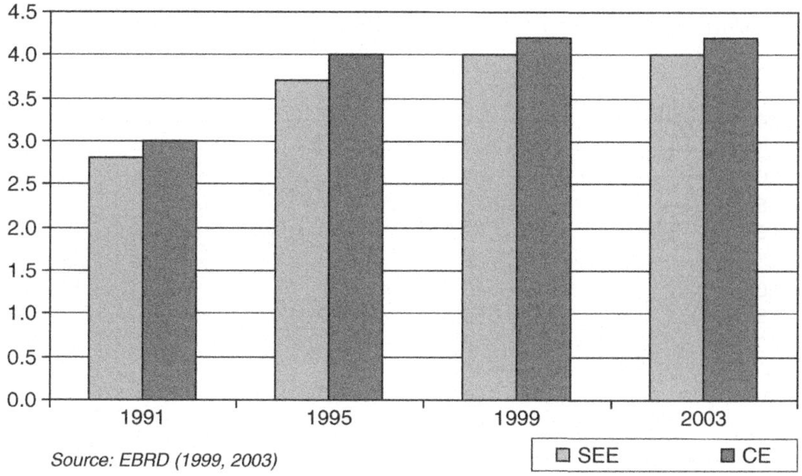

Figure 6.5 Price liberalization

mostly with respect to current account transactions. In most countries, however, the need for closer integration with the EU requires a further lowering of trade protection, particularly with respect to non-tariff barriers, as well as more uniform and lower tariff structures. As in the case of domestic prices, the average speed of external liberalization in SEE has been similar to that in CE. This is shown in Figure 6.6. As a matter of fact, being at a lower point relative to their counterparts of CE in 1991, the countries of SEE had almost reached the same level of reform in 1995. The inclusion of BH and SM slowed down the average progress of the region afterwards.

Multilateral commitments with well established institutions have played an important role in accelerating as well as sustaining the liberalization of trade and free access to foreign exchange. In particular, the eagerness of most of the particular economies to become members of multilateral trade organizations and to establish international trade agreements strongly reinforced their dedication to liberalization measures. For instance, the discipline imposed by EU Association Agreements and World Trade Organization (WTO) negotiations provided a very effective boost to the effort to sustain liberalization. In particular, except for BH and SM, all the other countries of the region have joined WTO. FYROM was the last one to do so in April 2003. Next, with respect to the signing of Stabilization and Association Agreements with the EU, Albania, BH and SM are the countries that so far have not done so. Albania began formal negotiations in January 2003, while BH and SM are at the stage where the EU has begun conducting a Feasibility Study on their readiness for a Stabilization and Association Agreement.[9] Note, however, that the rapid price as well as trade liberalization was not always without setbacks. Bulgaria and Romania constitute two examples of temporary setbacks in the reform progress. In particular, Bulgaria backtracked on the price liberalization reforms in 1995 and 1996 following the return to power of the

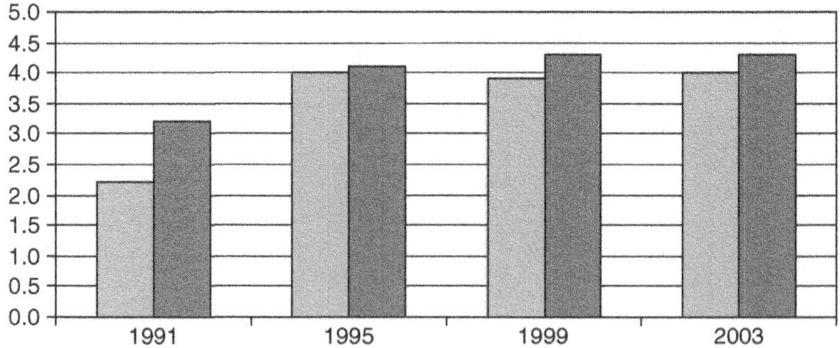

Source: EBRD (1999, 2003)

Figure 6.6 Trade and foreign exchange liberalization

former Communist Party. Soon, however, market liberalization was restored as a reform government was elected. A similar setback in trade liberalization occurred in Romania during 1996 (also in response to a change in government).[10]

All countries have to a certain extent developed legal and institutional frameworks to curb abuses of market power. In certain instances the progress in competition policy has primarily reflected the need for harmonization with EU policies. Overall, competition policy is an area of market liberalization where effective implementation has been difficult and this is reflected by the fact that the progress made in most countries of the region has been limited. More specifically, according to Table 6.3 (third row for each country), the progress made by most of them has been rather modest. Bulgaria, Romania and Croatia achieved a score of 2.3 in 2003, the highest in the region. At least for the first two countries, the progress made was largely driven by the need for their competition policy to become compatible with EU standards in the light of their bid for full membership in 2007. As a matter of fact, Bulgaria had managed to enact laws on competition as early as in 1991, which explains the fact that it had already achieved a score of 2.0 during the same year.[11] Note that all other countries had been lagging behind with corresponding scores equal to 1.0 (Table 6.3). Figure 6.7 compares the performance of SEE relative to CE. The average progress of the region has been lagging behind that of CE. It is interesting to note that during the early stages of transition (i.e., from 1991 to 1995) the region made no progress whatsoever on competition policy. This, in turn, reflected the fact that, except for Bulgaria, no other country had enacted an anti-trust law. The remaining countries, except for BH and SM, enacted laws regulating competition that came into effect after 1995.[12]

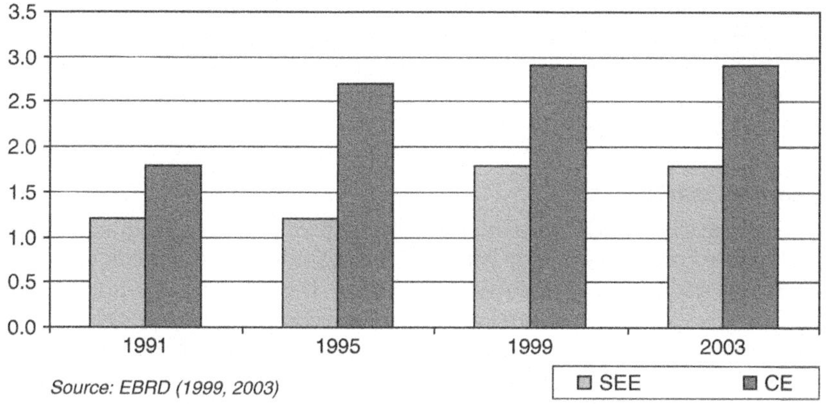

Figure 6.7 Competition policy

Financial market reform

Financial sector reform and the proper functioning of the financial markets has been essential for the efficient channelling of funds from savers to investors, a vital precondition for the growth prospects of the transition economies, but also for effective monetary management and hence stabilization. The slow financial and banking reform in the economies of SEE, in conjunction with delays in other reform measures such as privatization and enterprise restructuring, has a been a major cause of the financial crises, the stabilization setbacks and the overall poor performance of these countries. While passive finance and soft bank loans were standard features of central planning, a market economy requires financial discipline through the application of sound banking principles to function effectively. This re-orientation of the role and practices of the financial sector has been a particularly difficult challenge for the countries of SEE.

According to EBRD, financial market reform consists of two indicators: securities markets and non-bank financial institutions, and banking reform and interest rate liberalization. In Chapter 4 we examined some aspects concerning the functioning of financial markets in SEE during the first decade of transition. In particular, we looked at the role of the slow development of debt markets with respect to the effectiveness of stabilization policies and elaborated on interest rate developments in conjunction with the evolution of instruments of monetary control. In this section we will briefly consider the progress made on securities markets and non-bank financial institutions, and then we will focus on banking system reform. In most South East European economies state banks and former state banks remained dominant during the intermediate stages of transition. Their financial condition was impaired by the inherited stock of bad loans as well as by a flow of new non-performing loans due to the failure to apply sound banking principles. The analysis indicates that this weak loan portfolio, combined with an inefficient regulatory framework and the slow pace of enterprise reform, constituted major obstacles to effective stabilization and sustained growth prospects of these countries, while greatly contributing to the eruption of financial crises.

Securities markets

Securities markets and non-bank financial institutions remain small and illiquid in most countries of SEE. Although most South East European economies created stock exchanges early in transition, they became operational and regulated by securities commissions at the later part of transition. Overall, the stock exchanges remain quite underdeveloped with low capitalization and little liquidity.[13] Figure 6.8 clearly shows the low stock market capitalization of SEE by the end of 2003, expressed as a percentage of GDP, especially when compared with the countries of CE. Except for Croatia, the other countries

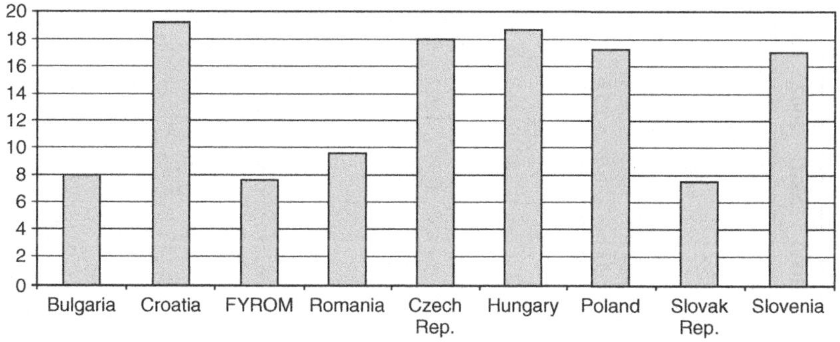

[a] There were no data available for Albania, BH and SM.
Source: EBRD (2004b)

Figure 6.8 Stock market capitalization in 2003[a] (% of GDP)

were well below the level of most Central European countries (the Slovak Republic was the only Central European country with very low capitalization). The underdevelopment of South East European stock markets reflects both a demand as well as a supply problem. The demand problem stems from the fact that there are few new investors and stocks are mostly traded between existing participants. Lack of confidence, low liquidity and insufficient legal protection for minority shareholders constitute some of the main reasons behind the investors' reluctance. The supply problem primarily reflects the lack of listing large companies with substantial free-floating shares. Most of the attractive large companies either are still state-owned or have been privatized through cash sales. Thus, South East European stock exchanges are largely inefficient since they do not serve as a reliable source of information or corporate evaluation.

Table 6.4 reports information on several indicators regarding financial market reform. More specifically, there are five rows for each country which refer to specific EBRD indices that capture progress on financial market reform. The first row corresponds to EBRD's indicator regarding progress on securities markets and non-financial institutions. This particular indicator verifies the slow progress of the economies of SEE. Croatia and, to a lesser extent, Bulgaria have made the most progress, achieving scores of 2.7 and 2.3 in 2003 respectively, while the other countries follow with scores of 2.0 or lower. Figure 6.9 compares the average progress of the region of SEE relatively to that of CE. The comparison reveals the considerable lagging of the former region relative to the latter. In particular, the countries of CE made considerable progress during the initial stages of transition, achieving an average score of 2.8 as early as in 1995. In contrast the progress of the South East European countries has been quite slow, reaching an average score of only 2.0 by 2003.

Table 6.4 Banking system reform

	1991	1992	1993	1994	1995	1996	1997	1998	1999	2000	2001	2002	2003
Albania													
EBRD index of reform of non-bank financial institutions	1.0	1.0	1.0	1.0	1.0	1.7	1.7	1.7	1.7	1.7	1.7	1.7	1.7
Number of banks (of which foreign owned)	n.a.	n.a.	n.a.	6(3)	6(3)	8(3)	9(3)	10(8)	13(11)	13(12)	13(12)	13(12)	15(13)
Asset share of state-owned banks (%)	n.a.	n.a.	n.a.	97.8	94.5	93.7	89.9	85.6	81.1	64.8	59.2	54.1	51.9
Bad loans (% of total loans)	n.a.	n.a.	n.a.	n.a.	34.9	40.1	91.3	35.4	32.7	42.6	6.9	5.6	4.6
EBRD index of banking sector reform	1.0	1.0	1.3	2.0	2.0	2.0	2.0	2.0	2.0	2.3	2.3	2.3	2.3
BH													
EBRD index of reform of non-bank financial institutions	n.a.	n.a.	n.a.	n.a.	1.0	1.0	1.0	1.0	1.0	1.0	1.0	1.7	1.7
Number of banks (of which foreign owned)	n.a.	n.a.	n.a.	n.a.	n.a.	n.a.	n.a.	n.a.	61(9)	56(14)	49(20)	40(21)	37(19)
Asset share of state-owned banks (%)	n.a.	n.a.	n.a.	n.a.	n.a.	n.a.	n.a.	n.a.	75.9	55.4	17.3	6.2	5.2
Bad loans (% of total loans)	n.a.	n.a.	n.a.	n.a.	n.a.	n.a.	n.a.	n.a.	58.7	15.8	20.7	11.5	8.3
EBRD index of banking sector reform	n.a.	n.a.	n.a.	n.a.	1.0	1.0	1.0	2.3	2.3	2.3	2.3	2.3	2.3
Bulgaria													
EBRD index of reform of non-bank financial institutions	1.0	1.0	1.0	1.0	2.0	2.0	2.0	2.0	2.0	2.0	2.0	2.3	2.3
Number of banks (of which foreign owned)	n.a.	n.a.	41(0)	40(1)	41(3)	42(3)	28(7)	34(17)	34(22)	35(25)	35(26)	34(26)	35(25)
Asset share of state-owned banks (%)	n.a.	n.a.	n.a.	n.a.	n.a.	82.2	66.0	56.4	50.5	19.8	19.9	14.1	0.4
Bad loans (% of total loans)	n.a.	n.a.	6.6	6.8	12.6	14.6	12.9	11.8	17.5	10.9	7.9	10.4	4.4
EBRD index of banking sector reform	1.0	1.7	2.0	2.0	2.0	2.0	2.7	2.7	2.7	3.0	3.0	3.3	3.3
Croatia													
EBRD index of reform of non-bank financial institutions	1.0	1.0	1.0	2.0	2.0	2.0	2.3	2.3	2.3	2.3	2.3	2.7	2.7
Number of banks (of which foreign owned)	n.a.	n.a.	43(n.a.)	50(n.a.)	54(1)	58(4)	61(7)	60(10)	53(13)	43(21)	43(24)	46(23)	41(19)
Asset share of state-owned banks (%)	n.a.	n.a.	58.9	55.5	51.9	36.2	32.6	37.5	39.8	5.7	5.0	4.0	3.4
Bad loans (% of total loans)	n.a.	n.a.	n.a.	12.2	12.9	11.2	8.2	12.6	20.6	19.8	15.0	11.5	9.4
EBRD index of banking sector reform	1.0	1.0	2.0	2.7	2.7	2.7	2.7	2.7	3.0	3.3	3.3	3.7	3.7

FYROM													
EBRD index of reform of non-bank financial institutions	1.0	1.0	1.0	1.0	1.0	1.0	1.0	1.7	1.7	1.7	1.7	1.7	1.7
Number of banks (of which foreign owned)	n.a.	n.a.	6(3)	6(3)	22(5)	22(5)	22(5)	24(6)	23(5)	22(7)	21(8)	20(7)	21(8)
Asset share of state-owned banks (%)	n.a.	n.a.	n.a.	n.a.	n.a.	0.0	0.0	1.4	2.5	1.1	1.3	2.0	1.8
Bad loans (% of total loans)	n.a.	n.a.	n.a.	n.a.	n.a.	66.1	59.5	50.3	62.6	46.5	44.4	35.7	34.9
EBRD index of banking sector reform	1.0	1.0	1.3	2.0	2.0	2.0	2.7	2.7	2.7	2.7	2.7	2.7	2.7
Romania													
EBRD index of reform of non-bank financial institutions	1.0	1.0	1.0	2.0	2.0	2.0	2.0	2.0	2.0	2.0	2.0	2.0	2.0
Number of banks (of which foreign owned)	n.a.	n.a.	n.a.	20(3)	24(6)	31(8)	33(13)	36(16)	34(19)	33(21)	33(24)	31(24)	30(21)
Asset share of state-owned banks (%)	n.a.	n.a.	n.a.	80.4	84.3	80.9	80.0	75.3	50.3	50.0	45.4	43.6	40.6
Bad loans (% of total loans)	n.a.	n.a.	n.a.	18.5	37.9	48.0	56.5	58.5	35.4	3.8	3.4	2.3	1.6
EBRD index of banking sector reform	1.0	1.0	1.0	2.0	3.0	3.0	2.7	2.3	2.7	2.7	2.7	2.7	2.7
SM													
EBRD index of reform of non-bank financial institutions	n.a.	n.a.	n.a.	n.a.	1.0	1.0	1.0	1.0	1.0	1.0	1.0	1.7	2.0
Number of banks (of which foreign owned)	n.a.	n.a.	n.a.	n.a.	112(3)	103(3)	106(3)	104(3)	75(3)	81(3)	54(8)	50(12)	47(16)
Asset share of state-owned banks (%)	n.a.	n.a.	n.a.	n.a.	94.7	92.0	89.8	90.0	89.0	90.9	68.0	35.6	34.1
Bad loans (% of total loans)	n.a.	n.a.	n.a.	n.a.	12.0	12.3	15.1	13.1	10.2	27.8	24.4	28.5	23.8
EBRD index of banking sector reform	n.a.	n.a.	n.a.	n.a.	1.0	1.0	1.0	1.0	1.0	1.0	1.0	2.3	2.3
SEE													
EBRD index of reform of non-bank financial institutions	1.0	1.0	1.0	1.4	1.6	1.6	1.7	1.8	1.8	1.8	1.7	2.0	2.0
EBRD index of banking sector reform	1.0	1.1	1.5	2.1	2.3	2.1	2.3	2.5	2.6	2.7	2.5	2.8	2.8

n.a. = not available.
Source: EBRD (1999, 2001, 2004b).

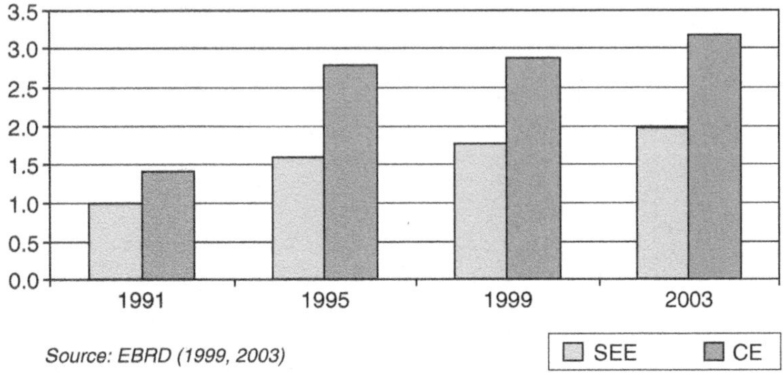

Source: EBRD (1999, 2003)

Figure 6.9 Non-bank financial institutions reform

Banking system reform

As pointed out, a common characteristic of the countries of SEE which posed a serious obstacle to better economic performance and to the effectiveness of macroeconomic policies referred to structural weaknesses due to the slow reform of their financial systems. The banking sector of the South East European countries remained largely underdeveloped, inefficient and, as a result, its performance in mobilizing funds was rather poor. Particularly during the first decade of transition, banks in the South East European counties were poorly capitalized with substantial portfolios of bad claims dominating the financial sector in most of these countries. As we have already seen, although this situation was shared by all the countries of SEE, it became more profound in Albania, Bulgaria and Romania where the common experience of the resurgence of inflation was accompanied by serious financial crises which constituted the manifestation of the chronic banking system fragility that characterized the particular economies. Thus, the development and the efficient functioning of the banking sector has been a fundamental challenge to an effective transition from a command to a market economy.

During the old regime the role of the banking system was passive since there was no need for financial intermediation. The system was based on a 'mono-bank' which was complemented by a few specialized banks whose prime task was to direct credit to state–owned enterprises (see Calvo and Kumar 1993). There was no need for adequate bank capitalization or for prudential regulations since credit flows were determined by the central plan and controlled by the mono-bank. This was particularly true for Albania, Bulgaria and Romania where the legacies of central planning were kept almost intact until the very end of the old regime. In the case of the former republics of Yugoslavia the situation was different since the two-tier banking system had already been introduced in the 1960s while it was much more decentralized. Due to the practices of central planning and the excessive dependence of banks on a small number of large state enterprises, these countries at the start of transition inherited a situation where there existed only a few state-owned banks whose portfolio of loans to enterprises already was (or had a high probability to become) non-performing.

Thus, banking reform constituted a vital challenge to the countries of SEE, as for all transition economies, for enhancing the growth prospects by effectively mobilizing funds from the savers to borrowers. As pointed out, however, despite its importance the pace of reform was slow, and as a result the banking system remained highly underdeveloped. The extent of underdevelopment was reflected in the low level of intermediation, the high cost of capital, the severe lack of financial discipline and the poor allocation of credit. In particular, with respect to the level of banking intermediation, it was particularly low even taking into account the low level of development of the particular countries. Figure 6.10 shows loans to the private sector as a percentage of GDP. As we can see, except for Croatia and Bulgaria, loans to the private sector stood at less than 15 per cent in all remaining counties in 2003. The corresponding average (unweighted) for the countries of CE was 30 per cent of GDP, while for the countries of the Eurozone it was about 110 per cent.[14]

The underdevelopment of the banking system affected the conduct of stabilization policies as well. This particularly referred to monetary policy, since an unsound banking system undermines the reliability of the transmission mechanism and makes it less effective, particularly when it relies on indirect instruments. Successful interest rate monitoring through indirect instruments requires, among other things, a sound and competitive banking sector. As pointed out in Chapter 4, the slow pace of banking sector reform was largely responsible for the prolonged reliance of most South East

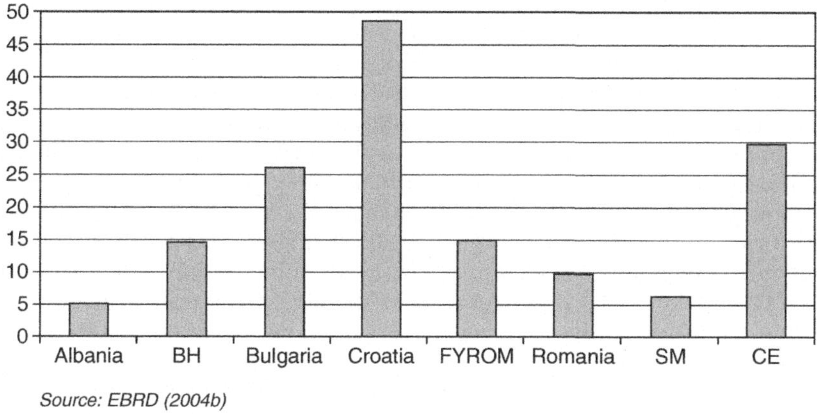

Figure 6.10 Domestic credit to private sector, 2003 (% of GDP)

European economies on direct instruments and administrative interest rate setting.

The three main challenges of banking system reform in SEE

There were three main problems facing commercial banks in SEE. The first referred to the lack of competition in the banking sector and its costs for effective intermediation, while the second concerned the number of bad loans in the balance sheet of commercial banks. The third was related to the institutional framework which dealt with issues such as capital adequacy and banking supervision. Table 6.4 displays information concerning the particular problems in each country of the region.

The first area of concern had to do with the limited competition which was primarily due to the dominant presence of state-owned commercial banks. In Table 6.4, the second and third rows for each country, referring to the number of banks and to the asset share of state-owned banks respectively, are indicative of the degree of competition in the banking sector. First, with respect to the number of banks, Albania and FYROM were the two countries with the smallest number of banks initially. Note, however, that a large number of commercial banks did not necessarily imply intense competition. In Bulgaria, for instance, the large number of banks initially was the result of the breaking-up of the former Bulgarian National Bank into a large number of small banks which, however, did not have a branch network. As a result competition remained weak (see Calvo and Kumar 1993). Next, Table 6.4 also reports high concentration with respect to the asset share of state-owned banks, particularly during the first decade of transition. In Bulgaria, seven state-owned banks held more than 50 per cent of banking system assets in 1999. Then, however, the asset-holding of state-owned banks fell sharply to about 0.5 per cent in 2003. In Romania, by the end of 1998, the banking system was dominated by heavily segmented state-owned banks, which held more than three-quarters of total bank assets. In 2003, their share was still standing high at about 41 per cent of total bank assets.

The situation was quite different in the former Yugoslav republics reflecting, in most cases, different initial conditions. More specifically, in Croatia the number of banks was already high at the beginning of transition, while in the case of FYROM, although low initially, it expanded rapidly. This was combined with the relatively low asset share of state-owned banks in both countries. In the case of Croatia it had stood at almost 60 per cent in 1993 but, after a moderate decline during the 1990s, it fell sharply to 5.7 per cent in 2000 and down to 3.4 per cent in 2003. In FYROM, the asset share of state-owned banks has always been negligible. This, however, did not prevent the banking sector from being highly concentrated in both countries. In particular, by the end of 1998, the two largest banks in Croatia controlled around 40 per cent of total banking assets, while in FYROM the share of the top three banks was about 60 per cent. By the end of 2002, the five largest banks had a share of about 63 and 74 per cent of total banking assets in Croatia and FYROM respectively (EBRD 2004a). The two late transition starters of the region, BH and SM, were initially characterized by a large number of banks as well as by the dominant presence of state-owned banks regarding their share of total bank assets. By 2003, however, there had been considerable improvement with respect to the latter, since the asset share of state banks fell to 5.2 in BH from almost 76 per cent in 1999, and to 34.1 in SM, from more than 90 per cent in 2000. Finally, in Albania the asset share of state banks was the highest in the region, standing at 52 per cent by the end of 2003. Furthermore, during the same year, the share of the five largest banks was almost at 86 per cent of total banking assets, the highest in the region as well.

The large share of bad (enterprise) loans in the portfolios of commercial banks was a common characteristic in all economies of SEE during the 1990s, which turned out to be a key obstacle inhibiting economic growth and financial sector development. This problem was inherited from central planning and kept mounting given the administrative allocation of financial resources and the soft budget constraints, which allowed enterprises to service outstanding loans through more borrowing. The delayed banking system reform and the rapid accumulation of bad loans were a reflection of the slow speed of structural reform and the prolonged reliance of enterprises on soft budget constraints. Thus banks, particularly state-owned ones, were engaged in loss-making lending which was also encouraged by the inadequate institutional framework that was reflected in insufficient banking supervision and a lack of accountability for bank bankruptcy. In Table 6.4, the fourth row for each SEE country reports bad loans as a share of total loans. This problem appeared to be particularly severe for Albania, BH, FYROM and Romania, and less so for Bulgaria, Croatia and SM. Note that this accumulation of bad debts took place although most of the countries had taken steps to alleviate some of the burden that the banking system inherited from central planning.

More specifically, most countries of SEE had been forced to take action at the beginning of the transition process. In Bulgaria, for instance, the government replaced some non-performing debt of enterprises with special state bond issues, while in Romania a substantial part of these loans was written off against government budget deposits in state-owned banks or replaced by government liabilities.[15] In Croatia, the government issued the so called 'big bonds' to large socially-owned companies which, in turn, were used by enterprises to repay their overdue obligations to banks.[16] Finally, following the information in Table 6.4, it is apparent that the situation improved considerably for most of the countries of the region during the period after the Kosovo War. In particular, Albania, BH and Romania made substantial progress, reducing the portion of bad loans quite sharply. However, FYROM has made moderate progress while in the case of SM the portion of bad loans has increased.

The accumulation of bad loans had very serious consequences for the particular economies as well as for the banking sector itself. First, it inhibited the enforcement of financial discipline on enterprises, delaying the imposition of reform measures. Second, banks shifted the credit risk burden into higher interest rates, which put profitable enterprises under financial pressure as well. This, as we saw in Chapter 4, was partly responsible for the large spread between nominal lending and deposit rates. Finally, the poor quality of loan portfolios seriously affected the solvency of commercial banks. This, on many occasions, forced central banks to undertake extensive refinancing of troubled commercial banks, undermining as a result the anti-inflationary stance of monetary policy. Furthermore, the bank insolvency problem significantly contributed to the eruption of financial crises by hindering the privatization prospects of commercial banks, while it was also responsible for the delaying of reforms.

Another issue that greatly contributed to banking sector fragility in the region concerned the weak institutional framework regarding the legal aspect of banking activities. As a matter of fact, commercial banks expanded rather quickly through the process of privatization and the opening-up to foreign institutions, while there was still insufficient regulation and weak supervision frameworks. The combination of weak loan portfolios and the absence of an effective regulatory and legal environment, together with the emergence of unfavourable macroeconomic shocks, led a number of banks to become insolvent causing, in some instances, serious financial crises. As a matter of fact, all the countries of the region, to a lesser or larger extent, faced serious bank insolvency problems which, in most instances, turned into overall financial crises, particularly in the cases of Albania, Bulgaria and Romania. In all these countries chronic financial fragility, which was manifested in the collapses of banks and pyramid schemes, was the common cause that led to financial crises. This, in turn, forced governments to take strong action aimed at strengthening the banking system.

The overall progress in banking sector reform, including interest rate liberalization, is captured by the corresponding EBRD index which appears in Table 6.4 (the last row for each country). Note that, among others, scores of 3.0 and above meant that there was 'substantial progress in establishment of bank solvency and of a framework for prudential supervision and regulation' (EBRD 2003).[17] It is interesting to note that, except for Croatia, all the other countries had a score below 3.0 by the end of 1999. As a matter of fact, by 2003, Bulgaria was the only one of the remaining countries that succeeded in reaching a score above 3.0. This is indicative of the slow overall progress in banking reform while, at the same time, it underlines the need for further progress in establishing bank solvency and strengthening regulation and supervision frameworks. Figure 6.11 compares the average progress made by the countries of SEE with that of their counterparts in CE. The progress of CE has been much more profound and quick. In particular,

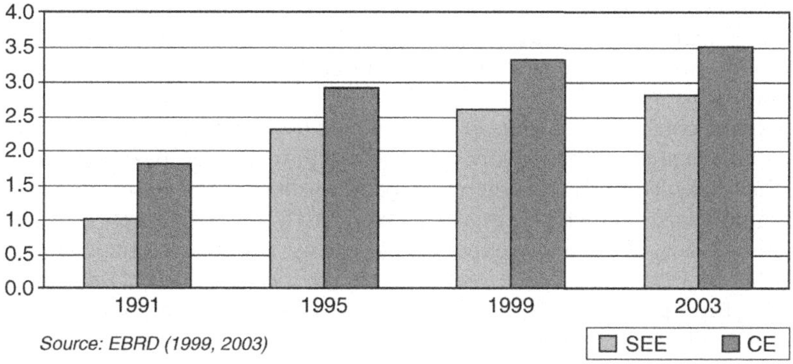

Source: EBRD (1999, 2003)

Figure 6.11 Banking sector reform

their average score had almost reached the 3.0 mark by 1995, which was still higher than the corresponding score of the South East European countries in 2003.

Country experience

In this subsection, we shall elaborate on individual country experience regarding banking reform. Starting with Albania, the slow pace of reform and the fundamental weaknesses with respect to the legal framework allowed the development of speculative investment schemes, which encountered spectacular growth during 1994–96 by promising excessive returns on deposits. These pyramid schemes eventually collapsed in early 1997, generating an acute crisis and public disorder. The crisis led to major legislative changes, which strengthened significantly the banking regulation and supervision frameworks. As a result, confidence in the banking sector has increased significantly. There were 15 banks operating in Albania in 2003 (Table 6.4). The Savings Bank was the only remaining state-owned one which, however, accounted for more than 50 per cent of all bank assets in Albania. After two unsuccessful attempts, it was eventually sold to an Austrian bank in 2003.[18]

In BH, the banking sector initially consisted of large and insolvent state-owned banks as well as private banks, which were small and undercapitalized. In both entities new banking laws were enacted to facilitate the financial restructuring, privatization and liquidation of state banks. Nevertheless, the process of privatization proceeded slowly. The number of banks increased to 61 at the end of 1999 and then fell moderately to 56 in 2000 (EBRD 2000). Also, despite the large number of banks, most banking assets were held by a small number of state banks. Effective consolidation in the sector started by mid-2001, and as a result there was a significant reduction in the number of banks. By the end of 2003, there were 37 banks, most of which operated in the Federation, while, bank privatization was essentially complete. Finally, adequate banking regulations, including supervision rules and prudential regulations, have been established in both entities (European Commission 2003).

Bulgaria constitutes a prime example where the combination of inefficient legal and regulatory framework and the accumulation of payments arrears by the banks led to the emergence of bank insolvency problems on a rather systematic basis, which eventually turned into a major financial crisis. As a matter of fact, the country experienced at least two major financial crises, the first in 1994 and a much more severe one towards the end of 1996 and the beginning of 1997. More specifically, there were three major reasons for the bank insolvency problems and the emergence of the financial crises. First, as pointed out, the root of the problem lay in the large portion of non-performing loans in the banks' assets portfolio, primarily as a result of the sluggish structural reform of enterprises. Second, despite the laws introduced in order to safeguard bank operations, new private banks operated under a rather lax supervisory environment and consequently the problem with the non-performing loans was aggravated.[19] Finally, the large depreciation of the domestic currency in 1994 contributed to an effective lowering of capital requirements, allowing more private banks to operate despite failing to meet the capital adequacy ratio requirement which stood at 8 per cent. In response to the lower liquidity of commercial banks, the central bank engaged in a large recapitalization of troubled banks, which, however, proved unsustainable, giving rise to a vicious circle whereby increasing financial support was accompanied by growing pressure on the exchange market. Eventually, the central bank could not avoid a large depreciation of the domestic currency in the spring of 1996 and an explosion in prices. The resulting decline in the confidence of the public reinforced the liquidity problems giving rise to a major financial crisis at the end of 1996, which eventually led to massive bankruptcy of banks and to their subsequent closure.[20]

As pointed out in Chapter 4, the implications of the financial crisis proved to be severe for the Bulgarian economy, since inflation increased sharply and economic activity declined considerably in 1997. As a result, following the advice of IMF, the government introduced a Currency Board regime for the exchange rate, together with a package of long overdue structural reforms. Particularly with respect to the banking system, a combination of closures, recapitalization, straitened supervision and the adoption of sound macroeconomic policies restored confidence. The privatization of the banking sector was largely completed after the sale of DSK Bank, the former savings bank and second largest bank in Bulgaria in terms of assets, in 2003. By the end of 2003, there were only two remaining non-private banks (which, held less than 1 per cent of the total banking assets).

In Croatia, besides the transition process, political developments such as secession from the Socialist Federal Republic of Yugoslavia and independence as well as war had an adverse impact on the banking system in the early 1990s. Furthermore, as in the other economies of the region, the accumulation of non-performing loans constituted a significant financial difficulty for the banking sector. To counteract these difficulties, the government enacted a bank rehabilitation law in 1994 and decided to rehabilitate four large banks, which together accounted for almost half of the total banking sector assets. The favourable macroeconomic conditions, following the successful launching of the stabilization programme, led to a rapid expansion of private banks which, however, due to deficiencies in banking regulations took high risks with respect to their lending practices and, as a result, encountered problems with the repayment of loans. The international financial crises of 1997–98, together with the tightening of macroeconomic policies, aggravated the situation and revealed the serious insolvency problems of several banks. The resulting loss of confidence led to a banking crisis, which contributed to a loss of official reserves and to a resurgence of currency substitution. The enactment of a new banking law, by the end of 1998, strengthened the supervisons authority of the central bank, enabling it to take stronger preventive action which eventually led to an overall improvement of the banking sector.[21] The run on Rijecka Bank in early 2002, however, highlighted the need for more efficient supervision and control mechanisms but, at the same time, successfully tested the resilience of the banking system. After that, a new banking law was adopted in 2002. Finally, by the end of 2003, there were only two remaining state-owned banks, which controlled about 3 per cent of the total banking assets.

The weaknesses of the banking system in FYROM did not differ from those of the other South East European economies. More specifically, the large share of non-performing loans in the portfolio of large banks, stemming from losses in the enterprise sector, was the key obstacle to financial sector development. Furthermore, the banking system was characterized by a particularly low level of intermediation and an insufficient legislative framework while, as indicated earlier, it was heavily concentrated. Two banks, namely Stopanska and Komercijalna Banka, accounted for more than half of total assets and about two-thirds of all deposits by the end of 1998.[22] A large rehabilitation operation took place in 1995, which involved the transfer of the operations of the 25 most indebted enterprises from the balance sheets of the banks to the Bank Rehabilitation Agency, which considerably improved bank liquidity.[23] The situation was further improved following the recapitalization and sale of Stopanska Banka which had become insolvent towards the end of 1998. The Kosovo crisis in early 1999 was the event that revealed major weaknesses in the banking sector. As a result, a new banking law was adopted in 2000. Also, the rapid economic recovery that followed, as well as the prompt central bank action towards reform, helped restore confidence in the banking system. In particular, in 2001, the central bank took firm steps to strengthen the regulatory and supervisory frameworks while strict capitalization requirements were introduced. By the end of 2003, the banking system was almost completely privatized, since there was only one remaining state-owned bank. As pointed out earlier, the quality of the banks' loan portfolio has improved moderately. This has been primarily due to the difficulties faced by several small banks.

In Romania, the reform of the banking system proceeded at a very slow pace. Despite repeated interventions by the government, bad debts continued to accumulate reflecting the lack of restructuring in the enterprise sector, which, in turn, was inhibiting structural change in the banking sector as well. The slow pace of reform in the banking system was manifested by the very high rate of concentration and the fact that the large state banks accounted for the bulk of deposits and banking assets (Table 6.4). The two insolvent state banks, Bancorex and Banca Agricola, were the main agents for quasi-fiscal support to the state enterprises and the agricultural sector prior to 1997, but the problem was largely alleviated by the accommodating nature of monetary policy. This, however, was changed as the new stabilization programme put forward in 1997, in collaboration with the IMF, called for a tightening of monetary policy and an end to the direct credits of the central bank (among other things).[24] As a result, the programme soon revealed the insolvency problems of the state banks in general, and of these two banks in particular, causing a serious banking crisis in late 1997. As a matter of fact, the government was forced to convert about US$1 billion of bad credits granted by the particular two banks into government bonds as a way of recapitalizing them.[25]

Romania's banking crisis proved to be less severe than the Bulgarian one, although it lasted longer, until 1999. Nevertheless, as a result of the crisis, inflation increased considerably, while GDP declined for three consecutive years. In 1998, the adoption of new central bank, banking and bank insolvency laws improved the legal environment of Romanian banking considerably. Furthermore, the ownership structure also improved following the privatization of two state banks (Romanian Bank for Development and Banc Post), the closure of Bancorex and the restructuring of Banca Agricola (see IMF 2001). The asset share of state-owned banks continued to remain significant in 2003. This largely was due to the failure of the government to sell Banca Comerciala Romana (BCR), the largest of the three remaining state-owned banks, which held about one-third of total banking assets (EBRD 2003). The BCR was partially privatized through the sale of 12.5 per cent to the International Finance Corporation and another 12.5 per cent to EBRD (see Stubos and Tsikripis, 2004).

As previously pointed out, the transition process in SM effectively started in 2001, following the political change that had occurred in October of 2000. At the beginning of 2001 there were 81 banks in Serbia and 11 in Montenegro. However, many banks were insolvent, while most assets were concentrated in six large, state-owned banks (EBRD 2001). Major steps, however, were taken to restore solvency as well as confidence in the banking sector. In particular, a number of banks were closed or put under supervision in Serbia during 2001. The central bank closed the four largest state-owned banks in January 2002, since all of them were found to be insolvent (EBRD 2002). In addition, towards the end of 2002, the Serbian government put about fifteen banks under state control with the purpose of offering them for sale after successfully completing the process of rehabilitation (European Commission 2003). In Montenegro, the largest state-owned bank was initially rehabilitated and then sold in July 2003. Overall, the number of banks in the country was reduced to 47 in 2003 since several were closed or merged or put into liquidation. Finally, the central banks of the two republics made considerable progress in strengthening banking supervision and regulation.

Some concluding remarks

Progress in structural reform constituted a major challenge faced by the transition economies since, in essence, it reflected the effectiveness of the transformation process towards the market system. In the case of SEE, the progress towards reform was particularly slow and this was clearly reflected in the disappointing economic performance of the region during the period 1991–98. The slow progress with respect to privatization and restructuring of the large state firms and the resulting persistence of soft budget constraints, together with the limited role of the banking system in mobilizing funds, were the main obstacles that largely contributed to substantial economic failures during the 1990s.

The progress made since the late 1990s has been quite remarkable. The renewed commitment of SEE to reform and the resulting acceleration have led to significant progress as well as to a considerable upturn in the economic performance of the region. Note, however, that despite the progress, SEE still lags considerably behind the Central European countries, and thus the role of the private sector must be strengthened further for them to be able to catch up with other countries effectively.

7
An Empirical Assessment of the Growth Determinants in South Eastern Europe

In the preceding chapters we examined different aspects of the transition process for the countries of SEE. More specifically, after presenting the basic facts of transition for the particular economies, our analysis focused on three broad determinants which greatly affected transition and thus the economic performance of the particular countries: initial conditions, macroeconomic stabilization and structural reforms. A common conclusion regarding conditions and developments with respect to these three broad factors referred to the fact that they were not as favourable in the case of SEE.

First, initial conditions were examined in Chapter 3. As explained, they primarily refer to the extent of structural and macroeconomic distortions inherited by central planning at the start of transition. Our analysis indicated that the countries of SEE faced quite adverse initial conditions, particularly in comparison with the experience of the economies of CE. Macroeconomic stabilization and performance were analysed in Chapters 4 and 5. Our analysis, particularly in Chapter 4, demonstrated the lack of credible macroeconomic policies by most countries in the region which, in turn, was primarily responsible for their failure to curtail inflation and generate favourable conditions for sustained economic growth during the first decade of transition. Finally, in Chapter 6, we considered the progress made with respect to structural reforms. The slow progress in most areas of reform was a common characteristic in almost all the countries under consideration, which was manifested by their serious lagging behind the countries of CE, especially during the past decade. Thus, as a result of the adverse impact of these three broad factors, the economic consequences of transition became much more severe for the economies of SEE. This was primarily reflected in the poor economic performance of the region, particularly relative to the economies of CE.

In this chapter, our aim is to take the analysis a step further by attempting to verify empirically the relative importance of these three groups of factors in explaining the output performance of SEE. In particular, we will attempt to quantify their contribution to the economic performance of the region while, at the same time, trying to ascertain how they compare relative to corresponding results concerning the Central European region. Before proceeding, we should mention that output growth may be considered as a relatively narrow concept to measure the overall progress of a country during the transition process. Nevertheless, it must be pointed out that, besides the fact that progress in other dimensions which also capture the extent of a country's moving forward to the market system may not always be easily measured, growth may serve as a very good *ex post* proxy since it constitutes the final link in a long and complex process (Havrylyshyn 2001).

Literature review

There has been an enormous body of literature which examines differences in growth performance among transition economies.[1] These studies rely on cross-country statistical analysis and mostly concentrate on the first decade of transition. Most of the studies followed similar specifications and have made important contributions by establishing definite conclusions about the main determinants of growth performance in transition economies. In particular, they provided substantial evidence to confirm the importance of variables capturing the impact of initial conditions, as well as macroeconomic and structural reform policies. The broad conclusions reached by the majority of these studies, to a larger or lesser extent, agree that these three broad factors constitute the primary determinants of the transition economies' growth performance.[2] In particular, while their importance may differ depending on the countries or the period under consideration, the results, in most studies, agree that greater output growth was associated with more favourable initial conditions, and faster and more effective macroeconomic stabilization, as well as more rapid progress in structural reforms.

First, with respect to structural reform, a wide body of research suggests that countries with deeper and more vigorous reforms were the ones that experienced an earlier output recovery and a faster reduction of inflation. More specifically, most studies verify the results initially reached by De Melo, Denizer and Gelb (1996), according to which there is a strong and positive impact of structural reform on growth. Studies by Fischer, Sahay and Vegh (1996, 1998), Havrylyshyn, Izvorski and van Rooden (1998), Aslund, Boone and Johnson (1996), Hernandez-Cata (1997), Wolf (1999), and Berg, Borensztein, Sahay and Zettelmeyer (1999), together with the importance of initial conditions and stabilization, confirm the positive impact of structural reform on output growth. Note, however, that a number of studies find reforms to have initially caused a decline in output growth rates, presumably due to adjustment costs. This, however, is then offset by a strong positive impact during the years following the introduction of reforms. In particular, supporting evidence for this 'J-curve effect' of structural reforms was found in several studies such as the ones by De Melo *et al.* (1997), Falcetti, Raiser and Sanfey (2000), Auslund, Boone and Johnson (1996), Havrylyshyn, Isvorski and van Rooden (1998), Hernandez-Cata (1997) and Wolf (1999). However, Berg, Borensztein, Sahay and Zettelmeyer (1999), by separating out the public and private sector, concluded that the impact of structural reforms is positive from the beginning of transition: that is, a possible decline in the state sector in response to reforms is more than offset by the positive reaction of the private sector (see also Havrylyshyn 2001).

Turning to macroeconomic stabilization, a firm conclusion (reached by virtually all studies) confirms its importance as a vital precondition for output recovery during transition. Most studies indicate that effective disinflation and lower fiscal deficits are associated with higher growth rates. More specifically, while all studies agree about the negative impact of inflation on growth, the results with respect to fiscal policy are not clear-cut. There are studies which find a positive impact of fiscal consolidation on growth, as for instance Fischer, Sahay and Vegh (1996, 1998) and Wolf (1999), while others reach opposite conclusions, such as a study by Lougani and Sheets (1997). Finally, some studies consider the role of the exchange rate. In particular, Fischer, Sahay and Vegh (1998), Papazoglou (1999a) and Papazoglou and Pentecost (2001) found a fixed exchange rate regime to have a significant negative impact on inflation and a positive one on growth. Note, however, that, as implied by the particular studies, the impact of the exchange rate on growth is indirect, primarily operating through its effect on inflation stabilization.

Finally, with respect to initial conditions, it is generally accepted that they constitute important determinants of growth, although the extent of their significance varies in different studies. As pointed out in Chapter 3, De Melo, *et al.* (1997) were the first to consider the impact of initial conditions, and found their role to be substantial. Other studies, however, indicate that the effect of initial conditions diminishes over time.[3]

Data and specification

Our sample consists of ten countries, five from SEE (BH and SM are excluded as they started the transition process much later) and the five countries of CE. Our data extend from 1991 to 2003, which means that the total sample consists of 130 observations. The annual growth of real output constitutes the dependent variable. With respect to the explanatory variables, in line with the vast majority of previous empirical studies, we employ variables largely capturing the three broad determinants of growth, namely initial conditions, macroeconomic stabilization and structural reform.

More specifically, with respect to macroeconomic stabilization, our analysis (following most previous empirical studies) relies on two variables: inflation and fiscal balance. Inflation constitutes the main proxy for stabilization and we expect it to affect output growth negatively, since lower inflation constitutes a vital precondition for output growth. Fiscal balance constitutes the prime policy tool reflecting the extent of a country's commitment to stabilization. We expect lower fiscal deficits or higher surpluses to be associated with higher output growth. Besides the indirect impact, after controlling for inflation, it is also expected to affect growth directly, either through crowding-out or through a short-run stimulus on aggregate demand.

Turning to structural reform, our analysis relies on the indices developed by De Melo, Denizer and Gelb (1996). In particular, we updated their liberalization index (LI) until the year 2003, using information on the more recent progress in structural reforms from the 2003 EBRD *Transition Report*. The LI consists of three subcomponents. The first refers to an index of internal liberalization (LII), which is based on the price liberalization and competition policy indicators of EBRD. The second includes an index for external liberalization, which is based on the trade and foreign exchange system indicator of EBRD. Finally, the third subcomponent represents an index of private sector development which measures progress in privatization and banking reform. In particular, it consists of EBRD's indicators on small- and large-scale privatization, governance and enterprise restructuring, banking reform and interest rate liberalization, and securities markets and non-bank financial institutions. All these indicators of EBRD are reported in Tables 6.1, 6.3 and 6.4. Note that following De Melo, Denizer and Gelb (1996), we normalized these indicators in such a way that their values range between 0 and 1, with an EBRD score of 4.3 (or 4+) to correspond to a value of 1. Following the previous literature, we expect liberalization to have a strong positive impact on output growth. Furthermore, we examine the behaviour of liberalization over time. In particular, we expect the impact of liberalization on output growth to diminish as the transition process progresses. Thus, we expect the interaction of the liberalization indicator with the time trend to affect growth negatively, implying a decreasing trend in the impact of liberalization over time.

With respect to initial conditions we use the 'index of distortions', which we constructed in Chapter 3, following the methodology used by De Melo *et al.* (1997). In particular, we employ the first of the two principal components which we calculated in Chapter 3. The first factor explains almost 50 per cent of the total variance over all initial conditions. Furthermore, if you recall from our analysis in Chapter 3, the resulting country scores for the specific factor were negative for all the countries in both regions. As explained, the higher the score (in absolute value) the more favourable the initial conditions. Thus, in our growth equation, a positive sign with respect to initial conditions would imply an adverse impact of the latter on output growth. In addition, an interesting issue refers to whether the effect of initial conditions is increasing or decreasing over time. Following Falcetti, Raiser and Sanfey (2000), we interact our index of initial conditions with the time trend. Thus, the overall impact of initial conditions on growth is captured by these two terms.

Finally, we use three additional variables to explain output variation. First, we use a variable capturing the distance of each country from Dusseldorf.[4] This variable is used as a proxy to underline the importance of close economic relations with the EU to growth performance of these countries. The lower economic integration of SEE with the EU, as compared to that of the Central European countries, to a certain extent is a reflection of the fact that the South East European region is geographically less favourably positioned than the Central European region. Second, the time trend is included to capture whether there is a trend in output growth over time. Finally, a dummy variable is used to test for the empirical importance of war or conflict episodes on growth. This could constitute an initial condition as well, but it is considered separately in order to capture the fact that the region of SEE went through a number of wars and ethnic conflicts which primarily stemmed from the break-up of the former Socialist Federal Republic of Yugoslavia.

Thus, from the preceding analysis, the basic equation to be estimated has the following form:

$$\begin{aligned} RGDPG_{it} = {} & \alpha_i + \alpha_1 LINF_{it} + \alpha_2 FB_{it} + \alpha_3 LI_{it} + \alpha_4 LI_{it} \times TIME + \alpha_5 INC_{it} \\ & + \alpha_6 INC_{it} \times TIME + \alpha_7 LDIS_{it} + \alpha_8 TIME + \alpha_9 WD_{it} + u_{it} \end{aligned} \tag{7.1}$$

where subscripts i and t are indices for country and time respectively; *RGDPG* is the average annual rate of real GDP growth; *LINF* is the natural log of the annual average inflation rate; *FB* is the fiscal balance expressed as percentage of GDP (a minus sign stands for deficit and a plus sign for surplus); *LI* is the liberalization index; *INC* refers to initial conditions; *LDIS* is the natural log of the distance of each country (capital city) from Dusseldorf; *WD* corresponds to war dummy (takes the value 1 in case of war and 0 otherwise); *TIME* captures the time trend; and finally, u is the error term. According to the above discussion, we expect the following signs for the coefficients of the above equation: $\alpha_1 < 0, > 0, \alpha_2 > 0, \alpha_3 > 0, \alpha_4 > 0, \alpha_5 > 0, \alpha_6 < 0, \alpha_7 < 0, \alpha_8 > 0$ and $\alpha_9 < 0$.

Output growth, initial conditions, liberalization and inflation: a graphical analysis

Before we proceed with the empirical analysis we can detect graphically the relationship between the output evolution, on the one hand, and the three broad determinants of output growth on the other. The figures which follow portray the closeness of the relationship between the particular variables during the first decade of transition (i.e., until 1998). A striking similarity in all cases refers to the largely distinctive performance between the countries of the two regions: despite the relative diversity in the circumstances in each of the ten countries, the performances of the countries in each region are clustered together, with the countries of SEE performing consistently worse than the ones of CE.

Figure 7.1 is a scatterplot graph relating the degree of output recovery, captured by the ratio of 1998 to 1989 output levels, to the level of initial conditions. Note that, as explained earlier, the initial conditions (which appear on the vertical axis) refer to the first principal component which was calculated in Chapter 3. Recall that higher negative scores correspond to more favourable initial conditions. Figure 7.1 clearly indicates the negative relationship between adverse initial conditions and output growth. The correlation coefficient between the two variables is about 0.55. In particular, with the possible exception of Poland, greater output recovery in 1998 relative to the 1989 level is associated with more favourable initial conditions. The less favourable conditions for most of the South East European countries tend to be associated with lower output recovery.

Figure 7.2 captures the relation between the extent of output recovery and liberalization. In particular, Figure 7.2 clearly shows the strong positive association between output recovery in 1998 relative to 1989 and the Cumulative Liberalization Index (CLI) since 1989. The correlation coefficient between the two variables is equal to 0.73. In addition, Figure 7.2 clearly demonstrates the considerable difference in the performance between the two regions: the countries of CE are the ones where high CLI is associated with more pronounced output recovery, while in SEE a slower output recovery is connected with lower scores for CLI.

Figure 7.3 displays the relationship between output recovery and stabilization. In particular, it captures the extent of association between

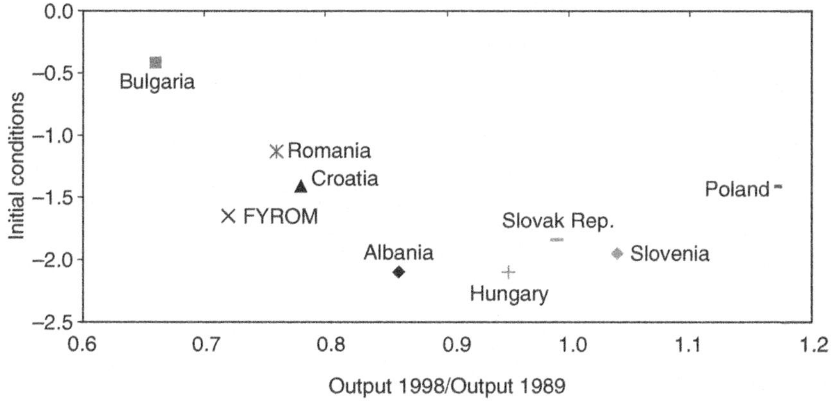

Figure 7.1 Initial conditions and output growth

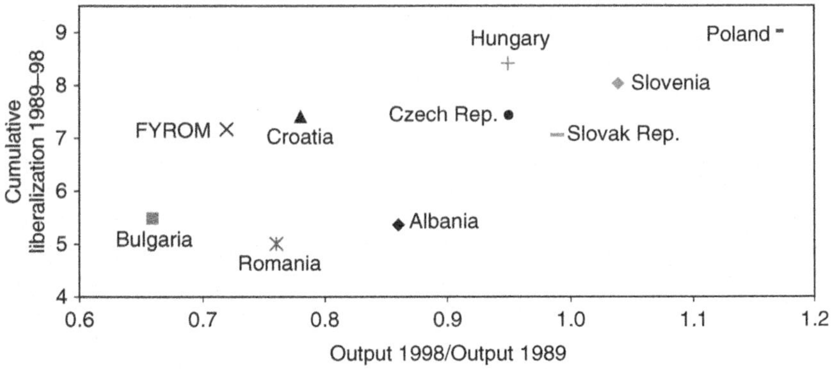

Figure 7.2 Growth and liberalization

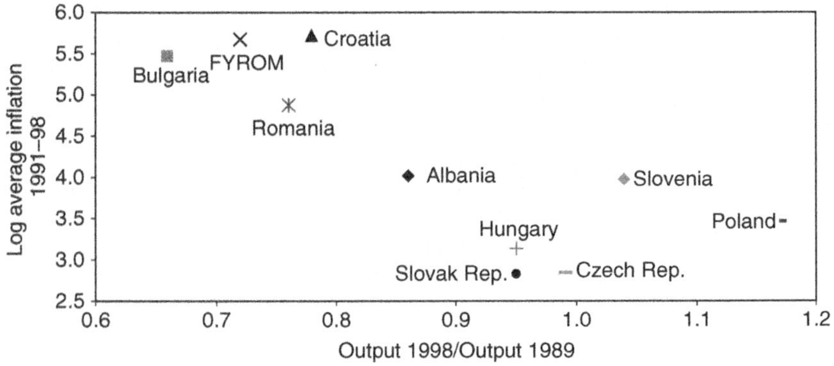

Figure 7.3 Growth and inflation

the average rate of inflation during the 1991–98 period (in log) and the extent of output recovery in 1998 as compared to the 1989 level. According to Figure 7.3, a strong negative relationship between the two variables is revealed, which is also verified by the fact that the corresponding correlation coefficient is about 0.8. Thus, the countries which were more successful in reducing inflation appear to be the ones with the better output recovery. Again, the countries of SEE were clearly outperformed by their counterparts in CE.

Finally, Figure 7.4 depicts the relationship between inflation and liberalization. After all, both inflation and output growth are considered to be dependent on liberalization policy. Figure 7.4 depicts a negative relationship between CLI scores and the average rate of inflation during the period 1991–98. However, this relation does not appear as strong as in the case

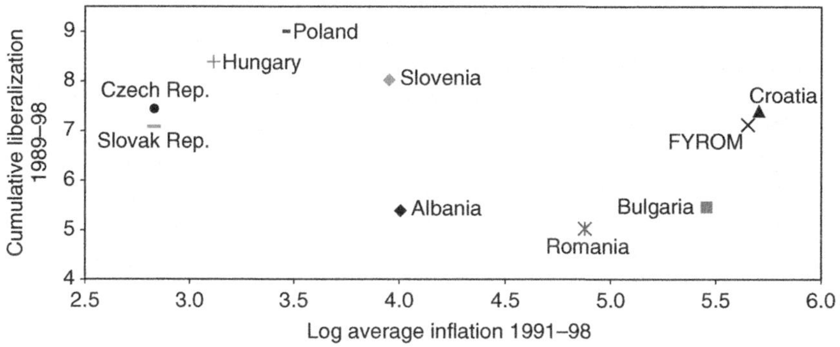

Figure 7.4 Inflation and liberalization

of reform and growth (the correlation coefficient takes the value of 0.43). A significant reason for that may be due to the fact that Croatia and FYROM, which as part of the former SFR of Yugoslavia started the transition process with a considerable degree of liberalization, faced particularly high inflation rates during the early stages of transition.

The empirical results

Tables 7.1 and 7.2 report the estimation results. In particular, Table 7.1 reports the results for the whole sample as well as for each region separately over the entire period. Equation 1 includes all ten countries of the sample, Equation 2 refers to five countries of SEE, and finally Equation 3 corresponds to five countries of CE. Table 7.2 reports the results for the same three equations but it refers to the first decade of transition (i.e., 1991–98). All equations were estimated using panel regression with a common constant. Our overall results are in line with most of the studies reviewed earlier concerning the empirical determinants of output performance in transition economies. In particular, the variables used to capture the impact of the three basic determinants of growth under transition – initial conditions, liberalization and stabilization – are statistically significant and have the correct signs. Note that for the explanatory variables that were not statistically significant the estimated coefficients are not reported. The reported coefficients correspond to estimation results, after the removal of the not statistically significant variables.

Let us begin our analysis by making some general observations. First, the 'explanatory power' of the particular equations appears to be high for this type of data, ranging from 0.63 to 0.73. Note that the equations for the period 1991–98 have stronger explanatory power than the corresponding ones for the period 1991–2003. This primarily reflects the importance of the

Table 7.1 Regression results, 1991–2003

Dependent variable: real output growth			
Independent variables	**Equation 1 All sample**	**Equation 2 SEE**	**Equation 3 CE**
Inflation	−0.92	−1.15	−1.80
	(−3.1)	(−3.2)	(−3.8)
Fiscal balance			0.41
			(3.2)
Liberalization (LI)	42.7	52.4	28.8
	(9.7)	(8.1)	(5.8)
(LI)×(time)	−6.6	−3.6	−4.6
	(−6.2)	(−3.7)	(−5.2)
Initial condition (IC)	7.5	14.2	6.6
	(6.0)	(7.1)	(5.7)
(IC)×(time)	−0.78	−1.0	−0.75
	(−4.6)	(−2.6)	(−4.7)
Time	3.8		7.1
	(3.9)		(3.9)
Distance	−1.7		
	(−3.7)		
Adjusted R^2	0.63	0.68	0.64
F-statistic	37.6	34.2	19.9
Observations	130.0	65.0	65.0

Note: Numbers in parentheses are t-statistics.

factors which predominantly affect output behaviour during transition (stabilization, structural reform and initial conditions). Thus, as we move further away from the initial date of the sample and the transition process progresses further, the explanatory power of the particular factors is weakened. As a matter of fact, the corresponding regressions were estimated for the period 1998–2003 and the empirical results indicate that all the explanatory variables are not statistically significant.[5] This, in turn, explains the fact that stabilization, liberalization and initial conditions appear to exert a greater impact during the period 1991–98, in comparison to 1991–2003. Turning to the estimation results for the separate equations for each region, we notice that the explanatory power of the equations for SEE is bigger than the one for CE. This may be due to the fact that, from the outset of the sample period, the countries of CE were already at a more advanced stage of the transition process than the SEE ones (our estimation is based on calendar time and not on 'transition' time).[6] A related issue refers to the fact that the impact of liberalization and initial conditions appears to be greater in magnitude in the case of SEE, while stabilization has a larger effect on the countries of CE. More specifically, inflation has a stronger impact on the Central European

Table 7.2 Regression results, 1991–98

Dependent variable: real output growth **Independent variables**	**Equation 1** **All sample**	**Equation 2** **SEE**	**Equation 3** **CE**
Inflation	−1.4	−1.23	−2.6
	(−2.7)	(−2.6)	(−2.9)
Fiscal balance			0.58
			(3.1)
Liberalization (LI)	46.0	72.4	35.3
	(7.1)	(7.3)	(4.3)
(LI)×(time)	−9.6	−10.1	−2.6
	(−4.5)	(−4.1)	(−2.0)
Initial condition (IC)	9.4	18.7	7.1
	(5.1)	(7.2)	(4.1)
(IC)×(time)	−1.6	−2.8	−0.86
	(−3.6)	(−3.1)	(−2.1)
Time	4.2		
	(2.5)		
Distance	−1.2		
	(−2.0)		
Adjusted R^2	0.65	0.73	0.67
F-statistic	25.8	27.8	15.5
Observations	80.0	40.0	40.0

Note: Numbers in parentheses are t-statistics.

countries and fiscal policy appears to affect only these economies as well. Thus, the fiscal policy variable is not statistically significant in the case of SEE or for the equations for the entire sample, and therefore it is not included in the estimation results of the corresponding equations.

Let us now examine the impact of each explanatory variable included in our estimation, starting with macroeconomic stabilization which is captured by the impact of two proxy variables: inflation and fiscal balance. As a general observation, we may conclude that while it contributes to output growth, its quantitative impact is relatively small in size.[7] More specifically, the impact of inflation appears to be small relative to that of the other determinants of output growth, while fiscal policy appears to exert an even smaller effect which is statistically significant only in the case of the Central European countries. The latter result, as explained earlier in this chapter, is in line with the findings of other studies (see Havrylyshyn 2001). In addition, it should be noticed that the impact of inflation is even smaller in the case of the South East European countries. Overall, macroeconomic stabilization appears to be more effective in contributing to economic growth in the case of the Central European countries. As indicated, this may be associated with the fact that transition started earlier in some countries and thus vigorous initial steps towards reform may have strengthened the effectiveness of macroeconomic stabilization.

The impact of liberalization is captured by two terms. The first indicates the strong positive impact of structural reforms on output growth which, however, according to the second term (capturing the interaction of the liberalization indicator with the time trend) diminishes over time as the transition process advances. The two terms together represent the overall impact of liberalization on output growth. As pointed out earlier, the impact of liberalization appears to be greater during 1991–98 than over the entire period, thus demonstrating the importance of structural reforms to economic growth during the 'core' years of transition. In particular, for the countries of CE we could see that the impact of liberalization becomes negative during the later years of the sample period (see the equation for the period 1991–2003). This could reflect the fact, that for some particular countries, structural reforms were largely completed towards the end of the sample period, having no further effect on growth. In addition, liberalization appears to have a greater impact on SEE. This, as already indicated, may reflect the fact that the countries of CE started the transition process earlier. Finally, it is interesting to note that the impact of liberalization on growth during the period 1991–98, diminishes much faster for SEE compared with CE, so the contemporaneous impact of liberalization on growth, although stronger in the case of SEE during the early years of transition, appears to diminish at a faster rate. Thus, in the case of the South East European countries, given the worse initial position of the particular countries, an increase in reforms by a given 'amount' appears to exert a greater marginal impact on growth, the effectiveness of which weakens faster.

The impact of initial conditions on economic growth is also captured by two terms, the second of which reflects the interaction of initial conditions with the time trend. The overall impact of initial conditions on growth is captured by the summation of these two terms. As explained earlier, a positive sign for the coefficient of initial conditions corresponds to adverse impact on growth. Thus there is a negative impact of initial conditions on growth which, however, diminishes over time. First, according to our results, the impact of initial conditions appears to be greater in the equations referring to the period 1991–98, relative to the ones for the entire sample period. Thus initial conditions matter but, as expected, the magnitude of their effect gets smaller as we move further away from the starting date. Furthermore, the initial conditions exert a greater impact on growth in the countries of SEE compared with their counterparts in CE. However, as in the case of liberalization, their impact appears to diminish faster in the former economies. This is more profound with respect to our estimation results concerning the period 1991–98.

Let us now turn to the other explanatory variables. The time trend is included in the estimated regression equations and its coefficient is positive, implying an increasing trend for output growth over time. Note, however, that it is statistically significant in the case of the estimations concerning the entire sample for both time periods, and in the case of CE only in the equation concerning the period 1991–2003. The time trend is not statistically significant in both equations concerning the South East European region, implying that output follows neither an increasing nor a decreasing trend over time (the values of the corresponding coefficients are not reported). Distance from Dusseldorf, operating as a proxy for proximity to Western markets, appears to be statistically significant only in the case of our estimations concerning the entire sample for both time periods. Its impact is negative, meaning that the further away from the EU market, the lower the output growth. This variable is assumed to operate as a proxy for the overall impact of the EU on the growth performance of the countries involved, and it appears to be less favourable for the countries of SEE, since they are the ones that are further away from the European market. Finally, the war dummy we used to capture the impact of wars and ethnic conflict that took place in the SEE region was not statistically important in any of the estimated equations and, as a result, it does not appear in Tables 7.1 and 7.2.

Explaining the difference in output growth between the two regions

In this section we will combine the results of our estimation as well as the actual evolution of policies and differences in initial conditions to explain the different growth performance of the countries of SEE relative to the ones in CE. More specifically, we will decompose the relative influence of the three broad determinants of growth to explain the evolution of output in our regressions. We will use the results of the two separate regressions for the two regions for the period 1991–98.

Figures 7.5 and 7.6 simply plot the average fitted values with respect to the three major explanatory variables, for the years from 1991 to 1998, for the regions of SEE and CE respectively. A bar above the horizontal axis indicates a positive influence of the particular variable on growth, while a bar below the axis indicates a negative influence. The height of the bar represents the magnitude of the effect. Also, a line represents the actual average growth path for each region. Note that, from the particular equations, the three basic factors that affect output are common to both regions and refer to macroeconomic stabilization, liberalization and initial conditions. Macroeconomic stabilization in the case of Central European economies includes the impact of both inflation as well as fiscal balance, while the latter is not included in the case of SEE, since it was not statistically significant in the estimated regression equations. In addition, the error term component is also plotted, so that the entire variation in actual growth performance is captured.

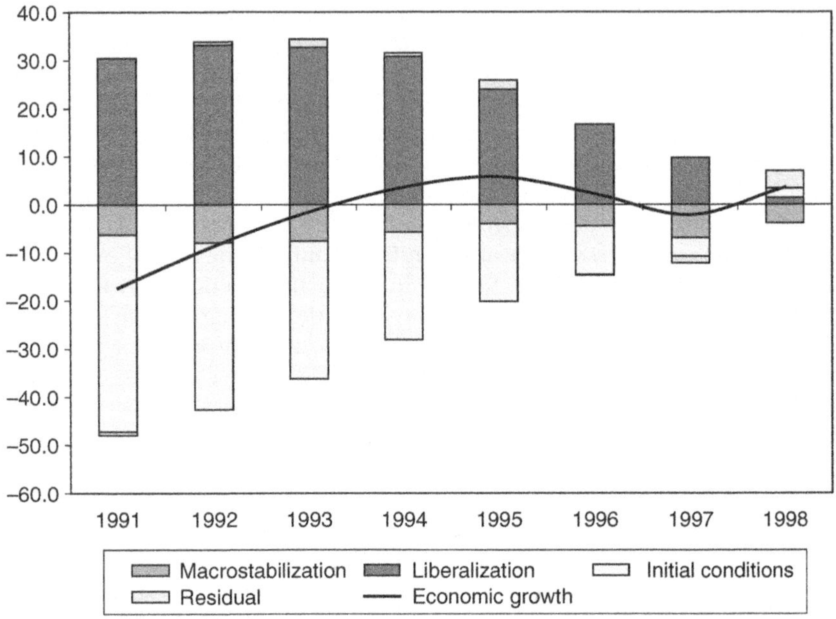

Figure 7.5 Determinants of growth in SEE

The two figures clearly show the impact of each determinant on growth. In particular, liberalization appears to have a strong positive impact in both regions, which diminishes as we move towards the later years of transition. The initial conditions and macroeconomic stabilization exert a negative impact. In the case of initial conditions the impact also weakens as we move away from the initial year. The impact of macroeconomic stabilization, primarily captured by the inverse relationship between inflation and output growth, is of smaller magnitude relative to other two determinants in both regions.

Finally, the two figures give a clear enough picture concerning the factors responsible for the relatively poorer output performance of the South East European region relative to the Central European one. First, we clearly see the adverse initial conditions to be the prime reason for the poor economic performance of SEE relative to CE during the early years of transition. The impact of liberalization initially appears to exert a greater effect on the South East European economies (possibly, as we explained, due to the fact that transition started earlier in the Central European countries). However, liberalization has a more lasting effect on economic growth in the case of the Central European countries. Finally, macroeconomic stabilization appears to exert a smaller effect on the South East European economies. As explained

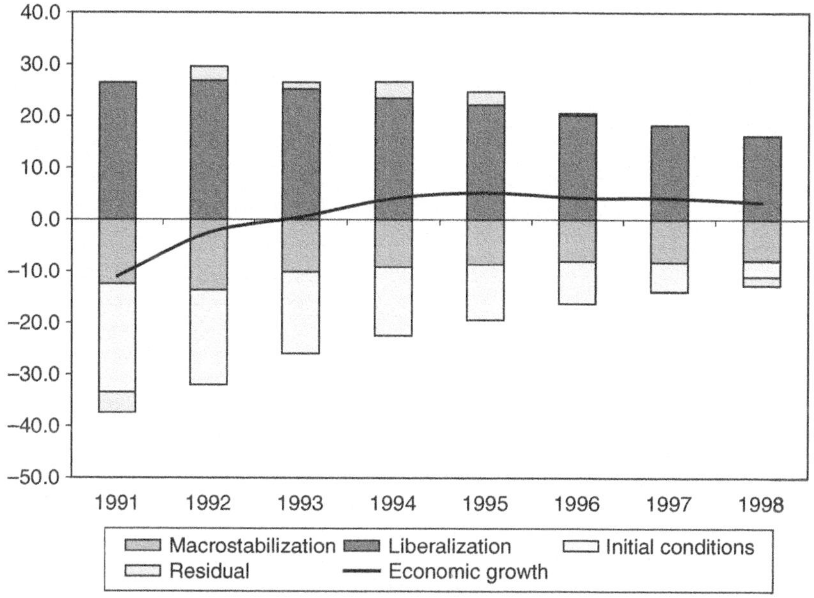

Figure 7.6 Determinants of growth in CE

earlier, the fact that by 1991, the starting date of our estimation, the transition process had already started in most Central European countries may have enhanced the impact of inflation and fiscal imbalances on economic performance. Finally, as shown in Figure 7.5, the adverse developments in macroeconomic stabilization appear to have been an important reason for the output reversal that occurred in SEE in 1997.

This page intentionally left blank

Part II
External Economic Relations

This page intentionally left blank

8
Trade Integration

Trade integration of the South East European economies with the rest of the world in general and with the EU in particular is of critical importance for their long-term growth prospects. For countries with the size as well as the extent of development as those in SEE, the prospects for strong and sustained economic recovery are closely linked to their ability to compete and thus attain access to foreign markets, especially those in developed countries such as the EU states. Thus, openness and greater trade integration of the countries in this region with the rest of the world is a vital precondition for growth and development. Furthermore, trade expansion and the removal of barriers would effectively enlarge the size of local markets and increase, as a result, their attractiveness to foreign investors, which would enhance the prospects for higher growth even further.

In this chapter we shall examine the geographical distribution and sectoral composition of the South East European countries' trade patterns. First we shall look into these patterns just prior to transition in order to appreciate the changes that took place during transition. Our analysis, with respect to changes in the geographical as well as structural patterns of trade, will focus on individual country experience as well as on the region as a whole.

Finally, an important issue that we shall examine in some detail is the particularly low level of trade among the countries of SEE. The low level of regional integration reduces the exporting potential of these countries and considerably weakens, as a result, their growth prospects. Our aim with respect to this matter will be twofold. First, we shall set up the map of bilateral trade flows among the countries of the region in order to obtain a clear picture concerning the participation of each country in intra-regional trading, and then we shall try to pinpoint the main factors which can explain the reasons for this low level of intra-regional trading.

Trade prior to transition

As in all centrally planned economies, the trade practices of the economies of SEE before the beginning of transition were largely confined within the CMEA: that is, they conducted most of their trading activity with their Eastern European counterparts and only a small portion of trade was directed towards the rest of the word. Table 8.1 reports the region's geographical composition of trade just prior to the beginning of the transition period, in 1989. Over 50 per cent of the region's total exports and imports were directed to, and originated from, the Eastern European countries.[1] As a matter of fact, Eastern Europe was the main trading partner for all the counties of SEE with the exception of the former SFR of Yugoslavia. Bulgaria appeared to be the country with the largest share of trade with other Eastern European countries. According to Table 8.1, about 83 and 73 per cent of Bulgaria's exports and imports respectively involved trading with Eastern Europe. The corresponding shares of the other countries were lower, but still substantial. The SFR of Yugoslavia had the lowest share, which largely reflected the fact

Table 8.1 Trade shares of South East European countries by direction, 1989 (%)

	Albania	Bulgaria	Romania	Yugoslavia	SEE
Exports					
Total	100.0	100.0	100.0	100.0	100.0
Industrial countries	33.0	5.9	41.6	49.8	29.9
of which EU	28.8	4.2	32.7	41.1	24.0
Eastern Europe	55.3	83.5	34.4	34.6	54.4
of which CE	21.8	9.6	8.8	8.3	9.1
SEE	24.3	3.3	3.6	2.3	3.2
Others	11.7	10.6	24.0	15.6	15.7
Total exports (in US$ mil.)	394.0	6,651.0	10,487.0	13,343.0	30,875.0
Imports					
Total	100.0	100.0	100.0	100.0	100.0
Industrial countries	30.9	14.5	18.7	53.6	30.5
of which EU	30.7	10.1	13.8	44.6	24.3
Eastern Europe	45.8	72.7	47.7	29.0	50.3
of which CE	18.2	11.0	11.8	9.4	10.7
SEE	19.1	3.0	4.8	2.2	3.3
Others	23.3	12.8	33.6	17.3	19.2
Total imports (in US$ mil.)	456.0	7,325.0	8,436.0	14,799.0	31,016.0

Source: WIIW annual database.

that it was not a member of CMEA and as a result it largely followed an independent trade policy.

Despite the heavy concentration of trading within the Eastern European bloc, the share of trade of the South East European states with the EU was rather significant.[2] About 24 per cent of the region's total international trade was conducted with the member states of the EU. Yugoslavia was the country with the largest trading ties with the West. In particular, the counties of the EU were its main trading partners with corresponding shares of exports and imports exceeding 40 per cent of the respective totals (see Table 8.1). The corresponding shares of Albania were considerable as well as Romania's exports. Bulgaria was the only country in the region which had very little trade with the West in general and the EU in particular.

An important feature of the geographical composition of trade of the South East European economies prior to transition (which, as we will see later on in this chapter, still remains a basic characteristic of the region) had to do with the very low level of regional integration (see also Petrakos and Totev 2000). According to Table 8.1, intra-SEE trading was just above 3 per cent of the region's total trade. More specifically, only Albania's trading with the other three countries of the region was significant, being about 24 and 19 per cent of its total exports and imports respectively. The corresponding shares of the remaining countries were considerably lower. Note, however, that the trading activity that occurred among the countries which belonged to the SFR of Yugoslavia is not accounted for.

Another aspect of the state trade practices by the centrally planned economies referred to the sectoral structure of trade. Trading within the Eastern European bloc primarily involved the exchange of natural resources and machinery instead of consumer goods. Overall, state trading led to a system of extreme specialization, where issues such as comparative advantage or transportation costs were of little concern.[3] This is verified in the case of SEE as well. According to Table 8.2, which reports the commodity breakdown of the exports and imports of the South East European countries in 1989, the trade patterns primarily involve the exchange of raw materials as well as machinery and equipment (Standard International Trade Classification, or SITC, 2, 3 and 7) and to a lesser extent consumer goods (SITC 0, 1 and 8). This was particular true for Albania, Bulgaria and Romania in which trade in the former three categories represented more than two-thirds of total trade. In Albania, the share of consumer goods was larger, reflecting the existence of a relatively larger agricultural sector. The pattern of international trade was not exactly the same in the case of Yugoslavia, due to that country's deviation from the strict central planning rules. According to Table 8.2, trade in manufactured goods and machinery and equipment (SITC 6 and 7) constituted the larger share of total trading in Yugoslavia.

Table 8.2 Trade shares of South East European countries by commodity in 1989, SITC groups (%)

	Albania	Bulgaria	Romania	Yugoslavia	SEE
Exports					
Total	100.0	100.0	100.0	100.0	100.0
Food, beverages, tobacco, and live animals (SITC 0,1)	19.5	11.6	4.3	11.8	9.3
Crude materials, inedible, except fuels (SITC 2)	14.4	4.0	4.1	5.3	4.8
Mineral fuels, lubricants, etc. (SITC 3)	54.4	7.7	32.1	1.4	13.9
Chemical products (SITC 4)	0.0	0.0	0.0	0.0	0.0
Animal and vegetable oils and fats (SITC 5)	0.6	3.4	9.5	13.3	9.7
Manufactured goods (SITC 6)	1.4	2.0	0.0	25.7	11.6
Machinery and transport equipment (SITC 7)	0.0	59.4	29.2	27.9	34.8
Miscellaneous manufactured articles (SITC 8)	9.7	11.1	18.1	14.5	14.9
Commodities not classified by kind (SITC 9)	0.0	0.7	2.6	0.0	1.0
Total exports (in US$ mil.)	394.0	6,651.0	10,487.0	13,343.0	30,875.0
Imports					
Total	100.0	100.0	100.0	100.0	100.0
Food, beverages, tobacco, and live animals (SITC 0,1)	9.9	1.6	1.5	7.9	4.7
Crude materials, inedible, except fuels (SITC 2)	15.1	9.2	5.4	9.3	8.3
Mineral fuels, lubricants, etc. (SITC 3)	26.1	35.1	56.0	15.8	31.5
Chemical products (SITC 4)	0.0	0.0	0.0	0.5	0.3
Animal and vegetable oils and fats (SITC 5)	12.1	5.0	5.5	14.0	9.6
Manufactured goods (SITC 6)	0.8	0.0	0.0	19.1	9.1
Machinery and transport equipment (SITC 7)	28.2	42.7	25.5	27.9	30.7
Miscellaneous manufactured articles (SITC 8)	7.8	5.2	3.4	5.4	4.8
Commodities not classified by kind (SITC 9)	0.0	1.1	2.7	0.0	1.0
Total imports (in US$ mil.)	456.0	7,325.0	8,436.0	14,799.0	31,016.0

Source: WIIW annual database.

Trade during transition

Let us now turn to trade performance of the countries of SEE after 1989. Table 8.3 reports exports (*X*) and imports (*M*) in millions of US dollars, together with the export to import ratio (*X/M*) for each of the South East European economies as well as for the entire regions of SEE and CE for the period 1989–2003. Table 8.4 contains similar information. It reports, more specifically, the evolution of exports and imports in index form during the same period in relation to the base year (1989 = 100).[4]

Looking at these two tables a number of observations can be made. First, with respect to exports, total exports were considerably reduced in the initial stages of transition and then recovered at a slow pace. Looking at Table 8.4, we can see that this was particularly true for Albania, Bulgaria and Romania, which experienced a substantial decline in exports, while the recovery, particularly for Bulgaria and Romania, was very slow. In the case of Croatia and FYROM the initial decline was much lower but the subsequent recovery was moderate as well, whereas in the case of FYROM it followed a rather unstable path. The seemingly spectacular increase in the exports of BH was the result of the very low export base of only US$36 million in 1993 as a result of the war. Overall, looking at the two regions, the growth of exports for SEE has been much lower than that for CE. In particular, total exports of the South East European countries increased only 75 per cent by 2002 relative to the 1990 level, and 123 per cent by 2003. The corresponding increase for the countries of CE was close to 400 per cent. In addition, it must be pointed out that SEE started from a much lower base relative to CE.

Turning now to imports, from the information in Tables 8.3 and 8.4 it can be seen that they followed the same trend of initial decline and subsequent increase as did exports. The difference, however, is that imports increased at a much faster rate. This is particularly true for Albania and BH, and to a lesser degree for Croatia and Romania. Overall, by 2003 the total imports of the South East European region had increased by about 200 per cent as compared to 550 per cent for CE. As in the case of exports, the increase in imports was more rapid for CE even though this region started from a much higher base. Note that the export and import performance of both regions in 2003 was affected by the considerable depreciation of the US dollar during that year.

The faster increase in imports led to an expansion of trade deficits. In Table 8.3 this is captured by the ratio of exports to imports (*X/M*). In particular, index values lower than one indicate trade deficits and thus limited potential to compete in the international markets. This ratio has been below or about half for most countries in SEE, and only in Bulgaria, FYROM and Romania did it stand above 0.5 in 2003. Overall, the ratio for SEE as a whole stood at 0.58 in 2003, being indicative of the poor competitive capacity of the region. In contrast, the countries of CE have shown a much greater potential in foreign trade. More specifically, despite the higher increase in imports

Table 8.3 Exports (*X*) and imports (*M*) for SEE (US$ mil.)

	1989	1990	1991	1992	1993	1994	1995
Albania							
Exports	394.00	322.00	73.00	70.00	122.00	141.00	205.00
Imports	456.00	456.00	281.00	541.00	604.00	601.00	680.00
X/M	*0.86*	*0.71*	*0.26*	*0.13*	*0.20*	*0.23*	*0.30*
BH							
Exports	n.a.	n.a.	n.a.	n.a.	n.a.	36.00	52.00
Imports	n.a.	n.a.	n.a.	n.a.	n.a.	775.00	950.00
X/M	*n.a.*	*n.a.*	*n.a.*	*n.a.*	*n.a.*	*0.05*	
Bulgaria							
Exports	6,651.00	5,232.00	3,434.00	2,444.00	2,282.00	3,359.00	5,220.00
Imports	7,325.00	5,584.00	2,715.00	4,345.00	4,462.00	4,670.00	5,469.00
X/M	*0.91*	*0.94*	*1.26*	*0.56*	*0.51*	*0.72*	*0.95*
Croatia							
Exports	n.a.	4,020.00	3,310.00	4,353.00	3,904.00	4,260.00	4,632.00
Imports	n.a.	5,133.00	3,811.00	4,346.00	4,666.00	5,229.00	7,510.00
X/M	*n.a.*	0.78	0.87	1.00	*0.84*	*0.81*	*0.62*
FYROM							
Exports	n.a.	1,113.00	1,095.00	1,199.00	1,055.00	1,086.00	1,202.00
Imports	n.a.	1,531.00	1,274.00	1,206.00	1,199.00	1,484.00	1,708.00
X/M	n.a.	0.73	0.86	0.99	*0.88*	*0.73*	*0.70*
Romania							
Exports	10,487.00	5,867.00	4,269.00	4,367.00	4,892.00	6,160.00	8,061.00
Imports	8,436.00	9,200.00	5,203.00	5,582.00	5,929.00	6,466.00	9,443.00
X/M	*1.24*	*0.64*	*0.82*	*0.78*	*0.83*	*0.95*	*0.85*
SM							
Exports	n.a.	n.a.	n.a.	n.a.	n.a.	n.a.	n.a.
Imports	n.a.	n.a.	n.a.	n.a.	n.a.	n.a.	n.a.
X/M	*n.a.*	*n.a.*	*n.a.*	*n.a.*	*n.a.*	*n.a.*	*n.a.*
SEE							
Exports	17,532.00	16,554.00	12,181.00	12,433.00	12,255.00	15,042.00	19,372.00
Imports	16,217.00	20,791.00	12,783.00	16,027.00	16,860.00	19,225.00	25,760.00
X/M	*1.08*	*0.80*	*0.95*	*0.78*	*0.73*	*0.78*	*0.75*
CE							
Exports	37,661.00	35,057.00	35,824.00	34,804.00	48,904.00	57,954.00	74,378.00
Imports	34,514.00	30,651.00	38,710.00	38,308.00	59,037.00	68,079.00	88,209.00
X/M	*1.09*	*1.14*	*0.93*	*0.91*	*0.83*	*0.85*	*0.84*

n.a. = not available.
[a]preliminary data.
Sources: WIIW database and EBRD (1997, 2001 and 2004b).

1996	1997	1998	1999	2000	2001	2002	2003[a]
210.00	159.00	208.00	275.00	256.00	305.00	329.00	450.00
909.00	694.00	812.00	943.00	1,084.00	1,321.00	1,499.00	1,850.00
0.23	*0.23*	*0.26*	*0.29*	*0.24*	*0.23*	*0.22*	*0.24*
336.00	381.00	511.00	650.00	1,100.00	1,050.00	1,110.00	1,360.00
1,882.00	2,400.00	2,548.00	2,600.00	3,100.00	3,025.00	3,800.00	4,580.00
0.18	*0.16*	*0.20*	*0.25*	*0.35*	*0.35*	*0.29*	*0.30*
4,781.00	4,314.00	4,150.00	3,755.00	4,760.00	5,062.00	5,631.00	7,445.00
4,891.00	3,880.00	5,044.00	5,220.00	6,362.00	7,182.00	7,831.00	10,750.00
0.98	*1.11*	*0.82*	*0.72*	*0.75*	*0.70*	*0.72*	*0.69*
4,512.00	4,332.00	4,557.00	4,226.00	4,071.00	4,543.00	4,842.00	6,170.00
7,787.00	9,100.00	8,327.00	7,724.00	7,688.00	8,918.00	10,464.00	14,150.00
0.58	*0.48*	*0.55*	*0.55*	*0.53*	*0.51*	*0.46*	*0.44*
1,148.00	1,237.00	1,311.00	1,192.00	1,319.00	1,155.00	1,115.00	1,360.00
1,625.00	1,774.00	1,915.00	1,796.00	2,085.00	1,690.00	1,995.00	2,300.00
0.71	*0.70*	*0.68*	*0.66*	*0.63*	*0.68*	*0.56*	*0.59*
7,645.00	8,387.00	8,315.00	8,509.00	10,367.00	11,386.00	13,868.00	17,620.00
9,058.00	10,129.00	10,802.00	9,637.00	11,868.00	14,139.00	16,200.00	22,155.00
0.84	*0.83*	*0.77*	*0.88*	*0.87*	*0.81*	*0.86*	*0.80*
1,842.00	2,368.00	2,858.00	1,497.00	1,723.00	1,900.00	2,075.00	2,477.00
4,102.00	4,799.00	4,849.00	3,296.00	3,710.00	4,820.00	5,615.00	7,320.00
0.45	*0.49*	*0.59*	*0.45*	*0.46*	*0.39*	*0.37*	*0.34*
20,474.00	21,178.00	21,910.00	20,104.00	23,596.00	25,401.00	28,970.00	36,882.00
30,254.00	32,776.00	34,297.00	31,216.00	35,897.00	41,095.00	47,404.00	63,105.00
0.68	*0.65*	*0.64*	*0.64*	*0.66*	*0.62*	*0.61*	*0.58*
76,860.00	85,366.00	97,404.00	97,231.00	1,09,255.00	1,21,306.00	1,37,708.00	1,71,300.00
1,01,607.00	1,11,606.00	1,24,810.00	1,23,332.00	1,32,763.00	1,41,146.00	1,56,120.00	1,99,500.00
0.76	*0.76*	*0.78*	*0.79*	*0.82*	*0.86*	*0.88*	*0.86*

Table 8.4 Export and import indices for SEE (1990 = 100)

	1990	1991	1992	1993	1994	1995	1996	1997	1998	1999	2000	2001	2002	2003
Albania														
Exports	100.0	22.7	21.7	37.9	43.8	63.7	65.2	49.4	64.6	85.4	79.5	94.7	102.2	139.8
Imports	100.0	61.6	118.6	132.5	131.8	149.1	199.3	152.2	178.1	206.8	237.7	289.7	328.7	405.7
BH														
Exports	n.a.	n.a.	n.a.	n.a.	100.0	144.4	933.3	1058.3	1419.4	1805.6	3055.6	2916.7	3083.3	3777.8
Imports	n.a.	n.a.	n.a.	n.a.	100.0	122.6	242.8	309.7	328.8	335.5	400.0	390.3	490.3	591.0
Bulgaria														
Exports	100.0	65.6	46.7	43.6	64.2	99.8	91.4	82.5	79.3	71.8	91.0	96.8	107.6	142.3
Imports	100.0	48.6	77.8	79.9	83.6	97.9	87.6	69.5	90.3	93.5	113.9	128.6	140.2	192.5
Croatia														
Exports	100.0	82.3	108.3	97.1	106.0	115.2	112.2	107.8	113.4	105.1	101.3	113.0	120.4	153.5
Imports	100.0	74.2	84.7	90.9	101.9	146.3	151.7	177.3	162.2	150.5	149.8	173.7	203.9	275.7
FYROM														
Exports	100.0	98.4	107.7	94.8	97.6	108.0	103.1	111.1	117.8	107.1	118.5	103.8	100.2	122.2
Imports	100.0	83.2	78.8	78.3	96.9	111.6	106.1	115.9	125.1	117.3	136.2	110.4	130.3	150.2
Romania														
Exports	100.0	72.8	74.4	83.4	105.0	137.4	130.3	143.0	141.7	145.0	176.7	194.1	236.4	300.3
Imports	100.0	56.6	60.7	64.4	70.3	102.6	98.5	110.1	117.4	104.8	129.0	153.7	176.1	240.8
SM														
Exports	n.a.	n.a.	n.a.	n.a.	n.a.	n.a.	100.00	128.6	155.2	81.3	93.5	103.1	112.6	134.5
Imports	n.a.	n.a.	n.a.	n.a.	n.a.	n.a.	100.00	117.0	118.2	80.4	90.4	117.5	136.9	178.4
SEE														
Exports	100.0	73.6	75.1	74.0	90.9	117.0	123.7	127.9	132.4	121.4	142.5	153.4	175.0	222.8
Imports	100.0	61.5	77.1	81.1	92.5	123.9	145.5	157.6	165.0	150.1	172.7	197.7	228.0	303.5
CE														
Exports	100.0	102.2	99.3	139.5	165.3	212.2	219.2	243.5	277.8	277.4	311.6	346.0	392.8	488.6
Imports	100.0	126.3	125.0	192.6	222.1	287.8	331.5	364.1	407.2	402.4	433.1	460.5	509.3	650.9

n.a. = not available.
Sources: WIIW database and EBRD (1997, 2001 and 2004b).

relative to exports, the exports to imports ratio was 0.86 in 2003, denoting a much higher value of exported goods per dollar of imported goods. A notable difference between the two regions, which clearly reflects the difficulty of the economies of SEE to effectively compete in World markets, refers to the fact that while, after the initial decline, the exports to imports ratio followed an increasing trend in CE, it kept falling in SEE throughout the entire period.

Initially, the larger decline of exports relative to imports and the widening trade deficits primarily reflected the collapse of the production systems of the transition economies and thus their limited capacity to compete in the international commodity markets. This was particularly true for the economies of SEE due to more adverse initial conditions (see Chapter 3). Also, the slow progress towards reform as well as the unstable political conditions and the outbreak of various armed conflicts, particularly during the period until the Kosovo War, contributed substantially to the poor exporting performance of these countries. An additional obstacle to SEE's export development was raised by the 'Association Agreements' of the EU which retained protection for a number of 'sensitive' products such as textiles, steel, iron and agriculture for which some of the participating countries had a capacity for effective competition.

Changes in geographical and structural trade patterns

The collapse of CMEA had a major impact on all transition economies, which were left with practically no trading patterns. The liberalization of trade that followed led to considerable changes in the geographical trade patterns of the particular countries. This primarily meant a fast and quite effective redirection of trade away from Eastern Europe and towards the West. More specifically, soon after the start of transition the EU became the dominant trade partner for all transition economies and for the South East European economies as well, replacing Eastern Europe. The sectoral composition of trade has also been changing, adjusting to specific resource endowments of the particular countries and thus reflecting their comparative advantages more closely. In this respect, it is interesting to see the extent to which the economies of SEE have shifted away from areas of specialization that were typical of the attitudes of central planning. This largely refers to the degree of increase of the consumer goods' share in total trading, as a result of the adjustment of their production systems to the opening of the economies and to trade liberalization. Note, however, that, by contrast to geographical patterns, the change in the sectoral composition proceeds more gradually since it takes time for the production patterns of the economy to adjust. Tables 8.5 to 8.12 report the geographical breakdown as well as the structural pattern of trade for the individual countries of SEE (Tables 8.5 to 8.11) and for the region as a whole (Table 8.12). Note that these Tables report information until 2003 and for every three years starting in 1993.[5]

Table 8.5 Albania: trade by direction and product groups

	1993		1996		1999		2002		2003	
	Exports	**Imports**	**Exports**	**Imports**	**Exports**	**Imports**	**Exports**	**Imports**	**Exports**	**Imports**
Trade by direction										
Total	100.0	100.0	100.0	100.0	100.0	100.0	100.0	100.0	100.0	100.0
Industrial countries	80.0	94.9	88.2	79.3	95.3	82.2	94.0	74.2	95.1	78.4
of which EU	73.0	87.3	86.0	76.3	93.6	80.2	92.2	70.9	94.3	75.6
Eastern Europe	17.0	2.8	8.7	17.6	4.2	16.4	5.5	20.4	4.5	16.2
of which SEE	13.1	0.5	3.8	10.1	2.9	6.6	2.2	6.2	3.2	6.6
Others	3.0	2.3	3.1	3.1	0.5	1.4	0.5	5.4	0.4	5.4
Trade by product (SITC classification)										
Total	100.0	100.0	100.0	100.0	100.0	100.0	100.0	100.0	100.0	100.0
Food, beverages, tobacco, and live animals (SITC 0,1)	14.0	20.1	8.9	32.0	6.7	24.8	8.0	19.0	5.6	18.2
Crude materials, inedible, except fuels (SITC 2)	24.0	0.7	16.9	1.2	7.3	4.1	5.0	4.2	8.7	1.5
Mineral fuels, lubricants, etc. (SITC 3)	8.3	3.3	4.1	2.6	2.8	4.7	2.0	9.1	1.0	8.6
Animal and vegetable oils and fats (SITC 4)	0.1	1.8	2.2	2.6	0.1	1.9	0.0	1.4	0.0	1.5
Chemical products (SITC 5)	4.3	12.4	1.4	5.9	0.7	7.6	0.8	8.0	0.6	7.3
Manufactured goods (SITC 6)	14.7	14.5	13.8	18.4	12.0	23.5	14.5	17.2	12.6	25.2
Machinery and transport equipment (SITC 7)	3.6	38.1	1.7	22.5	6.3	19.0	3.8	23.5	3.6	21.6
Miscellaneous manufactured articles (SITC 8)	31.0	9.1	51.0	14.4	64.1	14.4	65.9	17.6	67.9	16.1
Commodities not classified by kind (SITC 9)	0.0	0.0	0.0	0.4	0.0	0.0	0.0	0.0	0.0	0.0
Total (in US$ mil.)	122.0	604.0	210.5	909.0	275.0	943.0	329.0	1499.0	450.0	1850.0

Sources: WIIW database and IMF (2003).

Table 8.5 refers to the geographical and structural trade patterns of Albania. This country is the one with the greatest degree of integration with the industrial countries and the EU in particular. By 1993, some 80 per cent of Albania's exports were directed towards the industrial countries, while almost 95 per cent of its imports originated from these countries. In 2003, Albania's exports to the member states of the EU reached more than 94 per cent of total exports, while 76 per cent of its imports originated from the same countries. Significant changes have occurred with respect to the product composition of Albania's trade as well. Recall from Table 8.2 that most trade in 1989 concerned raw materials while imports of machinery and transport equipment were substantial. With respect to exports, a considerable shift has occurred in consumer manufactured products (SITC 8) which constituted about the two-thirds of total exports in 2003 (Table 8.5). At the same time, the SITC categories of food, beverages and raw materials (SITC 0, 1, 2, 3) which represented the bulk of Albanian exports in 1989 (Table 8.2) were reduced substantially. Turning to the import side, imports of foodstuffs, beverages and tobacco (SITC 0, 1) were increased while imports of raw materials were reduced. Finally, imports of manufactures (SITC 6, 8) increased considerably relative to the 1989 level, while imports in machinery and transport equipment (SITC 7) have not changed much.

Tables 8.6 and 8.7 report the geographical and structural patterns of trade for Bulgaria and Romania, which are very similar. Both countries directed their trade towards the industrial countries and the EU has become their main trading partner. Bulgaria appeared to have a lower degree of integration with the member states of the EU. In 2003, its exports to these countries reached 57 per cent of the total, while its imports were at 50 per cent of total imports. The corresponding shares for Romania were 68 and 58 per cent respectively. Trading with the countries of former Eastern Europe has been a significant part of total trade for both countries. Despite that, the degree of trade integration between these two countries and SEE has been very low. It should be noted, however, that it was low prior to transition as well (Table 8.1). With respect to product breakdown, recall from Table 8.2 that most trade concentrated on machinery and equipment as well as on raw materials, largely reflecting the extensive manufacturing sector in both countries under the old regime. The importance of these two categories has been gradually reduced while, at the same time, both countries have experienced considerable increase in their trading of manufactures (SITC 6 and 8).

Table 8.8 and 8.9 refer to BH and FYROM respectively. A common characteristic of the two countries has been the relatively large share of trade *vis-à-vis* the former Eastern European countries. This to a certain extent is explained by the fact that these two countries have had the largest share of intra-regional trade among all South East European countries. In some respects the two economies continue the tradition of heavy trading among the former Yugoslav republics that existed prior to the break-up of SFR of

Table 8.6 Bulgaria: trade by direction and product groups

	1993		1996		1999		2002		2003	
	Exports	**Imports**	**Exports**	**Imports**	**Exports**	**Imports**	**Exports**	**Imports**	**Exports**	**Imports**
Trade by direction										
Total	100.0	100.0	100.0	100.0	100.0	100.0	100.0	100.0	100.0	100.0
Industrial countries	43.2	41.3	51.6	42.3	66.2	57.9	76.8	67.2	75.2	68.6
of which EU	30.0	32.8	40.0	35.1	52.0	48.4	55.7	50.3	56.6	49.8
Eastern Europe	33.6	42.6	30.5	43.0	20.5	30.8	15.3	26.5	16.0	27.3
of which SEE	12.4	3.9	10.5	3.6	9.0	2.2	9.2	2.8	9.4	3.0
Others	23.2	16.1	17.9	14.7	13.3	11.3	7.9	6.3	8.8	4.1
Trade by product (SITC classification)										
Total	100.0	100.0	100.0	100.0	100.0	100.0	100.0	100.0	100.0	100.0
Food, beverages, tobacco, and live animals (SITC 0,1)	18.1	8.8	17.3	7.3	13.1	5.5	10.6	5.1	8.7	4.8
Crude materials, inedible, except fuels (SITC 2)	5.7	4.4	5.1	5.7	7.0	5.3	6.0	4.5	6.3	5.5
Mineral fuels, lubricants, etc. (SITC 3)	8.7	37.3	6.5	33.7	8.9	21.6	9.8	19.6	8.4	17.4
Animal and vegetable oils and fats (SITC 4)	0.8	0.3	0.4	0.3	0.6	0.3	0.3	0.6	0.1	0.4
Chemical products (SITC 5)	14.8	10.1	18.3	11.1	10.6	10.1	9.3	10.3	9.0	10.0
Manufactured goods (SITC 6)	25.1	13.2	26.5	16.4	23.5	18.1	22.6	20.5	24.7	21.1
Machinery and transport equipment (SITC 7)	17.2	19.6	12.5	16.0	11.2	29.0	12.4	27.6	13.0	28.7
Miscellaneous manufactured articles (SITC 8)	9.5	5.9	11.0	5.9	21.5	8.4	29.0	11.8	28.8	10.1
Commodities not classified by kind (SITC 9)	0.0	0.4	2.5	3.6	3.6	1.7	0.0	0.0	1.0	2.0
Total (in US$ mil.)	2282.0	4462.0	4781.0	4891.0	3755.0	5220.0	5631.0	7831.0	7445.0	10750.0

Sources: WIIW database and IMF (2003).

Table 8.7 Romania: trade by direction and product groups

	1993		1996		1999		2002		2003	
	Exports	**Imports**	**Exports**	**Imports**	**Exports**	**Imports**	**Exports**	**Imports**	**Exports**	**Imports**
Trade by direction										
Total	100.0	100.0	100.0	100.0	100.0	100.0	100.0	100.0	100.0	100.0
Industrial countries	48.7	55.8	62.2	60.1	72.2	67.5	74.6	64.4	74.0	63.7
of which EU	41.4	45.3	56.5	52.2	65.5	60.5	67.3	58.6	67.7	57.7
Eastern Europe	15.4	21.3	12.0	21.1	11.7	20.0	9.5	21.9	9.4	22.8
of which SEE	2.8	1.6	3.0	1.1	2.9	1.2	2.8	1.1	3.3	1.2
Others	35.9	22.9	25.8	18.8	16.1	12.5	15.9	13.7	16.6	13.5
Trade by product (SITC classification)										
Total	100.0	100.0	100.0	100.0	100.0	100.0	100.0	100.0	100.0	100.0
Food, beverages, tobacco, and live animals (SITC 0,1)	5.1	13.8	7.6	6.8	3.8	7.0	2.7	5.7	2.4	6.6
Crude materials, inedible, except fuels (SITC 2)	4.0	6.2	3.9	5.3	8.6	3.7	5.5	3.2	6.2	3.0
Mineral fuels, lubricants, etc. (SITC 3)	10.0	25.8	7.4	20.9	4.9	10.0	7.9	11.1	6.6	10.9
Animal and vegetable oils and fats (SITC 4)	1.3	0.2	0.9	0.2	0.6	0.2	0.1	0.4	0.2	0.3
Chemical products (SITC 5)	8.0	9.0	9.8	10.0	4.9	11.0	4.7	10.8	4.8	10.3
Manufactured goods (SITC 6)	27.4	15.7	22.8	21.3	20.5	28.6	18.8	29.1	19.3	28.0
Machinery and transport equipment (SITC 7)	17.1	22.3	13.6	25.6	16.6	27.3	21.2	28.2	21.5	29.5
Miscellaneous manufactured articles (SITC 8)	27.0	6.6	33.9	8.7	40.0	12.1	39.0	11.5	38.9	11.4
Commodities not classified by kind (SITC 9)	0.1	0.3	0.2	1.2	0.1	0.1	0.1	0.0	0.1	0.0
Total (in US$ mil.)	4892.0	5929.0	7645.0	9058.0	8509.0	9637.0	13,868.0	16,200.0	17,620.0	22,155.0

Sources: WIIW database and IMF (2003).

Table 8.8 BH: trade by direction and product groups

	1993		1996		1999		2002		2003	
	Exports	**Imports**	**Exports**	**Imports**	**Exports**	**Imports**	**Exports**	**Imports**	**Exports**	**Imports**
Trade by direction										
Total	n.a.	n.a.	100.0	100.0	100.0	100.0	100.0	100.0	100.0	100.0
Industrial countries	n.a.	n.a.	25.0	38.8	44.6	44.8	52.5	42.5	58.0	39.0
of which EU	n.a.	n.a.	22.1	31.7	42.3	37.6	51.1	39.0	55.9	35.9
Eastern Europe	n.a.	n.a.	70.9	60.5	50.8	54.0	44.2	50.2	40.0	54.4
of which SEE	n.a.	n.a.	67.0	41.6	42.9	32.8	37.4	32.0	32.0	32.5
Others	n.a.	n.a.	4.1	0.7	4.6	1.2	3.3	7.3	2.0	6.6
Trade by product (SITC classification)										
Total	100.0	100.0	100.0	100.0	100.0	100.0	100.0	100.0	100.0	100.0
Food, beverages, tobacco, and live animals (SITC 0,1)	25.4	43.3	11.6	31.0	8.7	20.6	5.3	19.2	5.3	22.5
Crude materials, inedible, except fuels (SITC 2)	6.0	2.3	28.8	1.1	3.9	2.1	16.3	3.3	6.5	2.4
Mineral fuels, lubricants, etc. (SITC 3)	0.9	9.8	3.3	7.0	5.2	6.4	6.7	6.3	9.2	11.2
Animal and vegetable oils and fats (SITC 4)	0.0	2.1	0.0	1.4	0.0	0.1	0.0	0.5	0.0	0.3
Chemical products (SITC 5)	6.6	6.4	2.9	8.5	2.8	8.9	2.0	8.6	3.6	14.1
Manufactured goods (SITC 6)	19.4	15.7	17.1	17.5	59.8	25.9	28.3	21.9	39.6	15.6
Machinery and transport equipment (SITC 7)	12.7	7.8	13.6	21.9	10.8	26.3	17.2	25.5	16.4	24.8
Miscellaneous manufactured articles (SITC 8)	27.2	8.3	21.8	9.7	8.2	5.6	23.5	12.9	17.9	8.6
Commodities not classified by kind (SITC 9)	1.7	4.4	0.9	1.9	0.7	4.1	0.7	1.8	1.5	0.5
Total (in US$ mil.)	85.0	424.0	336.0	1882.0	650.0	2600.0	1110.0	3800.0	1360.0	4580.0

n.a. = not available.
Sources: WIIW database and IMF (2003).

Table 8.9 FYROM: trade by direction and product groups

	1993		1996		1999		2002		2003	
	Exports	**Imports**	**Exports**	**Imports**	**Exports**	**Imports**	**Exports**	**Imports**	**Exports**	**Imports**
Trade by direction										
Total	100.0	100.0	100.0	100.0	100.0	100.0	100.0	100.0	100.0	100.0
Industrial countries	44.4	39.1	52.1	46.3	59.3	50.4	62.0	54.6	64.6	52.9
of which EU	34.5	33.5	42.8	38.7	44.7	40.1	51.1	44.8	54.7	43.7
Eastern Europe	50.2	50.0	44.1	41.2	35.8	43.3	36.2	38.6	33.1	39.7
of which SEE	16.8	21.1	29.2	21.0	30.6	20.0	32.3	19.7	30.0	19.8
Others	5.4	10.9	3.8	12.5	4.9	6.3	1.8	6.8	2.3	7.4
Trade by product (SITC classification)										
Total	100.0	100.0	100.0	100.0	100.0	100.0	100.0	100.0	100.0	100.0
Food, beverages, tobacco, and live animals (SITC 0,1)	20.5	19.8	21.1	14.5	19.0	13.7	17.9	13.3	16.7	12.8
Crude materials, inedible, except fuels (SITC 2)	6.1	5.6	5.9	4.8	4.3	3.2	3.3	2.5	2.9	2.6
Mineral fuels, lubricants, etc. (SITC 3)	0.2	15.9	0.9	9.1	1.9	9.1	2.2	13.2	5.4	14.0
Animal and vegetable oils and fats (SITC 4)	0.0	0.1	0.0	1.2	0.0	1.3	0.2	1.0	0.2	1.1
Chemical products (SITC 5)	4.5	15.5	6.1	10.5	4.6	10.4	6.2	10.6	5.1	11.1
Manufactured goods (SITC 6)	34.4	17.0	30.5	18.9	29.7	15.4	28.3	13.3	29.1	14.5
Machinery and transport equipment (SITC 7)	16.2	16.6	7.7	22.3	7.0	20.0	6.7	20.4	5.9	18.8
Miscellaneous manufactured articles (SITC 8)	18.1	6.6	27.8	10.7	31.3	5.5	34.9	5.7	34.5	5.6
Commodities not classified by kind (SITC 9)	0.0	2.8	0.1	8.0	2.2	21.4	0.3	20.0	0.2	19.5
Total (in US$ mil.)	1055.0	1199.0	1148.0	1625.0	1192.0	1796.0	1115.0	1995.0	1360.0	2300.0

Sources: WIIW database and IMF (2003).

Yugoslavia. Turning to the redirection of trade, we can see that exports to and imports from the industrial countries have increased considerably in both BH and FYROM. In particular, the share of exports of BH to the EU increased from 22 per cent in 1996 to almost 56 per cent in 2003. The corresponding share for FYROM increased at a slower pace, reaching about 55 per cent in 2003 from 34.5 per cent in 1993. The share of imports from the EU has been rising in both countries but at a slower rate in the case of BH. More specifically, it increased from almost 32 per cent in 1996 to 36 per cent in 2003. In the case of FYROM, it rose from 33.5 per cent in 1993 to 44 per cent in 2003. At the same time the trade share of BH and FYROM with respect to former Eastern European countries has been declining at a slow rate. More specifically, the share of exports of the latter country towards the former Eastern European countries declined from about 50 per cent in 1993 to 33 per cent in 2003, while the corresponding share of imports dropped from 50 to 40 per cent. In BH, the share of exports fell from 71 per cent in 1996 to 40 per cent in 2003, while the corresponding share of imports declined from 60.5 to just below 55 per cent. Thus, with respect to imports, these countries still remained the main trading partners of BH as of 2003. Finally, as pointed out, trade with the rest of the South East European countries, although falling, is still important. As a matter of fact, FYROM is the only country in which the share of intra-regional trade has been rising.

Turning to product breakdown, in the case of BH, the share of exports in manufactured goods (SITC 6) has been rising quite significantly, while that of consumer manufactured products (SITC 8) and foodstuffs, beverages and tobacco (SITC 0, 1) has been declining. The share of the latter has been steadily falling with respect to imports as well, while imports in machinery and transport equipment (SITC 7) have increased considerably. Turning to FYROM, the export share of consumer manufactures (SITC 8) has been rising significantly while that of machinery and transport equipment (SITC 7) declined. With respect to imports, the most noticeable change refers to the increased share of commodities not classified by item (SITC 9), while most of the other categories exhibited minor decline.

In the case of Croatia the redirection of trade towards the industrial countries and the EU was rapid (Table 8.10). Already by 1993 more than 60 per cent of Croatia's total trading was conducted with the industrial countries. Thereafter, however, the share of trade with the particular countries has not changed considerably. As a matter of fact, the share of exports has been lower in 2002, primarily as a result of the lower export share *vis-à-vis* the EU. Croatia's trading with the countries of former Eastern Europe remains significant and has not declined much since 1993. Exports to other South East European countries have been rising and reached about 20 per cent of total exports in 2003, primarily due to exports to BH. On the other hand, imports from the other South East European countries have been particularly low. Turning to product breakdown of international trade, most of

Table 8.10 Croatia: trade by direction and product groups

	1993		1996		1999		2002		2003	
	Exports	**Imports**	**Exports**	**Imports**	**Exports**	**Imports**	**Exports**	**Imports**	**Exports**	**Imports**
Trade by direction										
Total	100.0	100.0	100.0	100.0	100.0	100.0	100.0	100.0	100.0	100.0
Industrial countries	60.2	61.1	54.2	66.2	55.4	64.8	58.3	64.6	61.8	65.4
of which EU	56.7	55.4	51.0	59.4	49.4	56.7	52.3	55.8	54.7	56.5
Eastern Europe	35.1	29.7	36.5	22.1	34.8	26.8	33.9	25.7	34.2	24.5
of which SEE	6.5	1.3	14.0	1.7	14.6	2.4	19.7	3.2	19.8	3.9
Others	4.7	9.2	9.3	11.7	9.8	8.4	7.8	9.7	4.0	10.1
Trade by product (SITC classification)										
Total	100.0	100.0	100.0	100.0	100.0	100.0	100.0	100.0	100.0	100.0
Food, beverages, tobacco, and live animals (SITC 0,1)	12.0	8.5	11.1	10.6	9.1	8.0	10.7	8.2	11.7	7.8
Crude materials, inedible, except fuels (SITC 2)	6.1	3.8	5.5	2.8	5.7	2.2	5.7	2.4	5.7	2.3
Mineral fuels, lubricants, etc. (SITC 3)	9.7	9.9	9.2	11.0	7.8	11.1	9.3	12.2	9.6	11.0
Animal and vegetable oils and fats (SITC 4)	0.1	0.3	0.2	0.5	0.2	0.3	0.2	0.3	0.2	0.3
Chemical products (SITC 5)	14.5	12.3	14.3	10.9	12.0	12.1	10.3	11.4	9.6	11.1
Manufactured goods (SITC 6)	13.5	17.2	13.2	17.8	13.4	16.1	14.7	19.4	14.1	18.7
Machinery and transport equipment (SITC 7)	14.1	24.1	21.4	27.3	29.2	34.8	28.5	34.4	29.4	37.0
Miscellaneous manufactured articles (SITC 8)	29.9	16.7	25.1	14.3	22.5	11.9	20.6	11.6	19.6	11.6
Commodities not classified by kind (SITC 9)	0.2	7.3	0.0	4.7	0.1	3.5	0.1	0.1	0.1	0.2
Total (in US$ mil.)	3904.0	4666.0	4512.0	7787.0	4226.0	7724.0	4842.0	10,464.0	6170.0	14,150.0

Sources: WIIW database and IMF (2003).

Croatia's imports and exports concern chemical products (SITC 5), manufactures (SITC 6 and 8) and machinery and equipment (SITC 7). Overall, no major changes have occurred to the product breakdown of international trade since 1993. The most noticeable change concerns the rising importance of machinery and equipment (SITC 7) in both exports and imports.

Finally, the geographical and structural patterns of trade for SM since 1996 are reported in Table 8.11. The extent of trade integration of SM with the industrial countries and the former Eastern European countries did not change considerably up to 2003. In particular, the share of exports to and imports from the EU has been averaging about 40 per cent per year during the period 1996–2003. The respective shares for the Eastern European countries have been following opposite trends. Export shares to these countries have been decreasing gradually, primarily reflecting the declining shares of SEE. Import shares, on the other hand, have been rising despite the falling trend in the share of SEE. Turning to the product breakdown, an obvious remark refers to the stability in the structural pattern of trade, at least for the period under consideration. The product shares of exports and imports exhibit minor changes, with foodstuffs, beverages and tobacco (SITC 0 and 1), manufactures (SITC 6 and 8) and machinery and equipment (SITC 7) constituting the most important export categories. The situation with respect to imports does not change considerably either. The share of machinery and equipment exhibited moderate increase while the categories of manufactured goods, chemical products and mineral fuels have retained their importance. Given that the transition period for SM in essence started in 2001, following the political change that took place in October 2000, one must anticipate more changes in international trade, particularly with respect to sectoral composition, to occur in the future.

Geographical and structural trade patterns: an overall regional assessment

Table 8.12 refers to geographical and structural patterns of international trade for SEE as a whole. First, with respect to the geographical breakdown of trade, there has been a substantial trade redirection towards the industrial countries and the EU. Recall from Table 8.1 that about 24 per cent of the total exports and imports of the region were directed to, and originated from, the EU's member states in 1989. This has increased considerably since, and by 2003 the corresponding shares for exports and imports were about 61 and 53 per cent respectively. As a result, the export and import shares *vis-à-vis* the countries of Eastern Europe have been declining and were reduced to about 19 and 29 per cent respectively in 2003. Another important conclusion derived from Table 8.12 concerns the low trade integration within the region of SEE. In particular, only about 11 per cent of total exports and 6.5 per cent

Table 8.11 SM: trade by direction and product groups

	1996		1999		2002		2003	
	Exports	**Imports**	**Exports**	**Imports**	**Exports**	**Imports**	**Exports**	**Imports**
Trade by direction								
Total	100.0	100.0	100.0	100.0	100.0	100.0	100.0	100.0
Industrial countries	43.7	51.6	46.1	51.0	50.0	51.3	50.0	52.6
of which EU	41.8	42.0	36.2	41.4	40.1	42.6	41.6	43.1
Eastern Europe	48.8	33.8	47.4	35.2	42.9	37.8	44.7	41.3
of which SEE	36.2	19.4	38.2	17.9	31.1	15.3	30.7	13.7
Others	7.5	14.6	6.5	13.8	7.1	10.9	5.3	6.1
Trade by product (SITC classification)								
Total	100.0	100.0	100.0	100.0	100.0	100.0	100.0	100.0
Food, beverages, tobacco, and live animals (SITC 0,1)	25.3	13.1	21.1	9.6	22.0	10.1	20.3	9.0
Crude materials, inedible, except fuels (SITC 2)	4.3	10.4	5.5	7.0	5.2	3.4	5.3	2.9
Mineral fuels, lubricants, etc. (SITC 3)	2.4	13.9	2.4	18.0	3.4	16.9	2.2	15.1
Animal and vegetable oils and fats (SITC 4)	0.5	0.3	0.5	0.2	0.8	0.3	0.6	0.2
Chemical products (SITC 5)	8.4	14.3	9.6	15.8	7.5	13.6	9.3	13.5
Manufactured goods (SITC 6)	31.8	19.8	31.2	20.5	31.3	20.0	31.6	20.1
Machinery and transport equipment (SITC 7)	11.2	19.4	12.3	21.7	11.2	25.7	11.7	28.5
Miscellaneous manufactured articles (SITC 8)	14.6	7.9	14.6	6.4	16.3	8.8	17.3	9.6
Commodities not classified by kind (SITC 9)	1.7	0.9	2.8	0.8	2.3	1.2	1.7	1.1
Total (in US$ mil.)	1842.0	4102.0	1497.0	3296.0	2075.0	5615.0	2477.0	7320.0

Sources: WIIW database and IMF (2003).

Table 8.12 Total SEE: trade by direction and product groups

	1993[a]		1996		1999		2002		2003	
	Exports	**Imports**	**Exports**	**Imports**	**Exports**	**Imports**	**Exports**	**Imports**	**Exports**	**Imports**
Trade by direction										
Total	100.0	100.0	100.0	100.0	100.0	100.0	100.0	100.0	100.0	100.0
Industrial countries	51.3	53.6	55.4	56.2	64.3	61.1	69.4	61.5	69.9	61.9
of which EU	43.9	45.5	49.1	48.6	55.8	53.0	59.6	53.0	60.9	52.8
Former Eastern Europe	28.1	30.6	27.8	30.0	23.4	29.2	19.4	28.3	19.2	28.8
of which SEE	7.1	3.5	12.7	8.0	12.1	7.3	11.3	6.9	11.2	6.7
Others	20.6	15.7	16.9	13.8	12.3	9.8	11.2	10.2	10.9	9.3
Trade by product (SITC classification)										
Total	100.0	100.0	100.0	100.0	100.0	100.0	100.0	100.0	100.0	100.0
Food, beverages, tobacco, and live animals (SITC 0,1)	11.1	11.7	13.1	11.4	9.0	9.3	7.7	8.5	7.1	8.6
Crude materials, inedible, except fuels (SITC 2)	5.4	4.8	5.2	5.0	7.0	3.8	5.9	3.3	6.0	3.2
Mineral fuels, lubricants, etc. (SITC 3)	8.8	22.9	6.7	17.4	5.9	12.5	7.8	13.1	7.2	12.6
Animal and vegetable oils and fats (SITC 4)	0.7	0.3	0.5	0.5	0.4	0.3	0.2	0.5	0.2	0.4
Chemical products (SITC 5)	11.0	10.8	12.3	10.8	7.7	11.3	6.6	10.9	6.7	11.0
Manufactured goods (SITC 6)	23.0	15.5	22.6	19.0	22.1	21.8	20.4	22.8	21.4	22.3
Machinery and transport equipment (SITC 7)	16.0	22.2	14.4	23.2	17.0	28.1	19.1	28.5	19.5	30.0
Miscellaneous manufactured articles (SITC 8)	24.0	9.3	24.5	9.9	29.8	10.0	31.9	11.3	31.6	10.7
Commodities not classified by kind (SITC 9)	0.1	2.4	0.8	2.8	1.1	2.8	0.3	1.2	0.4	1.3
Total (in US$ mil.)	12,255.0	16,860.0	20,474.0	30,254.0	20,104.0	31,216.0	28,970.0	47,404.0	36,882.0	63,105.0

[a] It does not include BH and SM.
Sources: WIIW database and IMF (2003).

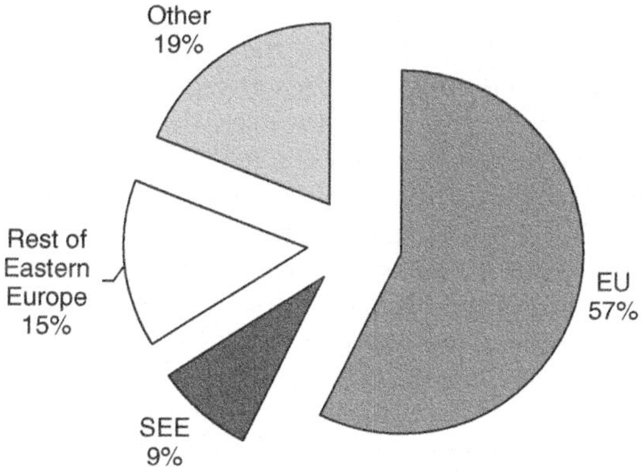

Figure 8.1 Trade shares of SEE in 2003

of total imports were directed to, and originated from, countries of the region in 2003. This is an issue we shall deal with later in this chapter.

It is interesting to examine how SEE compares to CE with respect to trade integration *vis-à-vis* the EU, but more generally in terms of trade openness. Figures 8.1 and 8.2 show the trade flows (exports plus imports), expressed as a share of total trade, of SEE and CE respectively during the year 2003. As indicated the trade integration with the EU has been greater in the case of CE. In particular, share of trade to total trade of SEE and CE *vis-à-vis* the EU were 57 and 65 per cent respectively. Note that the corresponding shares for SEE and CE in 1993 were about 45 and 56 per cent respectively, reflecting, on one hand, the rapid shift of trade towards the Western markets and, on the other, that the redirection of trade towards the EU has been an

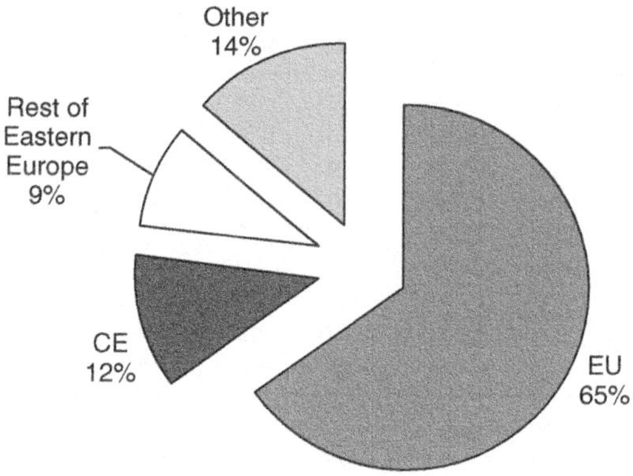

Figure 8.2 Trade shares of CE in 2003

ongoing process over the past decade. Another point of interest shown by these two figures refers to the fact that the share of intra-regional trade in the CE region, although higher than the corresponding one in SEE, could be considered rather low. In this case, however, their geographical proximity to the EU, as well as the fact that they reached the highest possible potential for integration by achieving full membership in 2004, significantly weakens the notion of 'region' for these particular countries.

Overall the degree of openness of the South East European economies, measured by the sum of exports and imports of goods expressed as a percentage of GDP, has been less than the corresponding one for the Central European economies. As a matter of fact, except for Poland which had a trade openness ratio of about 43 per cent, all the other Central European countries had ratios considerably higher than those of SEE. In particular, according to Table 8.13, the unweighted average ratio for the region increased to almost 67 per cent in 2003, as compared to 63.5 per cent in 1993, but it was still much lower than the 102,7 per cent for CE. Furthermore, according to the same information, trade plays a varied role in the SEE economies: the degree of openness varies greatly, with BH, Bulgaria and FYROM having a ratio of foreign trade to GDP of about 75 per cent and more, Croatia and Romania being next with ratios of about 70 per cent each, while SM and Albania follow with lower ratios. In addition, openness in SEE did not exactly follow an increasing trend over the past decade. This was the case in Croatia and FYROM after 1993 and in Bulgaria and Romania after 1996, mostly reflecting the impact of stabilization policies. Since 1999, however, the openness ratio has been rising steadily for most countries. Albania and BH constitute the two exceptions. Albania has to certain extent been continuing the tradition of low openness. In the case of BH the large drop in the openness ratio after

Table 8.13 SEE: trade openness[a]

	1993	**1996**	**1999**	**2002**	**2003**
Albania	38.4	42.9	35.3	37.6	36.2
BH	n.a.	55.6	106.0	74.3	74.8
Bulgaria	77.0	96.9	70.2	82.1	87.4
Croatia	78.4	64.0	60.7	68.7	71.1
FYROM	82.4	59.2	78.3	79.9	76.2
Romania	41.4	52.7	50.8	66.3	70.2
SM	n.a.	41.1	28.6	55.7	52.4
SEE[b]	*63.5*	*58.9*	*61.4*	*66.4*	*66.9*
CE[b]	*71.6*	*78.4*	*88.8*	*98.8*	*102.7*

n.a. = not available.
[a] The sum of exports and imports (% of GDP).
[b] Unweighted average.
Source: EBRD, *Transition Report* (2000, 2004b).

1999 was the result of the major decline in foreign official assistance, primarily from the EU.

As pointed out, the degree of openness has increased more steadily since the end of the Kosovo conflict. The previously low level, especially prior to the war, to a large extent reflected the fact that, on the one hand, trade figures were distorted by conflicts and trade blockades and, on the other hand, trade regimes of the countries of SEE were characterized by high protective measures. More specifically, with respect to the latter, trade policies were characterized by a significant level of protection that consisted of differentiated tariff structures which, in turn, resulted in high effective protection rates.[6] Furthermore, the overall slow progress towards reform and the establishment of free-market institutions which, among other things, would regulate and promote trade and formulate trade policies, led to slow integration of the particular countries into the world trade. During the years following the Kosovo conflict, however, a number of significant steps have been taken towards liberalization, which made the economies of the region more open. The EU played a major role in this by establishing trade agreements with the countries of SEE.[7] More specifically, pre-accession agreements with Bulgaria and Romania aimed at the liberalization of trade restrictions by both parties, while there were trade agreements with Albania, BH, Croatia and FYROM. In September 2000, within the framework of the stabilization and association process, the EU extended autonomous trade preferences (ATPs) to SEE, thus providing duty-free access to EU markets for almost all products originating from SEE. These preferences initially applied to Albania, BH and Croatia and then were extended to FYROM and SM (see Chapter 5).

Let us now turn to sectoral structure of South East European trade. Based on the data in Table 8.12 we can see that for the region as a whole there has been a rather moderate change in the structural pattern as compared to the situation prior to transition (Table 8.2). A main observation, particularly concerning the exports side, refers to the limited sectoral spread. As a matter of fact, three SITC categories together accounted for more than two-thirds of total exports in 2003. Indeed, from Table 8.12 it can be seen that manufactured goods (SITC 6), miscellaneous manufactured articles (SITC 8), and machinery and transport equipment (SITC 7) corresponded to about 21, 32 and 20 per cent of total exports respectively. Thus there was a much higher sectoral concentration of exports in 2003 compared to the situation in 1989 (Table 8.2) and 1993. Note that foodstuffs, beverages and tobacco (SITC 0 and 1) and mineral fuels, lubricants, and so on (SITC 3) were the next two categories, with a share of about 7 per cent each. Turning to the imports side, we observe a greater sectoral spread as compared to imports in 1989 (Table 8.2). Manufactured goods (SITC 6) have increased their share, while machinery and equipment (SITC 7) after the initial decline have also risen to 30 per cent in 2003, representing the largest importing category. Chemical products (SITC 5) as well as consumer manufactures (SITC 8) have both remained relatively stable after 1993 at around 11 per cent of total imports. By contrast, foodstuffs, beverages and tobacco (SITC 0 and 1) as well as mineral fuels, lubricants, and so on (SITC 3) have been declining steadily. This has been more profound in the latter category, whose share was reduced to one-third of what it was in 1989.

Regarding the sectoral breakdown of exports of the countries of SEE, an important observation refers to the fact that the share of exports of capital goods, which is primarily reflected by the share of the SITC 7 category, has increased only moderately, after the initial fall at the beginning of transition. This is in sharp contrast to the experience of the economies of CE. In particular, in the countries of CE the share of SITC 7 in exports increased from 25.4 per cent of total exports in 1995 to about 40 per cent in 2003.[8] In other words, while the structure of exports of CE converges towards that of industrial countries, the corresponding structure of SEE develops a rather diverging trend.[9] This, in turn, means that the industrial sectors for capital goods in South East European countries have not been able to recover, reflecting the fact that the particular countries primarily specialize in labour-intensive sectors, taking advantage of their low labour costs. This to a large extent was verified by the previous discussion on the sectoral composition of exports. Typical export products for the region are textiles and clothing, footwear and furniture, which are low value-added, labour-intensive products. Heavy manufacturing, consisting mostly of transportation equipment and basic metals, constitutes another important product category which is exported to the European markets.

Intra-regional trade integration

An issue which has received considerable attention refers to the low trade activity among the economies of SEE. Indeed, based on the data of Tables 8.1 and 8.12, the low degree of regional integration appears to have been the case during the period before as well as after transition. As pointed out earlier, the small portion of intra-regional trade prior to transition was to a certain extent due to the fact that Table 8.1 excludes all trade among the former Yugoslav republics. According to the World Bank (2003), about 53 per cent of the total exports of the former Yugoslav republics were directed to other former republics in 1987. This share fell significantly after the start of transition, contributing to the small portion of intra-regional trade.

Table 8.14 reports the bilateral flows of exports and imports within the region, as a share of total exports and imports respectively of each country for the year 2003 (see also Kyrkilis and Nikolaidis 2004). It is apparent that for most countries the trade flows from and towards their counterparts in SEE were rather low with respect to total flows. As a matter of fact, some countries

Table 8.14 SEE: bilateral intra-regional trade in percentage of total per country, 2003

	Albania		Bosnia and Herzegovina		Bulgaria		Croatia		FYROM		Romania		Serbia and Montenegro	
	Exports	**Imports**	**Exports**	**Imports**	**Exports**	**Imports**	**Exports**	**Imports**	**Exports**	**Imports**	**Exports**	**Imports**	**Exports**	**Imports**
Albania	...	...	0.0	0.0	0.2	0.0	0.4	0.0	1.5	0.3	0.1	0.0	0.4	0.1
BH	0.0	0.0	...	...	0.1	0.0	14.4	1.6	1.8	0.2	0.1	0.1	14.7	2.7
Bulgaria	0.0	2.5	0.1	0.3	...	...	0.4	0.4	1.7	6.5	1.5	1.0	2.0	2.9
Croatia	0.1	1.7	15.8	22.2	0.6	0.2	...	...	4.9	2.9	0.7	0.0	2.6	2.7
FYROM	0.7	0.9	0.4	0.5	2.1	0.2	1.3	0.5	...	...	0.1	0.0	8.3	3.5
Romania	0.1	0.9	0.0	0.5	3.1	2.3	0.3	0.9	0.1	0.6	...	...	2.7	1.8
SM	2.3	0.6	15.7	9.0	3.3	0.3	3.0	0.5	20.0	9.3	0.8	0.1	...	...
SEE	3.2	6.6	32.0	32.5	9.4	3.0	19.8	3.9	30.0	19.8	3.3	1.2	30.7	13.7

Source: WIIW database.

are not trading partners at all. Undoubtedly, ethnic and political disputes have played a considerable role in affecting the direction of trade flows within the region. Overall, historical factors have contributed significantly to both the absence as well as the persistence of trade, particularly with respect to former Yugoslav states.

More specifically, BH appears to be the country with the most intra-regional trade which, however, primarily concentrates on two countries, namely Croatia and SM, while trading with the remaining counties is quite low. Note, however, that trading of these two countries with BH primarily concerns their corresponding ethnic entities. FYROM and SM conduct a significant part of their trading within the region as well, a large portion of which is directed towards each other. Bulgaria and Croatia direct a considerable share of their exports to the region, while the corresponding portion of their imports is much lower. By contrast, in the case of Albania, the portion of imports originating from the other countries of SEE exceeds that of the exports directed towards the region. Finally, Romania appears to have the lowest degree of regional integration among the countries of the region. Note that trading between Romania and Bulgaria appears to be rather low despite their geographical proximity, and the fact that the two countries constitute, together with Croatia, the most developed countries of the region. As indicated, in addition the two countries are to become full members of the EU by 2007 which, in turn, means that their gradual shift to a situation of free trade has not affected their bilateral trade flows considerably.

Overall, it is apparent that regional integration, as reflected by the bilateral trade flows, has been low and in some cases practically non-existent. As a matter of fact, according to the preceding analysis, trade flows among the former Yugoslav republics have been essential in keeping intra-regional trade from falling even lower. So, although trade integration among these states has been much lower relative to pre-transition levels primarily due to political as well as ethnic considerations, it has on average been higher than any integration schemes involving the three remaining states of the region (i.e., Albania, Bulgaria and Romania).

The lack of sufficient intra-regional trade imposes a serious constraint on particular countries as regards development and growth; particularly for small countries, such as the majority of SEE, trade with neighbouring countries has essential advantages. For one thing, the short distance and the resulting low transportation costs would mean lower prices for the exporting countries and thus higher competitiveness. This is also encouraged by the similarity of consumer preferences in neighbouring countries. Furthermore, larger intra-regional trade leads to a more efficient use of the production system of the countries involved, primarily due to the emergence of internal and external economies of scale. This is particularly true for companies in small countries, such as the ones in SEE, which in order to survive need to generate the necessary economies of scale by ensuring a critical market size through operating in larger regional markets.

In addition, in cases in which there are close commercial ties among the countries of a greater geographical area, each country receives some of the benefits that result from the economic progress made by the others and this, in turn, contributes to faster development of the region as a whole.[10] A country can grow faster through the expansion of its exports to a rapidly growing neighbouring country. This is particularly important for the countries of SEE since the magnitude of their domestic trade is rather limited due to the small size of their economies. Furthermore, the poor export performance by SEE to the West would be compensated for by an increase in intra-regional trade.

Finally, the increase in intra-regional trade may be particularly beneficial to the industry structure of the countries in the region: the fact that most of the trade activity of the particular countries involves the member states of the EU means that it is of an inter-industry nature which, in turn, reduces the sectoral differentiation of their production systems, restricting them to a specialization in labour and raw material intensive industries.[11] Thus the development of a satisfactory level of intra-regional trade, to the extent that it is to a large extent of intra-industry character due to the greater similarities in their production structures, would assist the particular countries to maintain an adequate sectoral differentiation in their production systems (Petrakos 2003).

Besides the economic gains that would stem from greater intra-regional integration in SEE, there are broader reasons that have been examined in the literature. In particular, a common argument dealing with the reasons behind the need for regional economic integration in SEE stresses the political motives. More specifically, Uvalic (2001) argues that there are strong political reasons to promote closer economic integration in SEE. The political and security problems of the region of SEE create the need for stability, peace and development, to which the implementation of regional integration agreements can significantly contribute. Also, Anastasakis and Bojicic-Dzelilovic (2002) expand on the reasons why the international community and the EU advocate the central role of regional cooperation in SEE. The argument concerning the approach of the international community with respect to post-communist changes in Central and Eastern Europe emphasizes the role of regional cooperation to security and confidence building among neighbouring states. The EU internal argument, by taking into account the potential problems that could arise with the incorporation of post-communist states into the EU, advocates the development of sub-regional cooperation as a way of facilitating the integration process. For the countries of SEE, in particular, the regional argument emphasizes the need for these countries to prove their ability to cooperate with their neighbours before building stronger ties with the EU.

Explaining the low trade integration in South Eastern Europe

The low level of regional integration in SEE has been attributed to several factors, ranging from the limited capacities of the particular countries and trade policies to political developments, wars and ethnic conflicts. First, the limited capacities of the region, clearly reflecting the low level of development, impose significant limitations on the countries of the region arising from the demand as well as the supply side of their economies. In particular, as Kyrkilis and Nikolaïdis (2003) point out, demand-side limitations refer to small population size, slow output growth and low per capita incomes which undermine the demand stimulus for international trade. Thus, lack of adequate domestic (regional) demand favoured the direction of the bulk of the region's exports towards the EU market. Turning to the supply side, we pointed out earlier the similarity of the production structures of most South East European economies which tend to specialize in the rather low technology sectors and labour-intensive industries. Thus, as indicated earlier in this chapter, exports concentrate on consumer rather than on capital goods. On the other hand, the transformation process itself generates demand for technologically more advanced products, primarily capital goods, which cannot be produced by the countries of the region. Thus, as we saw, capital goods constitute the largest element of total imports in the region, which, in turn, makes the EU the major source of such imports (see Kyrkilis and Nikolaïdis 2004).

As pointed out, the similarity of production and export structures of the countries of SEE favours the establishment of intra-industry type of international trade within the region. Kaminski and Rocha (2003) have calculated the Grubel – Lloyd indices of bilateral trade between Albania, Bosnia and Herzegovina, Croatia and FYROM.[12] According to their findings, Albania's trade with both Bosnia and Herzegovina as well as with Croatia has a zero intra-industry content, while the intra-industry type of trade accounts only for 15 per cent, 15 per cent, and 9 per cent of the trade between Albania and FYROM, BH and FYROM, and Croatia and BH respectively. In fact, even these levels may be overestimated given the high level of aggregation (i.e., 2-digit SITC level) at which the analysis was conducted. This low level of intra-industry trade implies low potential for trade, at least until some new industrial capacities are installed that would expand the determinants of international trade within the region. Kyrkilis and Nikolaïdis (2004) explain that, given that intra-industry trade refers to high human skill and technology intensive products which are the result of similar but widely varied demand preferences while characterized by high income and low price elasticity of demand, it is rather apparent that most of the countries of the region are not in a position to produce such items. Thus there is not much scope for intra-industry trade within the region, which, in turn, constitutes another reason for the low intra-regional trade.

Trade policies may have also affected the extent of intra-regional trade. First, as pointed out earlier, trade policies in the region, particularly during the first decade of transition, were characterized by highly differentiated tariff structures, quotas and specific duties for various products, as well as licensing requirements in certain cases, which all resulted in significant levels of effective protection. In addition, the countries of the region failed to set up a Free Trade Area covering the whole region. Instead they negotiated a series of bilateral free trade arrangements which were uncoordinated and not always consistent with the WTO requirements.[13] These inevitably led to trade distortions as well as to non-transparent and complex trade policies, which in most cases were difficult to implement (see World Bank 2000b; Kyrkilis and Nikolaïdis 2004). The situation, however, has changed considerably since then and most of the countries of SEE have shifted to very liberal trade regimes. First, recall from Chapter 6 that the high scores of the particular countries with respect to the EBRD's index for trade and foreign exchange liberalization are indicative of the progress made in adopting liberal trade policies. More specifically, according to Table 6.3 most countries have achieved the highest possible score on this particular index. Furthermore, the successful trade liberalization in most South East European countries is underlined by the IMF's trade restrictiveness index for 2002.[14] According to that index, Albania, BH and Croatia apply a liberal trade policy having a rate of 1, while FYROM, Bulgaria and Romania (the last one to a lesser degree) use a rather liberal trade policy with ratings 2, 2 and 3 respectively. However, SM, with a score of 5, applies more restrictive trade policies than the other countries in SEE. Finally, five of the seven South East European countries have already become WTO members. BH and SM have applied as well and they are expected to become members in 2005 or later.

Furthermore, the role of the EU has been particularly important in promoting open trade regimes in the region. First, as we saw, within the framework of the Stabilization and Association Process the EU extended ATPs providing quite liberal access to EU markets for South East European exporters. In fact, according to EBRD (2003), the average tariff protection from the EU is much lower for the countries of SEE than for other transition countries.[15] However, it should be pointed out that, while the average may be low, goods that the countries of SEE typically export, such as textiles and agricultural products, face much higher tariffs (EBRD 2004a). Finally, an important development towards trade liberalization refers to the establishing of a Free Trade Zone in SEE. More specifically, the countries of SEE signed the Memorandum of Understanding on free trade in June 2001. The primary objective of this initiative has been the establishment of bilateral Free Trade Agreements (FTAs) among the countries of the region. By February 2003 21 bilateral FTAs were signed by all the countries of the region; these were intended to promote trade between the countries of the region and a more attractive business environment for foreign investors (EBRD 2004a). Of course, the effective implementation of these agreements still remains a major challenge.

Thus, while our analysis so far has shown that tariff protection cannot be considered responsible for the low intra-regional trade, the same cannot be said for the non-tariff obstacles. According to Gligorov, Holzner and Landesmann (2003) these include quantitative barriers, restrictive practices by governments, customs procedures and technical restrictions to trade (see also EBRD 2004a). Furthermore, low-quality infrastructure appears to be a major factor affecting the level of intra-regional trade adversely: the particularly poor condition of transport infrastructure makes trading difficult even between neighbouring countries. A rather typical example refers to the fact that there is only one bridge over the River Danube connecting Bulgaria and Romania (EBRD 2004a).

Finally, there are studies that give emphasis to political aspects regarding the obstacles to economic integration within the region. In particular, Anastasakis and Bojicic-Dzelilovic (2002) identified the establishment of 'illiberal' democracies, the limitations of social, human and institutional capital, the emergence of ethnic nationalism and border disputes as the main political limitations that restrain regional economic integration. In addition they emphasize the impact of the rapid expansion of organized crime and the informal sector. In particular, they argue that 'geographic proximity, the existence of many borders and the massive displacement of population have all conspired to facilitate intense regional cooperation in informal and largely criminalized activities'. The informal sector has hindered the normalization of relations between the countries of the region, undermined political and economic institutions and obstructed the process of regional integration. Finally, Lopandic (2001) emphasized the lack of tradition in multilateral cooperation of SEE countries.

Some concluding remarks

As expected, the fall of the previous regime brought about a major disruption in the direction as well as the structure of trade. During the past decade, and after the initial decline at the start of the transition process, the trade flows of the countries of SEE increased only moderately, mostly reflecting the limited progress in stabilization policies and reform measures, the reduction in the production base and the adverse impact of trade restrictions. Political instability and ethnic conflicts constituted major obstacles to trade expansion as well. Generally, for these economies the period of the 1990s was characterized by two major changes: the loss of their traditional trading partners and an almost immediate redirection of trade towards the industrial countries in general and the EU in particular. The structure of trade, however, did not shift much since, given the outdated technologies, they had to focus mainly on labour-intensive products. As a matter of fact, the sectoral composition of the region's exports declined, primarily concentrating on only a few products. Exports mostly consisted of consumer goods, as being labour-intensive, while capital goods, which are technologically more advanced, constituted the largest share of the region's imports.

While trade with the EU has expanded quickly, regional trade integration in SEE has been progressing at a very slow pace. A number of constraints, ranging from the limited capacities of the particular countries and non-comprehensive trade policies and institutions to political developments and the low quality of infrastructure, contribute to the diversion of exports to more promising markets than the regional one. Imports, on the other hand, are brought in from markets with an abundant supply of differentiated products and capital goods, which are necessary for the modernization and restructuring of the economies of the region.

Although higher intra-regional integration is important to the countries of SEE, one would expect that, given the low level of development of these countries, intra-regional integration would not generate the dynamic gains needed for faster growth and development. As Petrakos (2003) points out, international experience has shown that there is a limit to the benefits that can be derived from regional trade blocs involving less developed countries. On the other hand, however, the fact that trade between the countries of SEE and the EU is of inter-industry character, as a result of the technological gap between the two regions, attaches significant importance to intra-regional trade. So while trade with the EU is vital, since it provides access to technological progress, more intensive trade within the SEE region would provide a potential market for export recovery.

9

Foreign Direct Investment in South Eastern Europe

FDI has been of vital importance to the transition economies. Its importance primarily derives from its contribution to enhancing the growth prospects of the particular economies as well as the process of transformation towards the establishment of a market economy. In contrast to portfolio investment, which is primarily oriented towards short-term profit opportunities, FDI constitutes a long-term commitment which motivates investors to participate actively in the decision-making process contributing, as a result, to enterprise restructuring.

With respect to output growth, the importance of FDI derives not only from its contribution to a higher level of investment through financing for the acquisition of new plant and equipment, but also from the transfer of technology and organizational forms from relatively more advanced economies (UN/ECE 2001). A secondary effect stems from the fact that FDI is more productive than domestic investment generating, as a result, positive 'spillovers' to the local economy which enhance its growth prospects as well. Furthermore, it constitutes an important source of foreign exchange that helps to finance external imbalances while servicing the recipient country's foreign debt. Privatization-related FDI in particular has been an important source of financing fiscal imbalances. Thus FDI, by being a stable long-term source of financing either the current account or fiscal deficits, greatly contributes to macroeconomic stability. Several studies have established the relation between FDI and economic performance. More specifically, the positive impact of FDI on growth is verified by Borensztein, De Gregorio and Lee (1998), Baldwin, Braconier and Forslid (1999) and Lankes and Venables (1996), while Markusen (1995) found a strong relation between FDI and trade.

In addition, FDI has been essential at the firm level as well since it may be the main way through which advanced technology is transferred to these countries: as already pointed out, it contributes to enterprise restructuring and enhances firm performance by facilitating the introduction of new technology, know-how and managerial techniques. More specifically, in the case of developing countries such as the transition economies, it is likely that the higher efficiency of FDI would derive from the combination of advanced management skills and technology with domestic labour and inputs. This, in turn, explains the strong link between FDI and human capital, given that the contribution of FDI to economic growth is supported by its interaction with the level of human capital in the host country. It is in this respect that FDI contributes to growth in a larger measure than domestic investment. The strong positive link between FDI and enterprise restructuring has been shown by a considerable number of studies.[1]

In this chapter we shall examine the performance of SEE in attracting FDI. In particular, we shall first highlight the overall performance of the region and compare it with that of the countries of CE. Next, we shall explain the factors that have been primarily responsible for the rather weak performance of the particular economies relative to their counterparts in CE. Finally, we shall briefly look into the FDI performance of each country of the region separately.

Trends of FDI inflows in South Eastern Europe

The beginning of the transition process in the early 1990s signalled the start of foreign investment into the transition economies. FDI inflows initially increased modestly but then accelerated, mostly towards those countries that had made significant progress in speeding up privatization and which were more successful in improving investment climate. Thus, as we will see in this section, although the transition countries of SEE have succeeded in attracting some foreign investment, their effectiveness has been rather limited, particularly when compared to that of their counterparts in CE.

Table 9.1 reports the FDI inflows (in part 9.1A) and inward FDI stock (part 9.1B) for the countries of SEE during the period 1993–2003. As we can see from Table 9.1A, FDI inflows started up at a very modest pace but then, after 1996, increased considerably. In particular, FDI inflows increased from just below US$1 billion in 1996 to more than US$3 billion in 1997, primarily reflecting the acceleration of privatization in Bulgaria, Croatia and Romania. Then, for the years until 2002 they averaged around US$4 billion yearly, while in 2003 they reported a significant increase that reached close to US$7 billion. A major part of the higher inflows during 2003 was related to privatization, predominantly in the case of SM. Greenfield investment in small and medium-size projects in Bulgaria and Romania represented a substantial part of the total inflows in 2003 as well.[2] This increase in FDI inflows into the region during 2003, in conjunction with the decline in the corresponding inflows into the CE, as we shall see below, may designate a more permanent shift of foreign investment towards the countries of SEE.

In general, the distribution of FDI inflows among the countries of the region has been quite uneven. According to Figure 9.1 it is clear that Bulgaria,

Table 9.1 FDI inflows and inward stock in SEE (US$ mil.)

	1993	1994	1995	1996	1997	1998	1999	2000	2001	2002	2003[a]
A FDI inflows											
Albania	58	53	70	90	48	45	41	143	174	207	178
BH	n.a.	n.a.	n.a.	n.a.	n.a.	67	177	146	119	265	381
Bulgaria	40	105	90	109	505	537	819	1,002	813	905	1,419
Croatia	120	117	121	516	533	932	1,467	1,089	1,561	1,124	1,956
FYROM	n.a.	19	9	11	16	118	32	176	442	77	95
Romania	94	341	419	263	1,215	2,031	1,041	1,037	1,157	1,144	1,560
SM	n.a.	n.a.	n.a.	n.a.	740	113	112	50	165	475	1,260
SEE	**312**	**635**	**709**	**989**	**3,057**	**3,843**	**3,689**	**3,643**	**4,431**	**4,197**	**6,849**
B Inward FDI stock											
Albania	78	131	201	291	339	384	425	568	786	929	1,107
BH	n.a.	n.a.	n.a.	n.a.	n.a.	67	244	390	515	774	1,155
Bulgaria	141	247	337	446	951	1,597	2,403	2,257	2,758	3,662	5,000
Croatia	120	238	359	874	1,425	1,903	2,578	3,560	4,706	6,711	11,351
FYROM	n.a.	24	33	45	75	203	235	410	851	928	1,023
Romania	211	402	821	1,097	2,352	4,418	5,469	6,480	7,638	9,022	12,764
SM	n.a.	n.a.	n.a.	n.a.	740	853	965	1,015	1,180	1,655	2,915
SEE	**550**	**1,042**	**1,751**	**2,753**	**5,882**	**9,425**	**12,319**	**14,680**	**18,434**	**23,681**	**35,315**

n.a. = not available.
[a] Preliminary data.
Source: WIIW annual database.

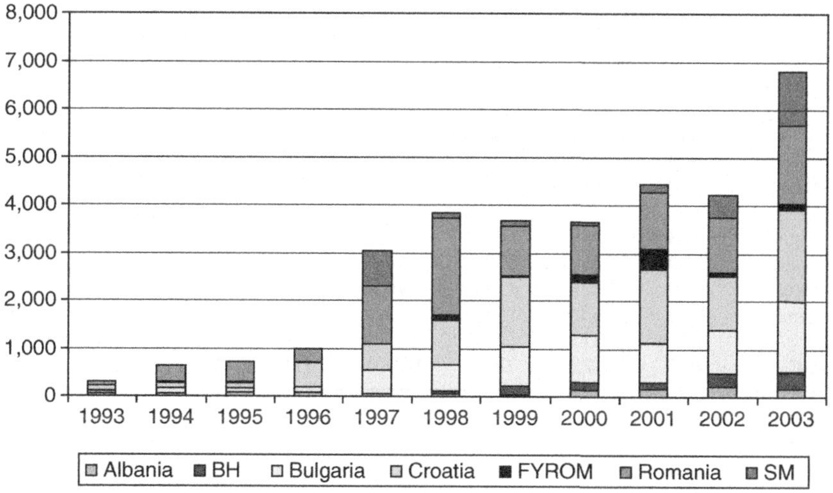

Source: WIIW annual database

Figure 9.1 The distribution of FDI inflows in SEE

Croatia and Romania have been attracting the bulk of FDI inflows into the region. More specifically, the FDI inflows into these three countries have been consistently about 75 per cent or more of the total inflows into the region. Note, however, that these three economies are the most developed in the region and the ones that have made the fastest progress towards reform.

Table 9.2 reports the FDI inflows into the region adjusted for the size of the economy (i.e., in per capita terms as well as in terms of GDP percentage). Both measures verify the increasing trend of FDI during the period under consideration. In particular, for the region as a whole, FDI per capita increased from an annual (unweighted) average of about US$20 during 1993–96 to US$150 in 2003. In addition FDI, expressed as a percentage of GDP, went up from an average of 1.4 during the same period to 4.8 in 2003. Bulgaria and Croatia are the two countries that have had the highest shares in the region.

According to Table 9.1B, the total stock of inward FDI into the region exceeded US$35 billion at the end of 2003. The increase in the FDI stock has been significant during recent years and it almost doubled in 2003 relative to its 2001 level. The biggest increase took place in 2003, reflecting the considerable rise in FDI inflows during that year. The uneven distribution of the inflows in the region can also be confirmed by the fact that about 80 per cent of the total FDI stock was concentrated in Bulgaria, Croatia and Romania. Finally, Table 9.3 reports the inward FDI stock of the region in per capita terms as well as in terms of GDP percentage. FDI per capita increased

Table 9.2 FDI inflows to SEE, adjusted for the size of the economy

	FDI per capita in US$ (annual average)				FDI in per cent of GDP (annual average)			
	1993–96	**1997–99**	**2000–02**	**2003[a]**	**1993–96**	**1997–99**	**2000–02**	**2003[a]**
Albania	21.0	13.0	55.3	56.6	3.5	1.6	3.8	2.9
BH	n.a.	25.5	51.3	98.7	n.a.	2.2	3.5	5.4
Bulgaria	10.3	75.3	114.3	182.0	0.8	5.8	5.3	7.2
Croatia	48.0	235.0	287.0	440.2	1.3	6.4	5.0	6.9
FYROM	7.0	27.7	114.0	46.3	0.4	0.7	6.8	2.0
Romania	12.3	63.3	50.0	73.9	0.9	3.1	2.7	2.8
SM	n.a.	31.3	26.7	151.8	n.a.	2.1	1.8	6.5
SEE	**19.7**	**67.3**	**99.8**	**149.9**	**1.4**	**3.1**	**4.1**	**4.8**

n.a.=not available.
[a] Estimates.
Source: WIIW annual database.

Table 9.3 Inward FDI stock in SEE, adjusted for the size of the economy

	Inward FDI stock per capita in US$				Inward FDI stock in per cent of GDP			
	1996	**1999**	**2002**	**2003[a]**	**1996**	**1999**	**2002**	**2003[a]**
Albania	89.0	126.0	300.0	352.0	10.1	10.7	18.1	17.4
BH	n.a.	51.0	223.0	299.0	n.a.	5.1	14.2	16.2
Bulgaria	53.0	282.0	446.0	641.0	4.5	19.7	21.3	24.7
Croatia	195.0	895.0	1,419.0	2,555.0	4.4	13.7	27.1	36.2
FYROM	20.0	101.0	467.0	499.0	1.0	6.0	24.3	25.5
Romania	55.0	246.0	415.0	587.0	3.1	16.3	17.9	20.1
SM	n.a.	115.0	206.0	351.0	n.a.	8.5	10.2	13.9
SEE	**82.0**	**259.4**	**496.6**	**754.9**	**4.6**	**11.4**	**19.0**	**22.0**

n.a.=not available.
[a]Estimates.
Source: WIIW annual database.

from an average (unweighted) US$82 in 1996 to almost US$500 in 2002, and to US$755 at the end of 2003. Finally, the FDI stock increased from 4.6 per cent of GDP in 1996 to 22 at the end of 2003. In both cases, Croatia is the country with the highest ratios in the region.

Figures 9.2 and 9.3 show how the total FDI stock of the entire region was distributed in terms of the main country investors and by sector of economic activity respectively at the end of 2003. Note that the particular shares do not include SM due to the unavailability of data. Also the figures for Albania are only approximations since the corresponding shares were available only

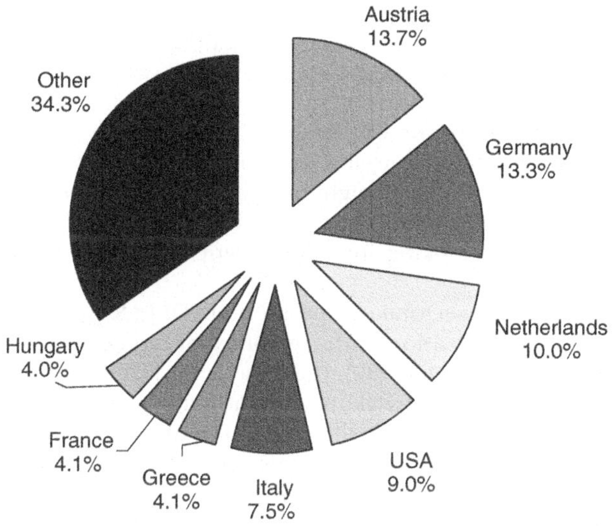

Figure 9.2 Inward FDI stock in SEE by investing country, 2003 (% of total)

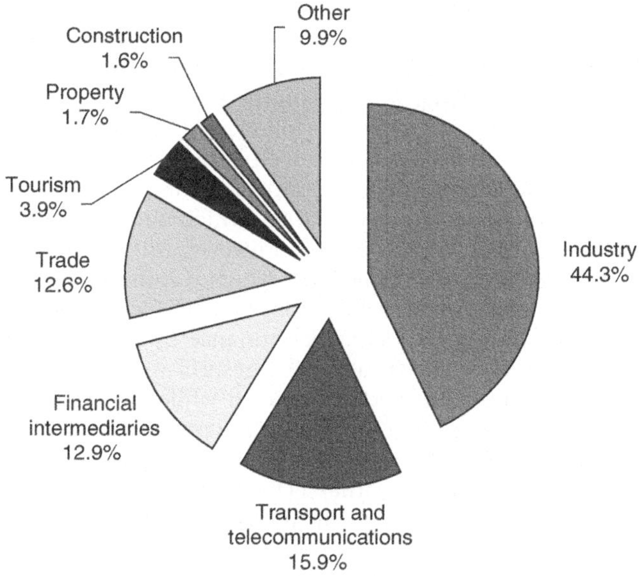

Figure 9.3 Sectoral composition of FDI stock in SEE, 2003 (% of total)

until 2002. What we did then was to apply the shares for 2002 for the particular country to the corresponding amount regarding the FDI stock at the end of 2003.[3] First, with respect to the main investors, we see that Austria and Germany are the leaders in the region with shares of 13.7 and 13.3 per cent respectively. In addition, the Netherlands, the USA, Italy and Greece constitute important investors as well. Geographical proximity appears to have played a significant role since neighbouring developed countries have contributed a significant portion of the total FDI to the region. This will become clearer as we shall be looking into the experience of individual countries below.

Figure 9.3 shows the sectoral composition of FDI in SEE. The sectoral destinations give some indication of the reasons that foreigners invested in the region. Following Dunning (1980), the reasons for FDI can be characterized as market-seeking, efficiency-seeking and natural resource-seeking. The fact that industry has been attracting the bulk of FDI inflows reflects the importance of the efficiency-seeking motive. More specifically, privatization in the particular sector was the vehicle through which foreign manufacturing companies moved to the region in order to take advantage of the lower labour costs. Transport and telecommunications, trade and financial intermediaries received significant amounts of foreign investment, which underlines the importance of the market-seeking motive. Tourism and agriculture, despite their importance for some countries, have attracted just a small share of foreign investment. Overall, the fact that most of the FDI has been privatization related means that the extent of FDI attracted in each sector has been mostly the result of the progress made on the privatization front.

While FDI inflows into SEE have been following an increasing trend during the recent years, the overall performance of the region has been lagging considerably behind that of the CE countries. Figure 9.4 shows the annual FDI inflows into the two regions since 1993, which underlines the relatively poor performance of SEE. As pointed out, however, while there was a drastic drop of FDI inflows into CE during 2003, which was in line with the global trend, the region of SEE experienced considerable increase. This, in turn, may be the start of an even better performance by the countries of SEE in the near future. More specifically, with respect to the countries of CE, the privatization process has been completed while, at the same time, all potential benefits to foreign investors from their prospective EU membership have been largely exhausted, since that process ended once they became full members. This could mean that FDI inflows into most countries of that region will start to follow global trends. By contrast, privatization in most countries of SEE has still some way to go, and thus the speeding-up of the process, as well as the expected future bids for EU accession by other countries beside Bulgaria and Romania, may significantly contribute to higher FDI inflows into the region. Furthermore, the countries of SEE have a considerable advantage relative to their counterparts in CE regarding

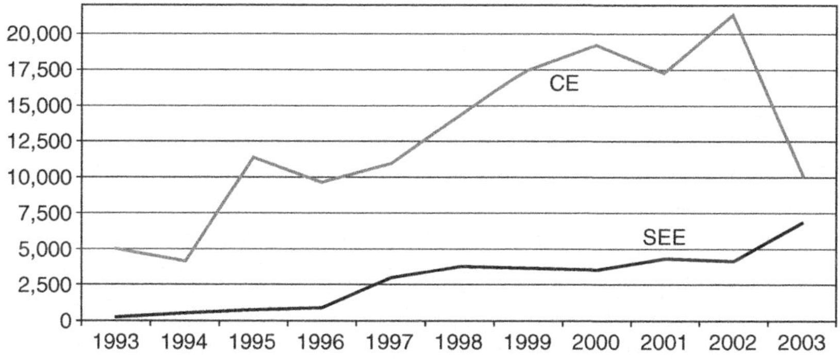

Source: WIIW database

Figure 9.4 Annual FDI inflows (in US$ mil.)

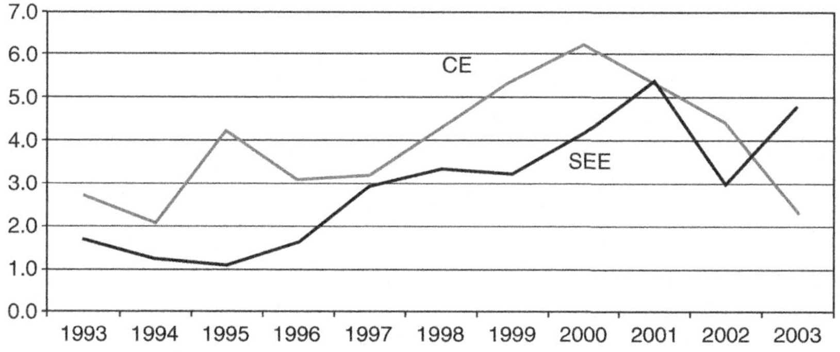

Source: WIIW database

Figure 9.5 Annual FDI inflows (% of GDP)

labour costs. Except for Croatia, gross average earnings in the economies of SEE are about one-third of those in most Central European countries.[4]

Figure 9.5 shows the FDI inflows into the two regions adjusted for the size of GDP. The FDI to GDP ratio has been higher in SEE in 2003 as a result of the much lower GDP level of the particular countries. Finally, the overall better performance of the CE region has been reflected in the size of the inward FDI stocks in the two regions. At the end of 2003, according to Figure 9.6, the inward FDI stock in SEE was just above US$35 billion, amounting to about one-fifth of the corresponding figure for CE. This figure, adjusted for the size of the economy, stood at 21.5 per cent of GDP in SEE, in comparison to 35 per cent in CE (Figure 9.7).

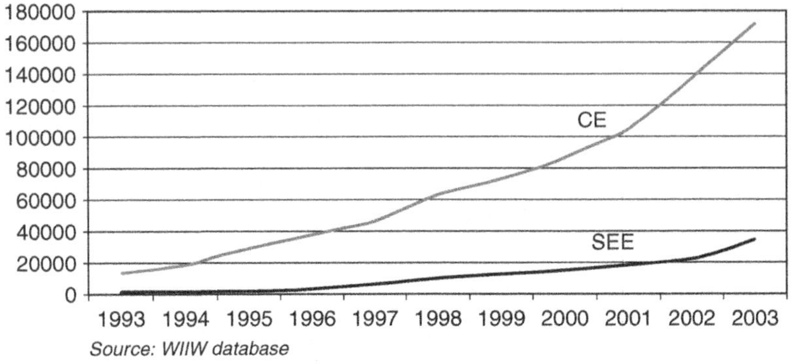

Figure 9.6 Inward FDI stock (in US$ mil.)

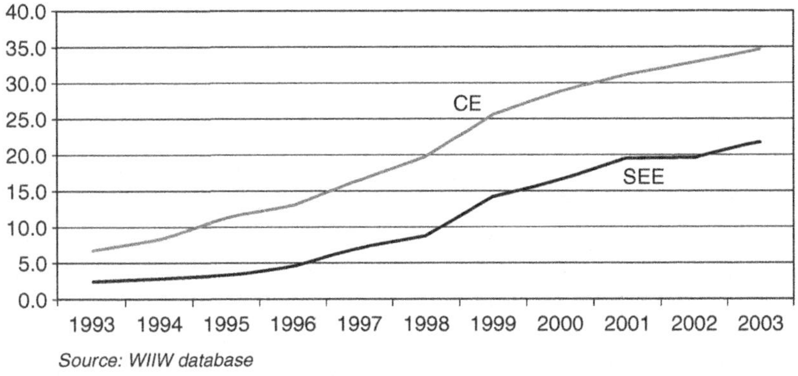

Figure 9.7 Inward FDI stock (% of GDP)

The determinants of FDI inflows in SEE

From the previous analysis we have seen that the transition economies of Central and Eastern Europe have been receiving considerable amounts of FDI, which, however, has been highly concentrated: the bulk of FDI inflows have been directed to the countries of CE, while the countries of SEE have been lagging behind.

In order to ascertain the main reasons for the poor performance of the countries of SEE in attracting FDI inflows, one has to look into what determines the flow of FDI into a particular country.[5] Overall, countries which have achieved a higher degree of macroeconomic as well as political stability are the ones that attract larger amounts of FDI. Good infrastructure and skilled labour, as well as an adequately liberalized external trade sector, constitute additional conditions that contribute to making a country more attractive to foreign investors. Moreover, location, market size and natural resources play a significant role as well. Finally, as far as the transition economies are concerned, progress in the transformation process has been of vital importance in determining the ability of the particular countries to attract FDI. The fact that FDI inflows to the countries of SEE have been considerably lower than those directed towards CE to a larger or lesser extent is explained by these factors. There has already been a great deal of discussion about the factors that determine the FDI inflows towards transition countries. The existing literature includes a large number of case studies (see, for instance, Holland and Pain 1998). In general, they conclude that the main factors which have affected the magnitude of FDI flows directed towards the transition countries include, among other things, the need to secure market access, the opportunity to participate in large-scale privatization processes and the degree of political and economic stability achieved in the host countries.

First, with respect to political factors, the emergence of a series of conflicts following the break-up of the former SFR of Yugoslavia generated a particularly unstable political environment which constituted a major obstacle to potential investors. Overall, especially during the past decade, SEE was considered as a high-risk area which was dominated by regional as well as internal conflicts. Together with the impact of political instability, the weak legal and institutional environment in most of these countries has played a significant role in the poor performance of SEE; so while forming the legal basis of a market economy became a priority task in all transition countries from the very beginning of the reform process, with legal changes starting at the beginning of 1990s, the degree of progress was not always satisfactory. In particular, the old regime's legislation still prevailed in most of the transition countries of SEE in the second half of the decade in important sectors of economic activity, such as banking and finance and international trade. This, in turn, generated a rather hazy investment environment. Overall, the impact of the investment climate on foreign direct investment has been highlighted by several studies which compare the weak performance of the South East European economies and other less advanced transition countries to that of the more advanced ones in CE.[6]

Turning to economic factors, a major impediment to FDI inflows into SEE has been the persistent macroeconomic instability and the slow progress of the transition process. The issue of macroeconomic stability constitutes a key factor which greatly affected FDI inflows in these countries. As we saw in Chapter 4, their macroeconomic environment during the past decade was characterized by continuing inflationary pressures and a decline in output, which primarily reflected inconsistencies in policy measures resulting (in some cases) in severe economic crises. Thus for most foreign investors the combination of macroeconomic and political instability in the region generated a rather hostile environment for investment.

The slow pace of structural reform constituted another obstacle, which was no less important, to foreign investment. In particular, as we saw in Chapter 6, the slow progress in privatization, as well as the methods primarily used, in contrast to the corresponding experience of the Central European countries, have been a key element that has significantly contributed to the limited involvement of foreign strategic investors. Overall, the lack of a firm commitment to reform made foreign investors especially cautious about moving into these particular countries. Furthermore, the fact that FDI is also an important aspect of the transition process itself, and therefore of the business environment for investing firms, may have created vicious circles. More specifically, there is growing evidence that enterprise productivity, research and development expenditure, innovation and company performance are higher in foreign-owned firms, both in the transition economies and in the West (Holland and Pain 1998; Barrell and Pain 1999). This then gives rise to the possibility of vicious circles in the transition process, with one group of countries with negative initial conditions attracting low levels of FDI, such as the ones in SEE, which further differentiates their business environment from their more advanced transition neighbours (i.e., the countries of CE).

Prospects for EU membership can be viewed as a determining element of the operating business environment, and this may have further influenced the lagging of the South East European economies behind the Central European ones. The fact that the countries of CE were the first ones to establish association agreements and adopt free trade provisions gave them a clear advantage *vis-à-vis* their counterparts in SEE in attracting foreign investors. Moreover, their candidacy for EU accession meant that they would eventually endorse EU rules and regulations, further reducing investment risk and thus attracting more FDI than the non-accession groups since firms, primarily from the EU, are encouraged to take advantage of the lower labour costs and relocate production to CE. Overall, potential investors may view EU membership as reducing country risk, both because the need to meet the requirements for EU admission represents an external validation of progress in transition, and also because ultimate EU membership implies guarantees in terms of institutional and legal environment and macroeconomic and political stability.[7] By contrast, countries excluded from the EU, typically because of poor progress in transition (as is the case for most of SEE), are expected to receive lower levels of FDI which, in turn, would further limit their progress in transition relative to their more successful neighbours (Grabbe and Hughes 1998). The effect of this has been an increasing concentration of FDI in the more successful transition economies of CE, and also an increasing differentiation in per capita income within the regions which is associated with inclusion or exclusion from EU membership. Thus, prospective EU membership could be an important independent determinant of FDI in transition economies.

For most South East European economies, as for most transition economies, the key resource is labour, which is regarded as having relatively high levels of skills and training and a strong scientific base. This has been true even after adjusting for their lower productivity. For the countries of CE, labour cost advantages were rated as the most important motivations of foreign partner organizations when considering engaging in FDI during the past decade.[8] In the case of SEE, however, low labour costs were not as effective in attracting FDI since they have been associated with a climate of overall instability for investment. Other important factors that affected FDI flows and contributed to better performance by CE relative to SEE refer to geographical location and to corruption. Geographic location factors are based upon the proximity of the host country to potential export markets, the desire of the investor to be active in every country of the region, proximity to buyers and suppliers, and the general geographic location of the host country.[9] For the countries of CE, geographical proximity to EU markets has been a major advantage relative to South East European ones. Furthermore, corruption practices have been much more of a problem in SEE than in the countries of CE. Corruption is considered as a deterrent to FDI and has been a significant factor in discouraging foreign business from investing in SEE.[10] More specifically, according to the indices calculated by Transparency International, the average score of the Central European countries was considerably higher (better) than that of the South East European ones.[11]

Overall, with respect to the performance of SEE in attracting FDI inflows over the past decade, we may say that the adverse initial conditions, the lack of tradition in democratic institutions and the eruption of the various conflicts led to considerable delays in the launching of reforms and of credible macroeconomic stabilization programmes, as well as in achieving political stability. This, in turn, slowed down the development of market institutions, gave rise to corruption practices and postponed EU membership prospects for most of the countries under consideration here. All these factors contributed to the low effectiveness of the countries of the region in attracting foreign investors. Nevertheless, the beginning of the new century signalled a renewed effort and a firmer commitment by these countries to acceleration of reforms and to achieving macroeconomic and political stability. Thus, while considerable problems still remain, there has been a substantial improvement which has led to a significant increase in the FDI inflows over the years following the beginning of the new decade.

FDI inflow trends into the individual countries of the region

In this section we analyse in some detail the individual country experience with respect to FDI. More specifically, besides the overall trend of FDI, we will trace FDI inflows in each country by examining the main countries which have invested as well as their distribution over different sectors of economic activity. The data we use are from the annual database of the WIIW.

Albania

FDI inflows into Albania have been rather modest. In particular, they were mainly low during the past decade, primarily reflecting the slow progress towards reform as well as the deep political and economic crisis that occurred in 1997 following the collapse of the pyramid investment schemes. Due to the social turmoil, FDI dropped in 1997 by about 50 per cent while it was further reduced during the period 1997–99 (Table 9.1A). This is apparent in Table 9.2 as well, according to which there was a considerable fall in FDI during the period 1997–99, relative to period 1993–96, either in terms of per capita or as a percentage of GDP. However, inflows significantly recovered at the beginning of the new decade and this was primarily associated with the speeding-up of the privatization process (Hunya 2002). The increase in FDI inflows over the period 2001–03 has led to an almost doubling of Albania's FDI stock (Table 9.1B). Note, however, that the low level of greenfield investment so far could mean a significant drop in FDI inflows once privatization is completed.

According to Figure 9.8, Italy and Greece (the two neighbouring EU states) accounted for more than 80 per cent of Albania's inward FDI stock at the end of 2002. This, in turn, indicates that, unlike the experience of other South East European countries, foreign investment into Albania is of a vicinity type (Slaveski and Nedanovski 2003). In particular, most Italian investment activity is concentrated in north west Albania, while the bulk of Greek investment

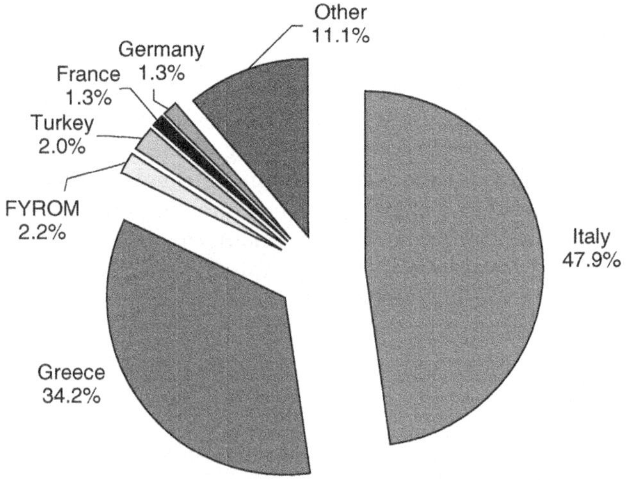

Figure 9.8 Inward FDI stock in Albania by investing country, 2002 (% of total)

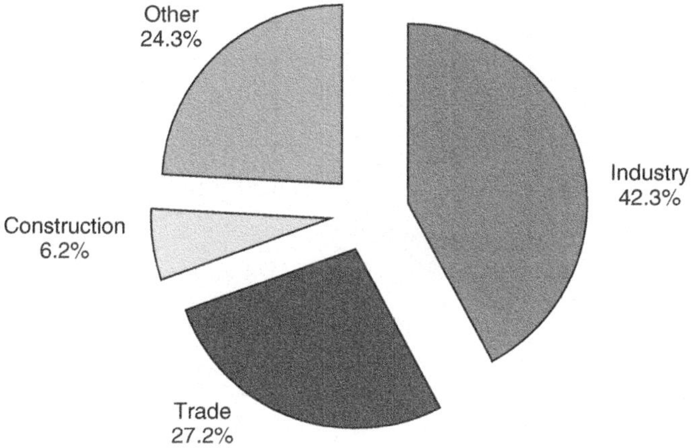

Figure 9.9 Sectoral distribution of FDI stock in Albania, 2002 (% of total)

has been directed to the south east part of the country. Turning to the sectoral composition of foreign investment in Albania, the majority of FDI has been directed to industry. More specifically, according to Figure 9.9, about 42 per cent of the total inward FDI stock went to industry. Trade absorbed a significant part of FDI (27 per cent of the total) while construction, tourism and agriculture attracted a smaller portion.

BH

The civil war, as well as the splitting of the country into two entities, made BH not very attractive to foreign investors. Until recently the markets in the two entities were largely segmented. Furthermore, despite the considerable efforts towards reform and harmonization of legal structures, the laws and regulations at state, entity or even municipality level are often contradictory or duplicative (Hunya 2002). Thus a rather hasty investment climate constituted the main reason for the weak FDI inflows. The low level of FDI is clearly shown in Table 9.1A. Note, however, that the situation has improved during the period 2002–03: total FDI inflows during these two years reached US$650 million, which is more than the cumulative FDI inflows during all previous years (Table 9.1B). Also, as Table 9.2 indicates, the increase in FDI when expressed in terms of GDP share was quite significant, primarily reflecting the speeding-up of the privatization process.

Turning to the main investor countries, Austria appears to be the top investing country in BH, accounting for about 29 per cent of the total inward stock at the end of 2003 (Figure 9.10). Croatia is second holding a share equal to 18 per cent. According to Figure 9.10, Germany, Slovenia and Kuwait

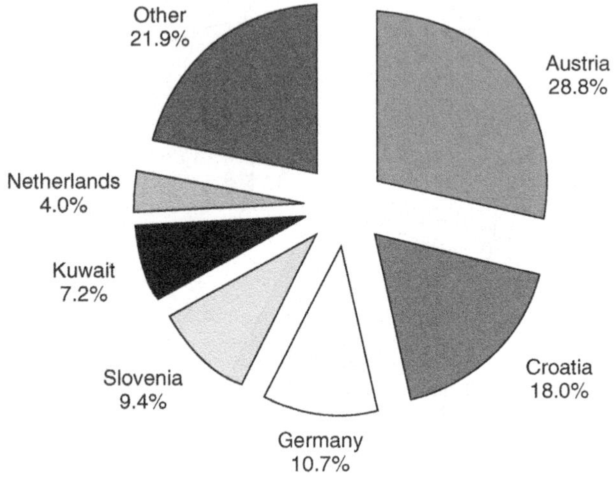

Figure 9.10 Inward FDI stock in BH by investing country, 2003 (% of total)

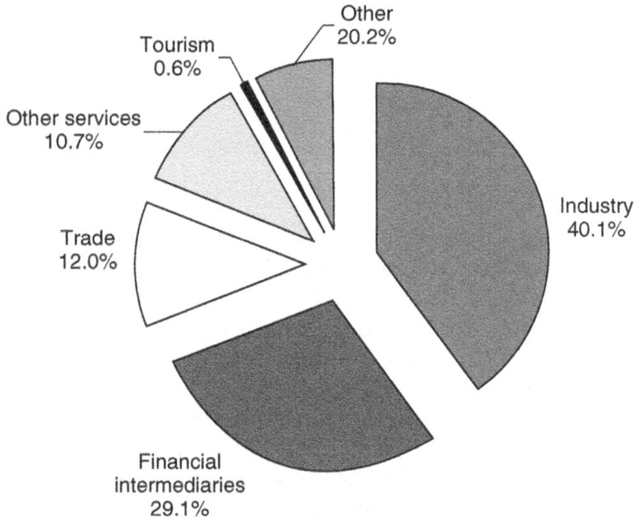

Figure 9.11 Sectoral composition of FDI stock in BH, 2003 (% of total)

constitute important investors as well. Turning to the sectoral distribution of the total FDI stock (see Figure 9.11), we see that industry has attracted by far the most FDI in BH. Also, a considerable amount of FDI has been directed to the banking sector, reflecting the recent progress in bank privatization.

Bulgaria

The low level of FDI inflows in Bulgaria, particularly until 1996, was strongly associated with the slow and superficial progress of this particular country towards reform as well as with the 'stop and go' macroeconomic policies. As explained in earlier chapters, the combined effects of delayed reform and growing enterprise losses led to a full-blown economic and political crisis towards the end of 1996. Inflation, government debt and the budget deficit spiralled out of control; commercial banks and financial markets essentially collapsed; and foreign reserves for defending the national currency were exhausted. The new stabilization programme that was endorsed in 1997, the central feature of which was the introduction of a currency board regime and the adoption of credible policies, together with the speeding-up of the reform progress led to a substantial recovery of the FDI inflows. Furthermore, conditions for foreign investors were improved as a result of the government's renewed effort to clamp down on corruption and to make the cumbersome bureaucracy more efficient (Panagiotou 2001).

Thus, according to Tables 9.1A and 9.2, FDI inflows to Bulgaria were at a low level during the period 1993–96, but they increased considerably in 1997 and remained at high levels until the end of the 1990s. Note that in 1997 alone Bulgaria attracted more FDI inflows than the four previous years taken together (Table 9.1A). Although FDI remained high during the period 2001–02, it declined moderately relative to its 2000 level, mainly reflecting the mixed results with respect to the progress regarding large-scale privatization. Note, however, that there was a substantial increase in FDI inflows during 2003, reaching about US$1.4 billion; this was due not only to privatization but also to a considerable amount of greenfield investment as well. At the end of 2003 the inward FDI stock reached US$5 billion, amounting to US$641 per capita and to about 25 per cent of GDP (Table 9.3).

The EU is by far the largest investor in Bulgaria since it held 63 per cent of the country's inward FDI stock at the end of 2003. With respect to individual countries, Greece is the largest investor in Bulgaria as of 2003, having invested about US$700 million, which represents about 14 per cent of the total FDI stock (Figure 9.12). Note, however, that Greece's participation may be underestimated since a large part of Greek investment has been taking place through Cyprus and Luxembourg (Panagiotou 2001). Italy, Germany and Austria follow with shares close to or above 10 per cent. Turning to sectoral composition at the end of 2003, according to Figure 9.13 the industrial sector has attracted the bulk of investment, some 32 per cent of the total, while the banking sector received about 21 per cent. Trade, and Tourism have received a significant part of the total FDI stock as well.

Overall, there has been substantial progress in attracting FDI over the past three years in Bulgaria. The speeding-up of reforms, particularly with

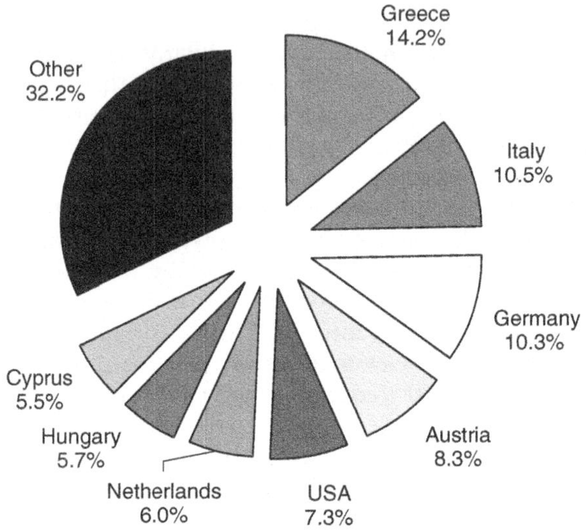

Figure 9.12 Inward FDI stock in Bulgaria by investing country, 2003 (% of total)

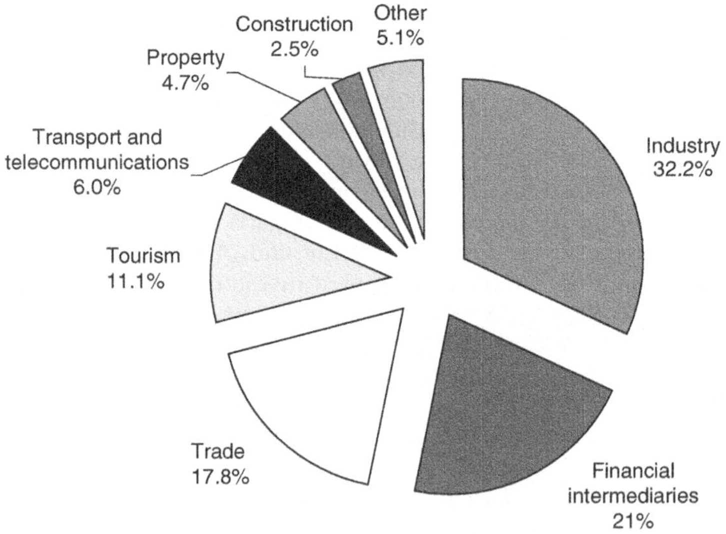

Figure 9.13 Sectoral composition of FDI stock in Bulgaria, 2003 (% of total)

respect to large-scale privatization, as well as the creation of an attractive environment for FDI have been particularly important to foreign investors. Furthermore their impact has been enhanced by other favourable factors, such as low labour costs, a skilled workforce and solid economic growth.

Croatia

Croatia constitutes the most developed country of the region which, in comparison to the other economies, progressed faster towards reform as well as improving its business climate. The break-up of Yugoslavia and the war that followed in the early 1990s temporarily put on hold Croatia's transition to the market system. Nevertheless, as soon as the war ended and the transition process began, FDI inflows started recovering, at a relatively slow pace at first but then, after 1996, picking up considerably (Tables 9.1A and 9.2). Croatia has been the most successful country of the region in attracting foreign investment. The cumulative inward FDI stock at the end of 2003 exceeded US$11 billion (see Table 9.1B), representing a share higher to 30 per cent of the total FDI stock of the region. Given the small size of the economy, Croatia has accumulated by far the largest FDI stock of the region, in per capita terms or as a percentage of GDP (Table 9.3).

According to Figure 9.14, Austria and Germany are the largest investors in Croatia, accounting for about 26 and 22 per cent respectively of the total

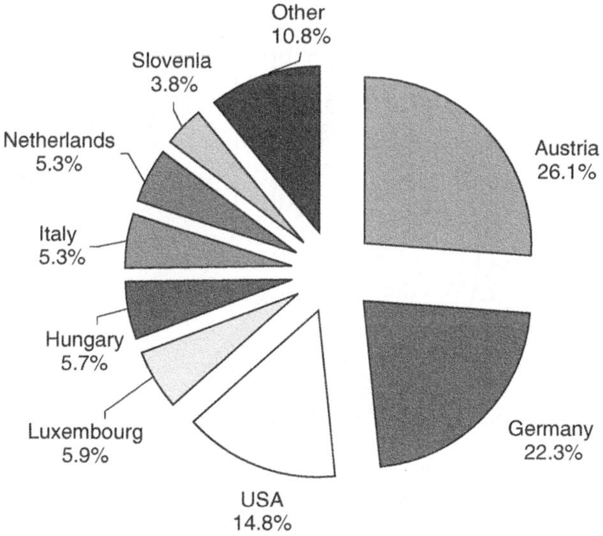

Figure 9.14 Inward FDI stock in Croatia by investing country, 2003 (% of total)

FDI stock at the end of 2003. The USA, and to a lesser extent Luxembourg, Hungary, Italy and the Netherlands, also hold significant portions of Croatia's FDI stock. Overall, the EU member states are by far the largest investors, holding about 70 per cent of the total FDI stock at the end of 2003. Looking at the sectoral composition of FDI as of 2003 (see Figure 9.15), we see that industry has attracted the largest part of cumulative FDI inflow, which amounts to about 39 per cent of the total. The banking sector, and transportation and telecommunications have received significant portions as well, each accounting for 23 per cent of the total. Surprisingly enough, tourism, one of the most important sectors of the Croatian economy, has thus far only attracted less than 5 per cent of the country's total FDI stock.

Finally, it must be pointed out that while Croatia has been the leading economy in attracting FDI inflows among the other countries of SEE, its performance has lagged behind its counterparts in CE, particularly during the past decade. In addition to the war and the overall political instability of the region, the lack of trade associations with the EU has hurt Croatian exports to Western markets, which, in turn, has affected FDI inflows adversely. In other words, foreign investors were reluctant to invest in Croatia as long as there were no association agreements with the EU, meaning that the risk of investing remained relatively high (Sonje and Vujcic 2001). Thus, the fact that Croatia received EU candidate status in June 2004 is expected to affect

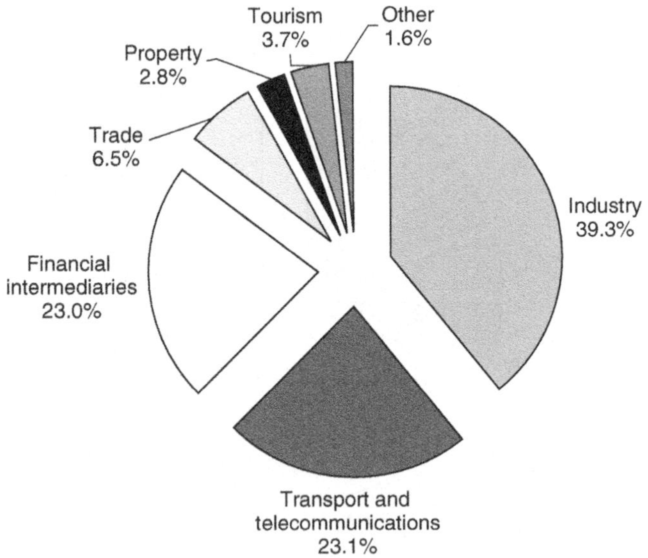

Figure 9.15 Sectoral composition of FDI stock in Croatia, 2003 (% of total)

the risk of investing favourably. In addition, substantial increases in labour costs may have affected FDI inflows negatively as well.

FYROM

FYROM has been the only republic of former Yugoslavia to have attained its independence peacefully. However, several events have affected the country adversely and account for its poor performance in attracting foreign investment. More specifically, the UN embargo on SM had a significant impact on the country's economy since this country was its main market and trade route. Then, in 1994 the Greek embargo on FYROM had an adverse impact as well. Later on, the Kosovo War of 1999, as well as the internal ethnic conflict in the first half of 2001, also had a severe impact on the country's economy and FDI inflows. In particular, the privatization process slowed down considerably as the sale of large firms was put on hold since for foreigners the risk of investing in FYROM increased dramatically. As we have seen in previous chapters, however, despite these adverse circumstances, FYROM managed to make significant progress in stabilization and reform which, in turn, exerted a positive influence on foreign investors.

According to Table 9.1A, FYROM has been attracting quite low FDI inflows, particularly during the previous decade. The inflows were low in terms of their absolute level as well as in per capita terms or in terms of their GDP share (Table 9.2). There was a temporary surge in 1998 which, however, fell off in 1999 as a result of the Kosovo crisis. Note that the large increase in FDI during the year 2001 was not the result of a boost of FDI inflows into the country but reflected instead the impact of a single deal. More specifically, the successful privatization of the state telecommunications company to a Hungarian strategic investor involved a cash payment equivalent to about 9 per cent of the country's GDP (see Slaveski and Nedanovski 2003). As Table 9.1A indicates, after this particular deal FDI inflows returned to their normal (low) levels in the period 2002–03. FYROM, together with Albania and BH, had the lowest inward FDI stock in the region, which stood at the US$1.0 billion mark at the end of 2003 (Table 9.1B).

According to Figure 9.16, Hungary and Greece are the largest investors in FYROM with shares equal to 35 and 25 per cent of the total FDI stock at the end of 2003. Note, however, that while Hungary's presence is associated with the buying of the telecommunications company mentioned earlier, Greece's investment has been much more diversified, involving a number of firms in different sectors. Cyprus, the UK, Switzerland and Germany constitute the next most important investing countries. The first one, however, may have been a country through which the transactions take place, which does not necessarily coincide with the actual country doing the investing. Turning to the sectoral composition of FDI, as of 2003 we can see that, according to Figure 9.17, transportation and telecommunications have attracted the largest part of cumulative FDI amounting to 37.4 per cent of

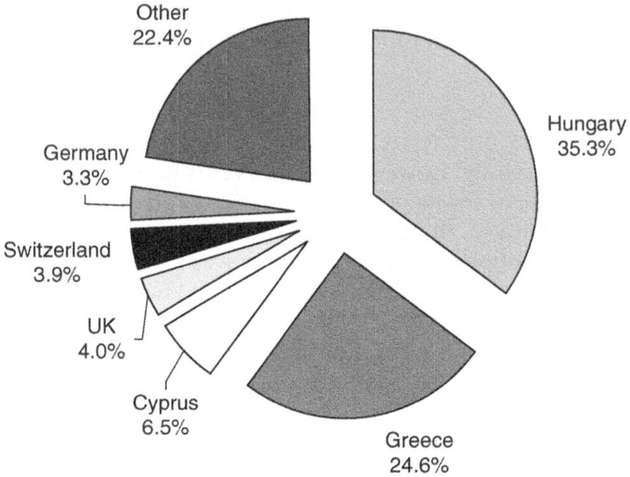

Figure 9.16 Inward FDI stock in FYROM by investing country, 2003 (% of total)

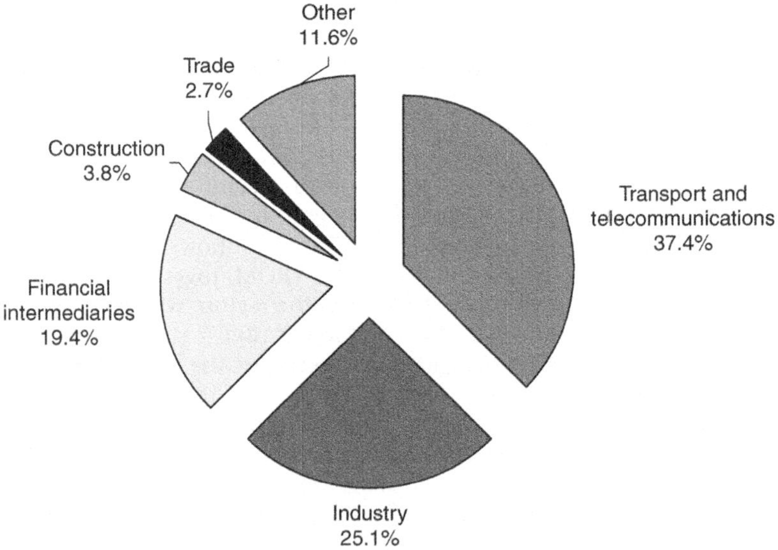

Figure 9.17 Sectoral composition of FDI stock in FYROM, 2003 (% of total)

the total. Industry and financial intermediaries have had significant participation as well, accounting for about 25 and 19 per cent of the total FDI stock respectively.

Romania

Romania is the largest economy of the region. Although it is rich in natural resources, it has not been as successful in attracting FDI inflows which have been low relative to the size of the country. This was mostly the result of the unfavourable initial conditions which primarily reflected the excessive focus of central planning on heavy industry and large infrastructure projects, the slow progress in structural reforms and the persisting macroeconomic instability. As explained earlier, this led to an overall economic deterioration and the re-emergence of inflation in 1997. Against this background of a risky investment environment, FDI inflows were understandably low. This was particularly the case during the period 1993–96, following which FDI started recovering, mainly as a result of the renewed efforts the country made towards reform and macroeconomic stabilization. Other key efforts that helped the country to attract higher FDI inflows included clamping down on corruption, reforming the bureaucracy to streamline decision-making and also promoting foreign investment by accelerating the adoption of the necessary legislation (Panagiotou 2001). Note that since 1997 FDI inflows have been averaging above US$1 billion. In 1998 they exceeded US$2 billion as a result of the successful privatization-related selling of state-owned companies during that year (Table 9.1A). According to Table 9.1B, at the end of 2003, Romania's total FDI stock almost reached US$13 billion, the highest in the region, which, however, when adjusted to the size of the economy stands below the region's average (Table 9.3).

As of 2003, the Netherlands appeared to be the largest investor in Romania, holding 18 per cent of the total FDI stock (Figure 9.18). Germany, France, Italy and Austria held significant shares as well. Overall, the member states of the EU held about 60 per cent of the total FDI stock at the end of 2003. Among the countries outside the EU, the USA held the largest portion. With respect to the distribution of Romania's inward stock by economic sector in 2003, industry attracted the largest share of about 55.5 per cent (Figure 9.19). Trade and transportation and telecommunications followed at some distance with 15.5 and 7.4 per cent respectively. Construction, tourism and agriculture received much less.

Romania has the potential to attract much higher levels of FDI given its geographic location, the large internal market, the rich and diversified natural resources as well as the low-paid but well educated labour force. So far the slow progress concerning reforms in general and privatization in particular have considerably limited the incentives to participate on the part of foreign investors. Furthermore, the persisting macroeconomic imbalances constitute another major obstacle. In any case, the fact that Romania is

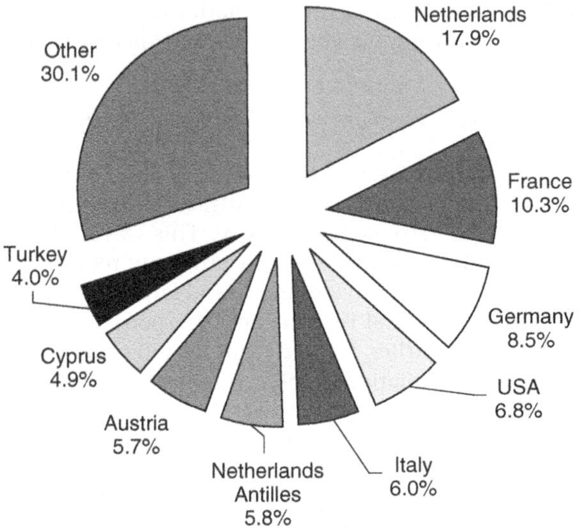

Figure 9.18 Inward FDI stock in Romania by investing country, 2003 (% of total)

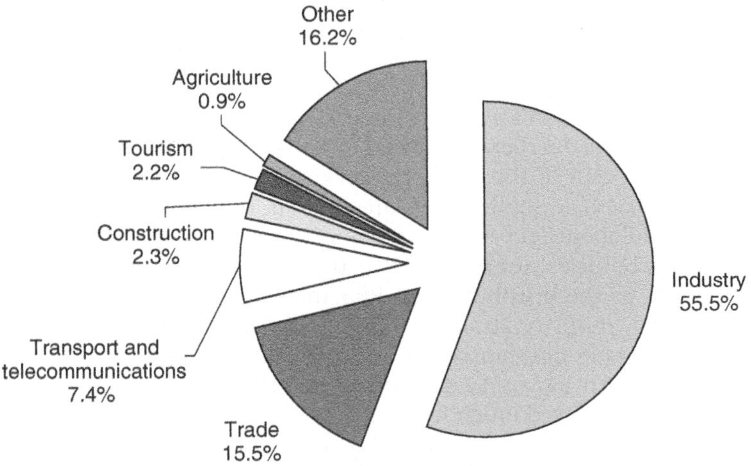

Figure 9.19 Sectoral composition of FDI stock in Romania, 2003 (% of total)

expected to join the EU (together with Bulgaria) in 2007 would mean that the investment climate will improve substantially leading, sooner or later, to further recovery of FDI inflows.

SM

As indicated in previous chapter, the transition process in SM started essentially only in 2001, after the political change that took place in October 2000. The slow progress in privatization kept FDI rather low during the period 2000–02. More specifically, according to Table 9.1A, a small recovery in FDI inflows occurred during 2001. A substantial recovery, however, took place in 2003. In particular, it increased to almost US$1.3 billion, a large part of which was linked to privatization. The increase was substantial when adjusted to the size of the economy as well (Table 9.2). This, in turn, led to considerable increase in the FDI stock which amounted to almost US$3.0 billion at the end of 2003 (Table 9.1B). Note that due to the unavailability of data we cannot examine issues regarding the main countries investing, or the sectoral distribution of FDI in SM.

Concluding remarks

After a slow start and a modest pace of increase during the past decade, FDI inflows to SEE appeared to have recovered significantly during the recent past and the region may become an important destination for foreign capital in the near future. The relative political and macroeconomic stability that was achieved by most countries, and the speeding-up of the reform process, have made the region more appealing to foreign investors. Furthermore, the low labour costs, particularly relative to their counterparts in CE, constitute another explanation for the attractiveness of the region as a destination for FDI, particularly from the EU member states.

EU member states are by far the most important investors. In particular, geographical proximity appears to be an important determinant since neighbouring countries such as Austria, Germany, Greece and Italy account for the greatest participation. Most FDI in the region is concentrated in industry, which is indicative of the significance of the low labour costs as their main comparative advantage relative to other emerging economies. The acceleration of the privatization process, especially with respect to large enterprises, has been the main driving force contributing to a higher level of FDI. Thus the ability of the region to attract more greenfield investment will greatly determine the course of FDI inflows over the longer run. Besides the low labour costs, greater trade integration is expected to be a crucial determinant as well since it will effectively contribute to the expansion of the size of the market.

10
The Euro and the Exchange Rate Regimes of the South East European Countries

As analysed in previous chapters, the countries of SEE have employed diverse exchange rate regimes, which were the result of different circumstances in each country. Among other things, these regimes reflect the extent of progress in the transition process, the preferred approach to stabilization as well as the authorities' reaction to economic shocks. As a matter of fact, with respect to current exchange rate arrangements, one can see that basically there are two types of exchange rate regimes in the region. More specifically, three countries have fixed regimes – Bulgaria, BH and FYROM – and the first two of these operate on a currency board arrangement while the third has a *de facto* peg arrangement. The remaining four economies prefer a managed floating regime. Furthermore, it must be pointed out that two territories of Serbia and Montenegro, namely Montenegro and Kosovo, have shifted to euroization, which essentially constitutes an irreversible peg; they have unilaterally adopted the euro as 'legal tender and the sole official currency'.[1] Overall, the chosen regimes manifest not only the degree of willingness but also the extent to which the economic circumstances in some countries allow the policy-makers to rely on greater exchange rate stability as a basic tool for macroeconomic stabilization.

The decision for monetary unification by most EU member states and the resulting shift to a common currency, the euro, constituted a major event for the international monetary system. Apart from its impact on the EU countries, it entails important implications for the global economy in general and the transition economies of Central and Eastern Europe in particular. However, as opposed to the economies of CE, which have already joined the EU and whose main concern with respect to the euro is their smooth transition to economic and monetary union, the role of the euro for the majority of the transition economies of SEE appears to be rather different. More specifically, it is primarily related to the stabilization question and the growth prospects of the particular countries. As a result, a legitimate question that arises refers to whether the euro would affect the effectiveness of existing exchange rate arrangements and thus induce the policy-makers to consider altering the exchange rate regimes already in place. The cases of Montenegro and Kosovo represent notable examples of changes in existing regimes caused by the launching of the euro.

Thus, a policy of greater exchange rate stability *vis-à-vis* the euro by the countries of the region may have quite favourable effects on the particular economies given the extent of trade and capital market integration between them and the EU. This would encourage even more economic integration with the member states of the EU, enhancing growth. Furthermore, the case of greater exchange stability, particularly when it takes the form of unilateral euroization, would lead to lower interest rates, which in turn would result in a lower cost of servicing public debt while leading to a higher level of investment and economic growth. It would also bring more credibility, primarily by imposing fiscal consolidation. By contrast, greater exchange rate stability would reduce the role of monetary policy as a stabilizing instrument. The significance of this, in turn, depends on the susceptibility of the countries in question to asymmetric shocks relative to the EU and the efficiency of mechanisms other than monetary policy for adjusting to these shocks. Following the pioneering studies of Mundell (1961), Kenen (1969) and Tavlas (1994), the susceptibility is reduced in the case of: (a) increased similarity in the structure of production between the particular countries and the EU, and (b) more flexibility in their wages and prices as well as greater mobility in their labour force.

In previous chapters we examined in some detail the macroeconomic situation of South East European countries, the progress of the transition process as well as the degree of economic integration (trade and FDI) with the EU. As indicated, some of these countries, despite their recent progress, still cope with considerable problems regarding the transition progress as well as getting their economies on track. Such an analysis could be particularly helpful for a critical evaluation of the possible implications of the euro for these economies. More specifically, in this chapter, we will attempt to examine possible effects of the euro on the exchange rate policies followed by the countries of the region. Given the current economic circumstances of each country as well as the corresponding policy priorities, we shall try to appraise the impact of the euro on the sustainability as well as the effectiveness of the existing exchange rate regimes. Taking into consideration the fact that the majority of these countries have some way to go until they are to be considered for accession, we shall discuss the appropriateness of an exchange rate policy that favours a euro-based exchange rate target as opposed to that of a greater degree of flexibility. The euro-based target refers not only to a conventional fixed peg or to a currency board arrangement but also to a situation of unilateral euroization. As a result, in the next section we will discuss some of the theoretical underpinnings concerning the effect of the euro on exchange rate policies. Then, by taking into consideration the current economic circumstances of each country, we will examine the possible implications of the euro for the effectiveness as well as the sustainability of the existing exchange rate arrangements in the region.

The euro and the choice of exchange rate regime: Some theoretical considerations

This section gives some theoretical insights with respect to the possible effects of the euro on alternative exchange rate regimes. More specifically, it focuses on two basic alternatives of exchange rate arrangements which, in a broad sense, reflect the existing regimes of SEE economies:[2]

1. A fixed nominal exchange rate regime *vis-à-vis* the euro, which can take the form of either a simple peg (FYROM) or a hard peg which refers to currency board arrangements (Bulgaria and BH) and euroization (Kosovo and Montenegro).
2. A more flexible nominal exchange rate regime, with the extent of flexibility being of varying degrees, so that the regime may take the form of a pre-announced crawl or crawling band, or that of a non-announced crawl (managed floating) or the form of a fixed peg with frequent discrete adjustments. The exchange rate arrangements of Albania, Croatia, Romania and SM are of this type and, more specifically, they can be described as managed floating regimes.

The extent to which the introduction of the euro strengthens or weakens some of the main characteristics of the two basic regimes would, in turn, affect their effectiveness positively or negatively respectively. As an initial remark, we should point out that it may be advantageous for small economies which have a high degree of openness to peg to the exchange rate of a much larger trading partner.[3] Indeed, empirical evidence indicates that small open economies represent the best candidates for a successful euroization/dollarization.[4] In the case of SEE, the fact that the euro is the currency of a large area which is of enormous importance to their economies would expand the advantages of a currency peg. It could, on the one hand, strengthen further the role of the EU as the dominant trading partner of the countries of the region, while, on the other, expanding the degree of their openness. This then would mean that for a country already operating successfully under a fixed regime, the shifting from, say, a DM peg to a euro peg would by itself reinforce the effectiveness of the system.

The desirability of a fixed exchange rate regime primarily stems from the gains in credibility since it provides a solid basis for monetary stability and low inflation. This is particularly true when the fixed regime takes the form of a hard peg such as a currency board or euroization.[5] The experience of transition economies that have adopted a fixed regime in the past has shown that it can become a very effective anti-inflationary instrument. Indeed, it constitutes a very simple policy rule, which has been most useful to the transition economies given the lack of other reliable nominal anchors, particularly during the early stages of transformation.[6] A crucial condition for a fixed regime to be effective during the process of disinflation is the consistency of other macroeconomic policies, which must be in line with the exchange rate policy. This, as we pointed out in Chapters 4 and 5, particularly refers to the need for restrictive fiscal policy, which, in turn, means lower external current account deficits and renders the system less vulnerable to speculative attacks. A regime fixed to the euro, which covers a much larger currency area, may impose greater discipline on the policy-makers to keep the other policy measures in line with the exchange peg. The fact that the domestic currency is tied to the corresponding one of a much larger currency area magnifies the costs of inconsistent macroeconomic policies.

Susceptibility and adaptability to asymmetric shocks

As pointed out, the sustainability of a peg crucially depends on the possibility of the country in question facing different shocks from those that are hitting the currency area to which it is linked. In particular, there are three types of measure of susceptibility to asymmetric shocks: direct correlation of shocks; correlations of growth rates of economic activity in order to depict both asymmetric shocks and asymmetric responses to symmetric shocks; and measures of structural features of the economies in question which make them either more or less prone to asymmetric shocks. First, with respect to correlation of shocks, two studies presented evidence pointing to low correlations of shocks between the countries of Central and Eastern Europe and the euro area.[7] In addition, correlations of GDP and industrial production growth rates were found to be low as well. Note that the particular results primarily concern the more advanced economies of CE which, in turn, implies that for the less developed countries of SEE the corresponding correlations would be even lower.

Turning to structural features, as pointed out previously, to the extent that the trade and economic structure of the particular countries is aligned with those of the anchor area the incidence of asymmetric shocks is reduced. Thus the extent to which the economies of SEE share a similar trade and output structure with the EU would positively affect the viability of an exchange rate regime tied to the euro.[8] This, in turn, means that the progress made in the transition process in general and in structural reform in particular would largely determine the extent to which the economic structures of the particular countries have been brought into line with that of the EU. Table 10.1 helps us make important observations about the output and export structures of the SEE region *vis-à-vis* the member states of the EU in 2003. First, with respect to output structure, the differences between the two regions are the ones normally expected between a developed and

Table 10.1 Output and export structures in 2003

	SITC[a]	Albania	BH	Bulgaria	Croatia	FYROM	Romania	SM	SEE	EU
Output structure (% of GDP)										
Agriculture		51.0	10.0	14.5	9.5	10.0	15.5	18.1	14.8	2.3
Industry + Construction		26.3	29.4	27.8	32.9	31.9	36.2	38.9	34.0	30.7
Services		22.7	60.6	57.7	57.6	58.1	48.3	43.0	51.2	67.0
Export structure (% of total exports)										
Agricultural products	(SITC 0, 1)	5.6	5.3	8.7	11.7	16.7	2.4	20.3	7.1	5.3
Crude material, energy and chemicals	(SITC 2, 3, 4, 5)	10.3	19.3	23.8	25.1	13.6	17.8	17.4	20.1	19.9
Machinery and transport equipment	(SITC 7)	3.6	16.4	13.0	29.4	5.9	21.5	11.7	19.5	45.4
Other manufactures	(SITC 6, 8)	80.5	57.5	53.5	33.7	63.6	58.2	48.9	53.0	27.0

[a] The numbers in parentheses refer to SITC product classification of international trade.
Sources: EBRD, *Transition Report* (2003); IMF, *International Financial Stastistics* (2001); and UN, Economic Survey for Europe (2003).

a developing region. The EU, the developed region, has a much larger services sector and a considerably smaller agricultural region than SEE, the developing region. Next, with respect to exports we see that the countries of SEE have a trade structure which differs considerably from that of the EU. In particular, the region of SEE displayed a large concentration of exports of manufactured products, which are mostly consumer goods, and a small one of machinery and transport equipment, which are primarily capital goods. By contrast, the EU exhibited a large concentration of capital goods and a much smaller one of consumer goods. Thus, with respect to the exports, SEE has developed a structure that is diverging from that of the EU (see also Petrakos 2003). This, of course, refers to the region as a whole and, as we will see in the next section, this may differ when one looks at each country separately.

Furthermore, the susceptibility to shocks could be seen in a dynamic rather than in a static context. Increasing trade integration may change a country's trade structure, making it either less or more susceptible to asymmetric shocks. More specifically, if it leads to greater specialization of production and more inter-industry trade, it would increase the susceptibility to asymmetric shocks (Artis 1991; Krugman 1991). By contrast, the susceptibility will be reduced if it leads to more intra-industry trade (Frankel and Ross (1996b)). Table 10.2 includes information about the share of intra-industry trade between the EU and SEE for the period 1993–2001. We employed the Grubel–Lloyd index (1975) using export and import data for 2-digit sectors. A common observation for all the countries of the region refers to a very low share of intra-industry trade with the EU, which in turn implies a very high share of inter-industry trade. Note that for the majority of the South East European countries considerably less than 50 per cent of their trade with the EU has been of an intra-industry nature, and only Bulgaria, Croatia and Romania reached a share that exceeded the 40 per cent mark in 2001.[9]

Table 10.2 Index of intra-industry trade between SEE and the EU

	1993	**1994**	**1995**	**1996**	**1997**	**1998**	**1999**	**2000**	**2001**
Albania	0.21	0.28	0.29	0.31	0.25	0.37	0.35	0.33	0.36
BH	0.23	0.15	0.19	0.16	0.19	0.24	0.25	0.24	0.27
Bulgaria	0.46	0.43	0.40	0.42	0.41	0.41	0.40	0.39	0.40
Croatia	0.37	0.38	0.45	0.45	0.42	0.40	0.42	0.45	0.46
FYROM	0.35	0.40	0.40	0.32	0.30	0.29	0.25	0.27	0.30
Romania	0.31	0.34	0.33	0.34	0.34	0.33	0.37	0.40	0.43
SM	n.a.	n.a.	n.a.	0.30	0.32	0.35	0.33	0.34	0.36
SEE[a]	0.28	0.28	0.29	0.33	0.32	0.34	0.34	0.35	0.37

n.a. = not available.
[a] Unweighted average.
Source: Eurostat (2002).

Given the high susceptibility of the countries of SEE to asymmetric shocks, our analysis turns to the question of adaptability to such shocks. This means that the viability of the system of greater exchange rate stability would depend on whether adjustment to asymmetric shocks could occur through other channels, such as wage and price flexibility. Thus, for the countries that have introduced more vigorous reforms and have removed structural rigidities, particularly with respect to labour markets, a higher degree of alignment of their exchange rates to the euro would be more justifiable. Labour market rigidities were inherited from the central planning system, reflecting the heavily regulated and protected formal sector. These regulations imposed considerable and quite inflexible barriers to employment and impeded labour mobility. Unfortunately in some countries of SEE labour markets still remain overregulated. This is particularly true for the countries of the former SFR of Yugoslavia where employment protection is still heavily regulated, while wage structures are quite inflexible.[10] The situation is relatively better in Bulgaria (and, to a lesser extent, in Romania). In Croatia, a new labour law was passed in 2003 which improved labour market flexibility considerably. Overall, labour markets in the region of SEE still remain quite inflexible.

Other considerations

Another challenge for the countries that pursue exchange rate stability refers to real exchange rate appreciation and the corresponding loss of competitiveness that may occur as a result of the exchange rate peg. Note that the euro peg would magnify the problem given the size of the currency area. The problem of real appreciation stems from two main sources. The first relates to the Balassa–Samuelson effect. More specifically, strong productivity growth in the traded sector as a result of the structural reform, would lead to an overall price increase, and thus to real appreciation given the fixed nominal exchange rate. In Table 10.3 we can see the cumulative real appreciation of the currencies of the South East European economies. Except in the case of SM and (to a much lesser extent) in Bulgaria, the appreciation of the real exchange rate was not as profound in the other economies during the period 2001–03. The real appreciation in SM rather reflects the response to initial undervaluation since the country is at a relative early stage of transition as well as reconstruction following the Kosovo War. The second source of real appreciation is associated with the role of large capital inflows. Strong capital inflows could cause monetary expansion and lead to real appreciation by undermining the disinflation process.[11] Overall, a high degree of financial openness cannot be easily reconciled with the need for stable exchange rates. Note that euroization constitutes the exception since it remains sustainable in case of large capital flows.[12] This, after all, constitutes an important feature of euroization which strengthens its attractiveness. Table 10.3 presents information regarding

Table 10.3 Competitiveness, Capital flows and foreign deposits

	Albania	BH[a]	Bulgaria	Croatia	FYROM	Romania	SM[b]
Real effective exchange rate[c]							
2001–03	0.0	−8.3	14.8	3.3	−0.5	6.3	76.4
Net capital flows (% of GDP)							
2001	6.7	20.0	8.9	13.6	7.9	7.8	7.7
2002	8.3	14.1	9.1	15.8	5.9	7.3	13.5
2003	7.5	19.0	10.5	7.5	6.7	4.6	7.2
Foreign deposits as percentage of total deposits							
End 2001	32.3	65.2	52.7	73.6	47.2	49.3	49.5
End 2002	32.2	57.0	49.8	67.7	48.0	44.7	56.8
End 2003	30.5	57.6	48.3	60.1	48.1	41.8	61.3

[a] The real exchange rate appreciation refers to the period 2000–02 and the net capital inflows include capital transfers for reconstruction.
[b] The foreign to total deposits ratio refers only to Serbia. The corresponding shares in Montenegro and Kosovo are 100%.
[c] Cumulative rate of appreciation.
Sources: WIIW database and IMF Country Reports.

the net capital inflows, expressed as a percentage of GDP, of the particular countries during the period 2001–03. As we can see, they do not constitute a significant threat in any of the countries of the region. Bulgaria and Croatia are the countries with the highest net inflows which are mostly FDI related.

As pointed out, the main argument against greater exchange rate stability *vis-à-vis* the euro refers to the fact that it reduces the effectiveness of monetary policy as a policy instrument. It must be pointed out, however, that in situations of low confidence in the domestic currency (which, at the same time, are accompanied by increasing use of foreign currencies for domestic transactions) the effective use of monetary policy is undermined. In particular, in such circumstances, the use of an independent monetary policy as a stabilization tool is either too costly in terms of output losses (Barro and Gordon 1983) or ineffective (Hausmann 1999; Jeanne and Wyplosz 2001). Thus it is interesting to see whether foreign currency deposits have grown enough to undermine the effectiveness of monetary policy in the economies in question. According to Table 10.3, we observe that foreign currency deposits have reached a considerable share of total deposits. More specifically, in most countries of the region they were at about 50 per cent or more of total deposits at the end of 2003. Croatia and BH had the highest shares of foreign deposits which stood at about 60 per cent of total deposits, while Albania had the lowest one in the region (about 30 per cent). Thus, for the countries of the region that still pursue an independent monetary policy, the effectiveness of such a policy could be undermined significantly.

Finally, in cases of low degree of credibility in domestic currency, sufficient financial openness and considerable use of the euro in domestic transactions, euroization may be particularly useful as a stabilization mechanism (Mazzaferro, Thimann and Winker 2002). The euro may be introduced *de facto* in circumstances of an already high degree of unofficial use which largely undermines the effectiveness of domestic monetary policy. Euroization, as with dollarization, corresponds to an extreme case of a hard peg and, as we pointed out, refers to the adoption of the euro as the official currency by countries or regions other than the eurozone. The implications as well as the necessary conditions for sustainability of euroization do not differ in any essential way from that of a CBA. In particular, a credible currency board arrangement largely has the same policy implications as euroization. There are, however, differences which, depending on the country-specific circumstances, may turn out to be important. First, euroization, by definition, constitutes a more permanent arrangement than a currency board arrangement and, as a result, provides even higher credibility. Euroization strengthens the economic links with the anchor country, leading to higher trade and financial integration. This, in turn, means better prospects for growth and development.[13] In addition, for countries where domestic monetary policy has not been as credible or as effective, euroization may be the preferred form of hard peg since it automatically provides credibility and thus restores confidence rather quickly. As indicated, Montenegro and Kosovo constitute the two territories that have already shifted to euroization.

The euro and the exchange rate arrangements of the individual countries

In this section we turn our attention to examining how the euro may affect the existing exchange rate policies of the South East European economies. The analysis relies on the theoretical analysis of the previous section as well as on the specific economic conditions of the particular countries that were examined in earlier chapters of the book. Specifically, with respect to the latter, our analysis in Chapters 5 and 6, concerning their recent progress in macroeconomic performance and transition process, are particularly useful in assessing the extent of vulnerability to speculation of the particular countries in the case of exchange rate policies that favour greater stability *vis-à-vis* the euro. In order to better facilitate the analysis, we include in Table 10.4 a summary of some basic external vulnerability indicators of the particular countries for 2003 that were examined in detail in Chapter 5.

Starting with Albania, we should point out that it may have the most liberal exchange rate system in the region in the sense that foreign exchange interventions are limited, aiming only at helping smooth excessive fluctuations in the exchange rate. Monetary policy primarily relies on inflation targeting and so far has been quite successful in reducing inflation considerably while maintaining high rates of growth. A future consideration for greater exchange rate stability as regards the euro would require

Table 10.4 A summary of external vulnerability indicators for 2003

	Albania	**BH**	**Bulgaria**	**Croatia**	**FYROM**	**Romania**	**SM**
Current account balance (% of GDP)	–8.4	–15.7	–8.3	–6.8	–5.4	–6.1	–11.6
Current account balance after official grants and FDI (% of GDP)	–3.1	–9.2	–1.6	–1.0	–3.3	–3.3	–4.5
External debt (% of GDP)	23.3	34.7	57.2	83.5	36.1	35.7	68.5
Gross official reserves (in months of imports of GNFS)	4.4	4.5	4.8	5.6	4.1	3.9	5.3
Short-term debt in (% of GIR)	4.7	n.a.	30.0	36.0	28.6	62.4	45.0
Exernal debt service (% of exports of GNFS)	5.1	9.3	12.2	16.6	12.8	17.4	13.4

n.a. = not available.
Source: Table 5.5 in Chapter 5.

significant reductions in the public as well as current account deficits otherwise it may be subject to speculative pressures. However, the current account deficit may be high but it remains sustainable primarily due to strong FDI inflows (Table 10.4). In addition, the level of international reserves is at a satisfactory enough level while external debt is not a problem as yet (Table 10.4). Furthermore, an obstacle to greater exchange rate stability has to do with the progress of reform. Despite the progress made, the Albanian economy needs to speed up structural reform and strengthen the flexibility of the system. Moreover, although the Albanian economy appears to have the largest degree of trade integration with the EU in the region, it presents the lowest trade openness in the region. Overall, we may say that the exchange rate policy so far followed has been quite effective and there seems to be no need for change. Most of the preconditions for greater exchange stability against the euro, as explained in the previous section, are not yet met, which means that such a regime cannot be sustained without the support of foreign aid.

Bosnia and Herzegovina also operates on a currency board arrangement *vis-à-vis* the euro. As in the case of Bulgaria, the regime has succeeded in bringing down inflation while there has been significant output recovery. The economic situation of the country, however, is totally different when compared to the Bulgarian case: given the more adverse economic conditions and the slow progress in structural reform, the viability of the currency board regime has been mostly the result of foreign official aid. The large external current account deficit has been primarily financed by grants, while the drop in external public debt ratio has been due to debt cancellation (Table 10.4). This, then, means that any attempt at greater exchange rate flexibility would run the risk of undermining market confidence, giving rise to speculation as a result. This could be facilitated by the high level of foreign currency deposits in relation to total deposits (close to 60 per cent as of December 2003: see Table 10.3). So far, even though the sustainability of the currency board arrangement relies on the support from foreign aid, it may be the only way for the domestic currency to gain credibility, given the current economic conditions of the country. Note, however, that foreign official assistance has been declining. More specifically, official EU assistance was considerably reduced from about 12.5 per cent of GDP in 1996 to only 1 per cent in 2003. As a result, BH must continue its reform efforts in order to attract higher levels of FDI and thus reduce its dependence on donor aid in order to preserve the sustainability of the CBA over the longer run.

Bulgaria has been operating under a currency board regime with its currency being tied to the euro. The currency board has been very effective in bringing down inflation and fostering growth. As noted, restrictive fiscal policy is in line with the currency board requirements, but the rise in the external current account deficit constitutes a concern. Note, however, that large enough capital flows, primarily related to privatization, help finance most of current account deficit (Table 10.4). The significant progress in structural changes includes the functioning of the financial sector and the enhancing of labour market flexibility, which are vital to the sustainability of the exchange rate regime. It must be pointed out, however, that further progress is needed in both fronts. Overall, the progress of the Bulgarian economy so far has been quite satisfactory and the euro appears to strengthen the functioning of the currency board.

FYROM has oriented its monetary policy towards the use of the exchange rate as a nominal anchor. The domestic currency is *de facto* pegged to the euro. This regime has maintained price stability. Note, however, that the worsening fiscal position, as well as the widening of the current account deficit, imposes a threat to the sustainability of the fixed regime. An additional challenge for maintaining the exchange rate peg to the euro was posed by the liberalization of capital and financial transactions in 2002. Thus, in the event of strong foreign inflows, and given the limited product and labour market flexibility, there might be serious consideration given to abandoning the fixed regime. The fact that the euro represents a larger currency area with strong economic and financial links to FYROM increases the possibility of such an outcome, and thus it may force the central bank of the country to take defensive measures such as temporary capital controls.

In Croatia, the inflation targeting is supported by intervention in the foreign exchange market to smooth seasonal exchange rate fluctuations which has helped keep inflation low. The easing of capital account transactions by mid-2001 made it harder for the central bank to maintain a balance between its objective of lowering inflation and reducing exchange rate variability. On the other hand, the new labour law introduced in 2003 has significantly improved flexibility in that particular market making the task of greater stability against the euro more feasible. Furthermore, the high level of international reserves together with the easy access to international capital markets makes foreign exchange market intervention feasible, at least over the short-run. By contrast, however, the emergence of large capital inflows, at least during the period 2001–2, constituted a point of concern. Finally, the high level of foreign deposits relative to total deposits (about 60 per cent in December 2003: see Table 10.3) affects adversely the effectiveness of the domestic monetary policy.

Romania belongs to the group of 'second-wave' countries for accession to the EU, as does Bulgaria. Romania's efforts to reduce inflation rely quite heavily on a policy of slow depreciation of the exchange rate. However, inflation has been declining at a rather slow pace, being the highest in the region in 2003. Overall, due to fiscal weaknesses as well as to external sector risks, the current framework of managed float seems more appropriate. This also satisfies the need for greater exchange rate fluctuation which is aimed at discouraging short-term capital inflows. As the macroeconomic environment improves and more flexibility is introduced into the system, however, a policy leading to greater exchange rate stability *vis-à-vis* the euro may be pursued. Note that since 2003, the central bank uses the euro as a reference currency in its decision on interventions in order to achieve greater stability *vis-à-vis* the larger trading partner of the country.

In Serbia and Montenegro a gradual and modest depreciation of the exchange rate has been thought as the more appropriate regime at this point so that the loss of competitiveness may be limited and the exit problems associated with an effective pegging of the exchange rate may be avoided. However, given the economic condition of the country, there is also concern about the impact that may have on market confidence, even with a policy of slow depreciation. Given that macroeconomic stabilization and structural reform are far from complete and the external position of the country is weak, even a limited degree of exchange rate flexibility may undermine the functioning of the domestic currency, making it quite vulnerable to speculation. Undoubtedly, the introduction of the euro increases the possibility of such an outcome occuring. Note that the consideration of these uncertainties forced the central bank to place the effectiveness of its exchange rate policy under review on a quarterly basis. Overall, although the economic circumstances of the particular country have been improving, a policy of greater stability of the exchange rate against the euro could not be sustained without the generous assistance of foreign official aid. The viability of such a policy would require a further improvement in the development of private sector activities in order to attract more foreign investors given the declining trend in donor aid, primarily from the EU.

The uncertainty surrounding the economic viability of SM as well as the sustainability of the current exchange rate policy have been the primary economic reasons for the high level of foreign deposits relative to total deposits (61 per cent in 2003, the highest in the region; see Table 10.3). The same reasons also explain the decision of Montenegro and Kosovo to move to euroization.[14] After all, by being territories and not having an autonomous monetary policy, the decision to adopt the euro involves no costs. The benefits, on the other hand, could be very significant considering their economic situation, since the official introduction of the euro favours the strengthening of economic ties with the anchor country fostering the growth prospects of the two territories while, at the same time, safeguarding stability.

Some concluding remarks

The euro has already had a major impact on the economies of SEE. This reflects, on the one hand, the substantial presence of the EU in world trade as well as the close political, economic and financial links developed between the two regions since the collapse of the previous regime. As pointed out, the specific characteristics of the particular economies, as reflected in the output and trade structures, the consistent macroeconomic policies and the progress in the transformation process, play a vital role concerning the impact of the euro on the existing exchange rate arrangements in the region.

The introduction of the euro does not necessarily mean that the countries in question must favour regimes that rely on greater exchange rate stability *vis-à-vis* the euro. As a matter of fact, the opposite may be the case. The fact that the euro is the currency of a much larger area which, at the same time, constitutes the dominant trading partner of the particular countries under consideration means that greater exchange rate stability would reveal (in a much more profound way) their economic as well structural weaknesses. Thus it would make it harder for most of these countries to sustain such a regime. This is a basic conclusion of our analysis which particularly applies to the countries in the southern Balkans. For some of these countries especially, exchange rate stability *vis-à-vis* the euro cannot be sustained without the support of foreign official sources of finance.

The analysis focused on three main factors in considering the desirable extent of exchange rate stability against the euro. The first factor is primarily related to the degree of similarity of production and trade structures between the two regions. Similar structures would make it less likely for countries to experience different terms of trade shocks or different world demand conditions for their exports. The second factor has to do with the consistency of the macroeconomic policies adopted as well as with the progress made in the transition process, and this was examined in earlier chapters. Note that the latter largely determines the degree of flexibility introduced in the labour, product and financial markets. The third factor refers to real appreciation, which is primarily associated either with the Balassa–Samuelson effect or with the impact of large capital inflows.

The analysis showed that, for the majority of the countries of SEE, the first two factors are the ones that make the sustainability of a fixed regime *vis-à-vis* the euro almost impossible, while the threat from capital inflows is not a major issue as yet. More specifically, the structure of the particular economies differs significantly from that of the EU while, given the slow pace of reform, not enough flexibility has been introduced into the system. As a matter of fact, only Bulgaria has made enough progress to achieve the sustainability of the currency board regime. Croatia has only recently taken initiatives to improve labour market flexibility, while Romania has followed a slower pace of reform. Both Croatia and Romania prefer a managed floating regime and this also reflects their concerns regarding the emergence of strong capital inflows. The remaining economies (i.e., the southern Balkan nations), despite the progress made recently with respect to stabilization and reform, cannot by themselves as yet sustain a fixed exchange rate against the euro. In the two countries that operate under a fixed regime, BH and FYROM, the sustainability of the peg, particularly in the former, has been largely due to the support from external official aid. Finally, the third factor does not currently represent a threat to the majority of these countries. The level of capital inflows is relatively low, while price competitiveness is not a major issue as yet, reflecting the low quality of domestic products.

Finally, euroization constitutes an alternative solution for a hard peg but it is rather early for the economies of SEE to attempt such a shift, given their state of development.[15] The situation is different with Montenegro and Kosovo, which are small territories with no independent monetary policy, in which case the choice between the euro and the domestic currency is rather obvious. There are, however, two points that must be taken into consideration when assessing the possibility of euroization in at least some of the South East European countries. The first refers to the high unofficial euroization that exists in some of these countries, meaning that the effectiveness of domestic monetary policy is already being undermined. The second concerns the prospect of future accession which is the ultimate policy objective for most of them. The combination of these two points, in conjunction with the dominant economic presence of the EU in the region, could very well mean that the case of *de facto* euroization may be an inevitable situation in the future for some of these economies.

Notes

1 Introduction

1 Note that SM is not included in the SEE region's average due to unavailability of data.
2 Johnson, Kaufmann and Shleifer (1997) examine the extent of the underground economy during transition.

2 The Stylized Facts of Transition in South Eastern Europe

1 The inflows of FDI and the reorientation of trade represented two very important facts of transition that were essential to economic performance. We shall discuss them in the following chapters. Stylized facts of transition are analysed by Campos and Coricelli (2002), World Bank (part 1, 2002) and Blanchard (1997).
2 The surprisingly large output decline constituted one of the most widely discussed issues concerning transition economies. This, as expected, led to the emergence of a considerable body of literature focusing on the possible explanations of the output fall. Some of the most popular explanations speak of the special circumstances of the 'transformational' recession (Kornai 1994); restrictive macro-policies (Rosati 1994); the impact of a credit crunch as a result of the reduction in state subsidies (Calvo and Coricelli 1992); the consequences of disorganization that emerged as the central planning collapsed (Blanchard 1997; Blanchard and Kremer 1997) and the dissolution of the Council for Mutual Economic Assistance (CMEA) in 1990 and the resulting complete breakdown of trade relations among its members.
3 A detailed analysis concerning the pattern of output growth in transition economies is given by Havrylyshyn and others (1999), Havrylyshyn (2001), Campos and Coricelli (2002), EBRD (1999), and Papazoglou and Pentecost (2004).
4 Note that the figures for the overall output growth in the two regions are weighted averages. They were calculated by using current nominal GDP, expressed in terms of US dollars, as weights. This is also the case with respect to the other variables considered in the chapter, except for inflation.
5 An analysis for the inflation developments in transition economies is included in Cottarelli and Doyle (1999), Begg (1998), and Ghosh (1997).
6 Similar information on all transition economies is given by Fischer and Sahay (2000).
7 See also Blanchard (1997) and Havrylyshyn and others (1999).
8 See also Havrylyshyn and others (1999).

3 The Impact of Initial Conditions

1 In which case it equals 1 and 0 otherwise. See also De Melo *et al.* (1997).
2 See EBRD (1999, box 2.1).
3 That is, the three Baltic states, plus Russia, Belarus, Ukraine and Moldova.

4 Macroeconomic Stabilization and Performance I: The Period Prior to the Kosovo War

1 See Gros and Steinherr (1995).
2 See Cottarelli and Doyle (1999).
3 The relationship between inflation and fiscal deficits in transition economies is strongly supported by empirical evidence. See Fischer (1996), Sahay and Vegh, Lougani and Sheets (1997), and Cottarelli, Griffiths and Moghadam (1998).
4 Buiter (1997) separates such operations when performed by the non-central bank financial sector to which he refers as contingent fiscal deficits.
5 For a detailed discussion of the basic features of quasi-fiscal operations see Mackenzie and Stella (1996), Buiter (1997), Markiewicz (1998, 2001) and Budina and van Wijnbergen (1996).
6 We must point out that our calculations constitute approximations of the true magnitude of the quasi-fiscal deficits.
7 For a more detailed analysis for the phenomenon of soft budget constraints, see Kornai (1999).
8 See Claessens and Peters (1997) and Mihov (2001).
9 See Budina and van Wijnbergen (1996) and Daianu (2001).
10 The two studies use the same approach. Actually the second study expands the first by including data from 1995 and 1996. Also, a similar simulation was carried out by Cottarelli and Doyle (1999) for the year 1997.
11 See Sonje and Vujcic (2001).
12 See also Bishev (2000).
13 For similar results which, however, refer to the 1992–94 period for selected transition economies, see UN/ECE (1995).
14 The average M1 and broad money to GDP ratios for the EU member states are about 25 and 70 per cent respectively.
15 Bulgaria also constituted an exception with respect to the broad money to GDP ratio which was high until 1996, while Croatia may be the only case where the broad money to GDP ratio for 1997 and 1998 was close to the average level that corresponds to countries with about the same per capita income.
16 This primarily refers to fiscal policy. Note, however, that Albania managed to reduce inflation without achieving fiscal consolidation. As we will see in more detail below, the strong recovery in money demand contributed to the reduction of inflation in spite of the large fiscal deficits.
17 See IMF (1999a).
18 See also Gomulka (1999).
19 In Bulgaria the initial devaluation took place in February 1991 and was combined with the launching of the first stabilization programme. In Romania, there were three major devaluations: in November 1990 (by 77 per cent), in April 1991 (by 66 per cent) and in November 1991 (by 240 per cent). The consecutive devaluations in Albania took place between September 1991 and January 1992. In Croatia there were

continuous depreciations from March 1992 until the introduction of the stabilization programme in October 1993. Finally, in FYROM the exchange rate depreciated sharply during the period from the introduction of the new currency in April of 1992 until the launching of the stabilization programme in January 1993.

20 In Albania, Croatia, FYROM and Romania currency convertibility initially had a much narrower scope since the foreign exchange market was operated by a limited number of licensed banks.

21 Bosnia and Herzegovina adopted a currency board as well in 1997. Macroeconomic stabilization in the particular country will be studied in Chapter 5.

22 The structural weaknesses with respect to the banking system will be examined in some detail in Chapter 6.

23 The particular classification of the exchange rate regimes in Croatia and FYROM was not explicitly announced by the authorities but rather was the result of the actual policies followed.

24 Also, it should be pointed out that it is difficult to access the impact of initial appreciation on external competitiveness. Due to the fact that the exchange rate systems of the transition economies were heavily regulated by the old regime, there were large discrepancies between PPP exchange rates and the prevailing ones.

25 See UN/ECE (1999).

5 Macroeconomic Stabilization and Performance II: The Period after the Kosovo War

1 An independent group of Yugoslav economists: see UN/ECE (1999), EBRD (1999) and Welfens (2001).

2 The two countries were host to about 700,000 refugees; see EBRD (1999) and Demekas *et al.* (2001).

3 See EBRD (1999).

4 See World Bank (2000a).

5 Bulgaria and Romania were excluded since they were already accession candidates.

6 For a detailed analysis on the Stability Pact and the role of the EU, see Bartlett and Samardzija (2000). See also European Commission (2000) and Welfens (2001).

7 See European Commission (2003).

8 See European Commission (2003).

9 For an overview of these indicators, see Berg, A., E. Borensztein, G. M. Milesi and C. Patillo (1999).

10 Such studies include Sachs, Tornell and Velasco (1996), Frankel and Rose (1996a), Kaminsky, Lizondo and Reinhart (1998) and Brussiere and Mulder (1999).

11 See, for instance, Brussiere and Mulder (1999).

6 Structural Reform

1 Where a score of 1 corresponds to conditions before reform with dominant state ownership of means of production, and a score of 4+ indicates that the country's structural characteristics are comparable to those prevailing on average in the advanced market economies.

2 The areas of structural reform that will be examined in this chapter by no means exhaust all the different aspects of reform. For instance, a different dimension of reform could include indicators with respect to the progress towards institutional reform. In particular, an institutional quality index was developed by

Weber (2000), which relied on six of the indicators of governance developed by Kaufmann, Kray and Zoido-Lobaton (1999a, 1999b). These six indicators of governance included: extent of establishing democratic rule, government effectiveness, political instability and violence, extent of regulation, rule of law, and graft.

3 See, for instance, Djankov and Murrell (2002), Megginson and Netter (2001) and EBRD (2002).
4 It is not by accident that there was growing public discontent over the fact that the transfer of state-owned assets into private hands was accompanied by widespread corruption. See SELDI (2001).
5 See also World Bank (2000a).
6 The information mostly comes form EBRD (1996, 1999, 2000, 2003) as well as from European commission (2003).
7 See also Zinnes, Eilat and Sachs (2001).
8 See Gros and Steinherr (1995).
9 As a matter of fact, in the case of BH the Feasibility Study was approved in November 2003. EBRD (2003, 2004b).
10 See EBRD (2000).
11 Two laws were enacted in 1991 by the Bulgarian authorities: the Law on Commerce eliminated *de jure* monopolies and the one on Protection of Competition established an anti-trust body. See EBRD (1995).
12 In particular, Albania adopted a competition law in December 1995, Croatia adopted one in the autumn of 1995, FYROM in 1999 and Romania one in 1995 that came in effect in 1997. See EBRD (1998, 2003).
13 See EBRD (2004a).
14 See EBRD (2004a).
15 See Barisitz (2001).
16 See Barisitz (2000).
17 It also corresponds to full interest rate liberalization as well as to significant lending to private enterprises and to significant presence of private banks.
18 See Stubos and Tsikripis (2004).
19 See IMF (1999b).
20 See Barisitz (2001) and UN/ECE (1997).
21 See IMF (1998b, 2000b) and Barisitz (2000).
22 See IMF (2000a).
23 See IMF (1998a).
24 See Barisitz (2001).
25 See Daianu (2001).

7 An Empirical Assessment of the Growth Determinants in South Eastern Europe

1 These include De Melo, Denizer and Gelb (1996), de Melo, *et al.* (1997), Fischer, Sahay and Vegh (1996, 1998), Havrylyshyn, Izvorski, and van Rooden (1998), Havrylyshyn and van Rooden (1999), Heybey and Murrel (1999), Selowsky and Martin (1997), Aslund, Boone, and Johnson (1996), Hernandez-Cata (1997), Wolf (1999), and Berg, Borensztein, Sahay and Zettelmeyer (1999).
2 A paper by Havrylyshyn (2001) provides an excellent review of empirical studies concerning the growth performance of transition economies.
3 See for instance Berg, Borensztein, Sahay and Zettelmeyer (1999) and Falcetti, Raiser and Sanfey (2000).

4 This variable was found in Ficsher and Sahay (2000). Recall that a dummy variable capturing geographical proximity to Western markets is included in the initial conditions as well (see Chapter 3). The fundamental role of EU to the growth prospects of these countries constituted the main reason for considering it separately.
5 The particular results are not reported.
6 'Transition' time refers to the date at which the communist regime collapsed and the country in question began to move towards the market system. Our estimations are based on calendar time meaning that in 1991, the starting date of our sample, some countries, particularly in CE, were ahead of others in the transition process. See also Fischer, Sahay and Vegh (1996) and Fischer and Sahay (2000).
7 See also Berg, Borensztein, Sahay and Zettelmeyer (1999) for a similar result.

8 Trade Integration

1 Eastern Europe includes all former CMEA member countries, as well as the SFR of Yugoslavia and Albania.
2 Then, the EU was called European Economic Community. Note that the trade shares with the EU in Table 8.1 refer to 15 current member states.
3 See EBRD (1999).
4 For a similar analysis see Petrakos (2003)
5 Except for SM where the starting year is 1996.
6 See Michalopoulos (1999) and World Bank (2000a).
7 See, Demekas *et al.* (2001).
8 According to the annual database of the WIIW.
9 See also Petrakos (2003).
10 For a more detailed analysis see Petrakos (2003).
11 In Chapter 10 below we will examine in some detail the structure of trade between the EU and the countries of SEE.
12 The Grubel–Lloyd index is the difference between unity and the quotient of absolute differences between exports and imports of a given sector and the total of imports and exports for the sector. The index assumes the value of 100 in the presence of two-way trade and zero when exports do not overlap with imports across sectors.
13 Croatia had a free trade agreement with Slovenia, FYROM and Bosnia and Herzegovina. In addition the latter had a free trade agreement with FYROM, while FYROM had another one with Bulgaria and Serbia and Montenegro. Bulgaria had a free trade agreement with Romania.
14 The index varies from 1 to 10. A higher score means a more restrictive trade policy. See EBRD (2004a).
15 On an unweighted basis this is 2.1 per cent for SEE, compared to 4.9 for Central Europe and the Baltic states and to 6.1 for the Commonwealth of Independent States.

9 Foreign Direct Investment in South Eastern Europe

1 See, for instance, Blanchard *et al.* (1991), Barrell and Holland (2000) and Holland and Pain (1998).
2 See Hunya and Stankovsky (2004).

3 At any rate, the FDI stock of Albania represented about 3 per cent of the region's total stock in 2003.
4 See EBRD (2004b).
5 See UN/ECE (2001).
6 For more details see UN/ECE (2001).
7 See, for example, Baldwin, Francois and Portes (1997).
8 Bevan and Estrin (2000) have found that unit labour costs in transition economies are a significant determinant of FDI inflows.
9 See Resmini (2000).
10 For a statistical analysis regarding the relation between corruption and FDI flows, see Wei (1997).
11 According to Corruption Perceptions Index for 2003, the average score of the South East European countries was 3.0, while that of the Central European countries stood at 4.4 (see www.transparency.de).

10 The Euro and the Exchange Rate Regimes of the South East European Countries

1 See Padoa-Schioppa (2002).
2 A third regime would refer to a freely floating exchange rate. However, this regime does not apply to the case of the transition economies. As a matter of fact, with the exception of the exchange rates between the three key currencies (dollar, euro and yen), there are almost no countries that have deliberately refrained from foreign market intervention. See Bofinger and Wollmershaeuser (2000).
3 See Corker *et al.* (2000).
4 See for instance, Rose and Engel (2000).
5 See Del Negro *et al.* (2001), Masson (1999) and Gulde, Kahkonen and Keller (2000).
6 See for instance, Papazoglou (1999b).
7 See Fidrmuc and Korhonen (2002) and Frenkel and Nickel (2002).
8 See Masson (1999) and Corker *et al.* (2000).
9 See also Petrakos (2003).
10 See, for instance, Rutkowski (1998, 2003).
11 See Gulde, Kahkonen and Keller (2000) and Corker *et al.* (2000).
12 See Calvo (2001).
13 See Rose (2001) and Frankel and Rose (2002).
14 Of course, political reasons played significant role as well.
15 Note, however, that the EU objects to the euroization in the case of candidate countries. The conversion rate between the currency of a candidate country and the euro is to be adopted by a unanimous decision of the EU Council.

References

Anastasakis, O. and V. Bojicic-Dzelilovic (2002), 'Balkan Regional Cooperation and European Integration', found on line at: www.lse.ac.uk/collections/hellenicObservatory/pdf/brie.pdf

Artis, M. J. (1991), 'One Market, One Money: An Evaluation of the Potential Benefits and Costs of Forming an Economic and Monetary Union', *Open Economies Review*, 2, pp. 315–21.

Aslund, A., P. Boone and S. Johnson (1996), 'How to Stabilize: Lessons from Post-Communist Countries', *Brookings Papers on Economic Activity*, 1 (Washington, DC: Brookings Institution), pp. 217–313.

Baldwin, R., H. Braconier and R. Forslid (1999), *Multinationals, Endogenous Growth and Technological Spillovers: Theory and Evidence*, Centre for Economic Policy Research (CEPR) Discussion Paper, No. 2155, London.

Baldwin, R., J. Francois and R. Portes (1997), 'The Costs and Benefits of Eastern Enlargement: The Impact on the EU and Central Europe', *Economic Policy*, 24, pp. 127–70.

Barisitz, S. (2000), 'The Development of the Croatian Banking Sector since Independence', *Focus on Transition*, No. 2, pp. 96–12 (Vienna: Oesterreichische Nationalbank).

Barisitz, S. (2001), 'The Development of Romania and Bulgarian Banking Sectors since 1990', *Focus on Transition*, No. 1, pp. 79–119 (Vienna: Oesterreichische Nationalbank).

Barrell, R. and D. Holland (2000), 'The Location of Foreign Direct Investment Activity, Country Characteristics and Experience Effects', *Journal of International Business Studies*, 11, pp. 9–22.

Barrell, R. and N. Pain (1999), 'Domestic Institutions, Agglomerations and Foreign Direct Investment in Europe', *European Economic Review*, 43, pp. 928–34.

Barro, R. J. and D. Gordon (1983), 'Rules, Discretion and Reputation in a Model of Monetary Policy', *Journal of Monetary Economics*, 12, pp. 101–21.

Bartlett, W. and V. Samardzija (2000), 'The Reconstruction of South East Europe, the Stability Pact and the Role of the EU: An Overview', *MOCT-MOST*, 2, pp. 245–63.

Begg, D. (1996), 'Monetary Policy in Central and Eastern Europe: Lessons After Half a Decade of Transition', IMF Working Paper, 96/108 (Washington, DC: International Monetary Fund).

Begg, D. (1998), 'Disinflation in Central and Eastern Europe: The Experience to Date', in C. Cottarelli and G. Snapary (eds), *Moderate Inflation: The Experience of Transition*

Economies (Washington, DC: International Monetary Fund and National Bank of Hungary).
Berg, A., E. Borensztein, G. M. Milesi-Ferretti, and C. Patillo (1999), 'Anticipating Balance of Payments Crises: The Role of Early Warning Systems', IMF Occasional Paper No. 186 (Washington, DC: International Monetary Fund).
Berg, A., E. Borensztein, R. Sahay and J. Zettelmeyer (1999), 'The Evolution of Output in the Transition Economies: Explaining the Differences', IMF Working Paper 99/73 (Washington, DC: International Monetary Fund).
Bevan, A. and S. Estrin (2000), 'The Determinants of Foreign Direct Investment into Transition Economies', London Business School, Centre for New and Emerging Markets Discussion Paper Series, No. 9, London.
Bishev, G. (2000), 'Monetary Policy and Transition in South-Eastern Europe', in V. Gligorov (ed.), *Balkan Reconstruction: Economic Aspects* (Vienna: The Vienna Institute for International Economic Studies).
Blanchard, O. (1997), *The Economics of Post-Communist Transition*, (Oxford: Clarendon Press).
Blanchard, O. and M. Kremer (1997), 'Disorganization', *Quarterly Journal of Economics*, 112(4), pp. 1,091–126.
Blanchard, O., R. Dornbusch, P. Krugman, R. Layard and L. Summers (1991), *Reform in Eastern Europe* (Cambridge, MA: MIT Press).
Bofinger, P. and T. Wollmershaeuser (2000), 'Options for the Exchange Rate Policies of the EU Accession Countries (and Other Emerging Market Economies)', CEPR Discussion Paper Series, No. 2,379, February, London.
Borensztein, E., J. De Gregorio and J. W. Lee (1998), 'How Does Foreign Direct Investment Affect Economic Growth?', *Journal of International Economics*, 45(1), pp. 115–35.
Brada J. (1996), 'Privatization "is" transition', *Economics of Transition*, 2(3), pp. 56–72.
Brussiere, M. and C. Mulder (1999), 'External Vulnerability in Emerging Market Economies: How High Liquidity can Offset Weak Fundamentals and the Effects of Contagion', IMF Working Paper, 99/88 (Washington, DC: International Monetary Fund).
Budina N. and S. van Wijnbergen (1996), 'Fiscal Deficits, Monetary Reform and Inflation: the case of Romania', Tinbergen Institute Discussion Paper, TI96-113/4.
Budina N. and S. van Wijnbergen (1997), 'Fiscal Policies in Eastern Europe', *Oxford Review of Economic Policy*, 13(2), pp. 47–64.
Buiter, W. (1997), 'Aspects of Fiscal Performance in Some Transition Economies Under Fund-Supported Programs', IMF Working Paper, 97/31 (Washington, DC: International Monetary Fund).
Calvo, A. C. and M. Kumar (1993), 'Financial Markets and Intermediation', in *Financial Sector Reforms and Exchange Arrangements in Eastern Europe*, Occasional Paper 102 (Washington, DC: International Monetary Fund).
Calvo, G. A. (2001), 'Capital Markets and the Exchange Rate', *Journal of Money, Credit and Banking*, 33(2), Part 2, pp. 312–34.
Calvo, G. A. and F. Coricelli (1992), 'Output Collapse in Eastern Europe: The Role of Credit', IMF Working Paper 92/64 (Washington, DC: International Monetary Fund).
Campos, N. F. and F. Coricelli (2002), 'Growth in Transition: What We Know, What We Don't, and What We Should', *Journal of Economic Literature*, 40(3), pp. 793–836.
Claessens, S. and R. Kyle Peters (1997), 'State Enterprise Performance and Soft Budget Constraints: The Case of Bulgaria', *Economics of Transition*, 5(2), pp. 305–22.
Coricelli, F. (1998), *Macroeconomic Policies and the Development of Markets in Transition Economies* (Budapest: Central European University Press).

Corker, R., Beaumont, C., Van Elkan, R. and D. Iakova (2000), 'Exchange Rate Regimes in Selected Advanced Transition Economies – Coping with Transition, Capital Inflows, and EU accession', IMF Policy Discussion Paper, PDP/00/3 (Washington, DC: International Monetary Fund).

Cottarelli, C. and P. Doyle (1999), 'Disinflation in Transition 1993–97', Occasional Paper (Washington, DC: International Monetary Fund).

Cottarelli, C., M. Griffiths and R. Moghadam (1998), 'The Nonmonetary Determinants of Inflation', IMF Working Paper, 98/23 (Washington, DC: International Monetary Fund).

Dabrowski, M. (1999), 'Disinflation, Monetary Policy and Fiscal Constraints. Experience of Economies of Transition', CASE, *Studies and Analyses*, No. 16, (Warsaw: Centre for Social and Economic Research).

Daianu D. (2001), 'Strain and Economic Adjustment: Romania's Travails and Pains', in M. Blejer and M. Skreb (eds), *Transition: The First Decade*, pp. 441–76 (Cambridge, MA: The MIT Press).

Davidson Institute, Data on Transition Economies (Davidson Data Center & Network), University of Michigan Business School, found on line at: www.wdi.bus.umich.edu/research/data_center.htm

De Broek, M., K. Krajnyak and H. Lorie (1997), 'Explaining and Forecasting the Velocity of Money in Transition Economies with Special Reference to the Baltics, Russia and other Countries', IMF Working Paper, 97/108 (Washington, DC: International Monetary Fund).

De Melo, M., C. Denizer and A. Gelb (1996), 'From Plan to Market: Patterns of Transition', Policy Research Working Paper 1564 (Washington, DC: World Bank).

De Melo, M., C. Denizer, A. Gelb and S. Tenev (1997), 'Circumstance and Choice: The Role of Initial Conditions and Policies in Transition Economies', Policy Research Working Paper 1866 (Washington, DC: World Bank).

Del Negro, M., A. Hernandez-Delgado, O. Humpage and E. Huybens (2001), 'Introduction: Context, Issues and Contributions', *Journal of Money, Credit and Banking*, 33(2), Part 2, pp. 303–11.

Demekas, G. D., J. Herderschee, J. McHugh and S. Mitra (2001), 'Building Peace in South East Europe: Macroeconomic Policies and Structural Reforms since the Kosovo Conflict', a joint IMF – World Bank paper for the *Second Regional Conference for South East Europe*, Bucharest, 25–26 October.

Djankov, S. and P. Murrell (2002), 'Enterprise Restructuring in Transition: A Quantitative Survey', *Journal of Economic Literature*, 40(3), pp. 739–92.

Dunning, J. H. (1980), *International Production and the Multinational Enterprise* (London: Allen & Unwin).

EBRD (1995), *Transition Report 1995: Investment and Enterprise Development* (London: European Bank for Reconstruction and Development).

EBRD (1996), *Transition Report 1996: Infrastructure and Savings* (London: European Bank for Reconstruction and Development).

EBRD (1997), *Transition Report 1997: Enterprise Performance and Growth* (London: European Bank for Reconstruction and Development).

EBRD (1998), *Transition Report 1998: Financial Sector in Transition* (London: European Bank for Reconstruction and Development).

EBRD (1999), *Transition Report 1999: Ten Years of Transition* (London: European Bank for Reconstruction and Development).

EBRD (2000), *Transition Report 2000: Employment, Skills and Transition* (London: European Bank for Reconstruction and Development).

EBRD (2001), *Transition Report 2001: Energy in Transition* (London: European Bank for Reconstruction and Development).
EBRD (2002), *Transition Report 2002: Agriculture and Rural Transition* (London: European Bank for Reconstruction and Development).
EBRD (2003), *Transition Report 2003: Integration and Regional Cooperation* (London: European Bank for Reconstruction and Development).
EBRD (2004a), *Spotlight on South-eastern Europe: An Overview of Private Sector Activity and Investment* (London: European Bank for Reconstruction and Development).
EBRD (2004b), *Transition Report 2004: Infrastructure* (London: European Bank for Reconstruction and Development).
European Commission (2000), *The EU and South-eastern Europe: The Stabilization and Association Process* (Brussels: European Commission).
European Commission (2003), *The Western Balkans in Transition*, Occasional Paper (Brussels: European Commission).
European Economy (2003), The EU Economy: 2003 review, 6 (Brussels: European Commission).
Eurostat (2002), *Intra- and Extra-EU Trade*, supplement 2-2002 CD (Luxembourg: European Commission).
Eurostat (2003), *External and Intra-European Union Trade – Statistical Yearbook*, (Luxembourg: European Commission).
Falcetti, E., M. Raiser and P. Sanfey (2000), 'Defying the Odds: Initial Conditions, Reforms and Growth in the First Decade of Transition', Working Paper No 55 (London: European Bank for Reconstruction and Development).
Fidrmuc, J. and L. Korhonen (2002), 'Similarity of Supply and Demand Shocks Between the Euro Area and the CEECs', *Jahrbuch der Wirtschaft Osteuropas*, 27(3), pp. 2–38.
Fischer, S. and R. Sahay (2000), 'The Transition Economies After Ten Years', IMF Working Paper 00/30 (Washington, DC: International Monetary Fund).
Fischer, S., R. Sahay and C. A. Vegh (1996), 'Stabilization and Growth in Transition Economies: The Early Experience', *Journal of Economic Perspectives*, 10, pp. 45–66.
Fischer, S., R. Sahay and C. A. Vegh (1998), 'From Transition to Market: Evidence and Growth Prospects', IMF Working Paper 98/52 (Washington, DC: International Monetary Fund).
Frankel, J. and A. Rose (2002), 'An Estimate of the Effects of Common Currencies on Trade and Income', *Quarterly Journal of Economics*, 67(2), pp. 437–66.
Frankel, J. and A. Rose (1996a), 'Currency Crashes in Emerging Markets: An Empirical Treatment', *Journal of International Economics*, 41, pp. 351–66.
Frankel, J. and A. Rose (1996b), 'The Endogeneity of the Optimum Currency Area Criteria', *National Bureau of Economic Research*, NBER Working Paper No 5700 (Cambridge, Massachusetts: National Bureau of Economic Research).
Frenkel, M. and C. Nickel (2002), 'How Symmetric are the Shocks and Shock Adjustment Dynamics Between the Euro Area and Central and Eastern European Countries?', IMF Working Paper No. 02/222 (Washington, DC: International Monetary Fund).
Ghosh, A. R. (1997), 'Inflation in Transition Economies: How Much? And Why', IMF Working Paper 97/80 (Washington, DC: International Monetary Fund).
Gligorov, V. and S. Sundstrom (1999), 'The Costs of the Kosovo Crisis', WIIW Current Analyses and Country Profiles, No. 12 (Vienna: The Vienna Institute for International Economic Studies).
Gligorov, V., M Holzner and M. Landesmann (2003), 'Prospects for Further (South)-Eastern EU Enlargement: From Divergence to Convergence?', Vienna Institute for

Economic Studies Research Reports, No. 296 (Vienna: Institute for International Economic Studies).

Gomulka, S. (1999), 'Macroeconomic Policies and Achievements in Transition Economies, 1989–1999', *Economic Survey of Europe* No. 2/3, Chapter 3 (New York, Geneva: UN/ECE).

Grabbe, H. and K. Hughes (1998), 'Enlarging the EU Eastwards', *Chatham House Papers*, The Royal Institute of International Affairs, London.

Greenspan, A. (1999), 'Currency Reserves and Debt', speech delivered at the World Bank Conference on *Recent Trends in Reserves Management*, Washington, DC: April 29, found on line at: www.bog.frb.fed.us

Gros, D. and A. Steinherr (1995), *Winds of Change: Economic Transition in Central and Eastern Europe*, (Longman: New York).

Gulde, A. M., J. Kahkonen and P. Keller (2000), 'Pros and Cons of Currency Board Arrangements in the Lead-up to EU Accession and Participation in the Euro Zone', IMF Policy Discussion Paper, PDP/00/1 (Washington, DC: International Monetary Fund).

Halpern, L. and C. Wyplosz (1997), 'Equilibrium Exchange Rates in Transitional Economies', *IMF Staff Papers*, 44(4), pp. 430–51.

Hausmann, R. (1999), 'Currencies: Should There be Five or One Hundred and Five?', paper presented at the seminar on *Alternative Exchange Rate Regimes for the Region*, Panama City, Panama, found on line at: www.iabd.org/OCE/exchangerate/5curr.pdf.

Havrylyshyn, O. (2001), 'Recovery and Growth in Transition: A Decade of Evidence', *IMF Staff Papers*, 48, pp. 53–87.

Havrylyshyn, O. *et al.* (1999), 'Growth Experience in Transition Countries, 1990–98', IMF Occasional Paper, No. 184 (Washington, DC: International Monetary Fund).

Havrylyshyn, O. and Ron van Rooden (1999), 'Institutions Matter in Transition, but So Do Policies', IMF Working Paper 00/70 (Washington, DC: International Monetary Fund).

Havrylyshyn, O., I. Izvorski and Ron van Rooden (1998), 'Recovery and Growth in Transition Economies 1990–97: Stylized Regression Analysis', IMF Working Paper 98/141 (Washington, DC: International Monetary Fund).

Hernandez-Cata, E. (1997), 'Liberalization and the Behavior of Output during the Transition from Plan to Market', *IMF Staff Papers*, 44, pp. 405–29.

Heybey, B. and P. Murrell (1999), 'The Relationship Between Economic Growth and the Speed of Liberalization During Transition', *Policy Reform*, 3, pp. 121–37.

Holland, D. and N. Pain (1998), 'The Diffusion of Innovation in Central and Eastern Europe: A Study of the Determinants and Impact of Foreign Direct Investment', NIESR Discussion Paper No.137 (London: NIESR).

Hunya, G. (2002), *FDI in South-Eastern Europe in the early 2000s* (Vienna: Vienna Institute for International Economic Studies), July.

Hunya, G. and J. Stankovsky (2004), *Foreign Direct Investment in Central and Eastern Europe with Special Attention to Austrian FDI Activities in this Region* (Vienna: Vienna Institute for International Economic Studies), July.

IMF (1998a), 'Former Yugoslav Republic of Macedonia: Recent Economic Developments', IMF Staff Country Report No. 98/82 (Washington, DC: International Monetary Fund).

IMF (1998b), 'Republic of Croatia: Selected Issues and Statistical Appendix', IMF Staff Country Report No. 98/90 (Washington, DC: International Monetary Fund).

IMF (1999a), 'Albania: Recent Economic Developments and Statistical Appendix', IMF Staff Country Report No. 99/96 (Washington, DC: International Monetary Fund).

IMF (1999b), 'Bulgaria: Recent Economic Developments and Statistical Appendix', IMF Staff Country Report No. 99/26 (Washington, DC: International Monetary Fund).

IMF (2000a), 'Former Yugoslav Republic of Macedonia: Recent Economic Developments', IMF Staff Country Report No. 00/72 (Washington, DC: International Monetary Fund).

IMF (2000b), 'Republic of Croatia: Selected Issues and Statistical Appendix', IMF Staff Country Report No. 00/22 (Washington, DC: International Monetary Fund).

IMF (2001), 'Romania: Selected Issues and Statistical Appendix', IMF Staff Country Report No. 01/16 (Washington, DC: International Monetary Fund).

IMF (2003), *Direction of Trade Yearbook*, Publications Services of International Monetary Fund (Washington, DC: International Monetary Fund)

Jeanne, O. and C. Wyplosz (2001), 'The International Lender of Last Resort-How Large is Large Enough?', IMF Working Paper No. 01/76 (Washington, DC: International Monetary Fund).

Johnson, S., D. Kaufmann and A. Shleifer (1997), 'The Unofficial Economy in Transition', *Brookings Papers on Economic Activity*, 2, pp. 159–239.

Kaminski, B. and Manuel de la Rocha (2003), 'Stabilisation and Association Process in the Balkans: Integration Options and their Assessment', World Bank Working Paper, No. 3108 (Washington, DC: World Bank).

Kaminsky, G., S. Lizondo and C. Reinhart (1998), 'Leading Indicators of Currency Crises', *IMF Staff Papers*, 45, pp. 1–48.

Kaufmann, D., A. Kray and P. Zoido-Lobaton (1999a), 'Aggregating Governance Indicators', World Bank Policy Research Working Paper, No. 2195 (Washington, DC: World Bank).

Kaufmann, D., A. Kray and P. Zoido-Lobaton (1999b), 'Governance Matters', World Bank Policy Research Working Paper, No. 2196 (Washington, DC: World Bank).

Kenen, P. (1969), 'The Theory of Optimal Currency Areas: an Eclectic View', in R. A. Mundell and A. K. Swoboda (eds), *Monetary Problems of the International Economy* (Chicago: Chicago University Press)

Kornai, J. (1994), 'Transformational Recession: The Main Causes', *Journal of Comparative Economics*, 90 (August), pp. 39–63.

Kornai, J. (1999), 'Hardening the Budget Constraint: The Experience of Post-Socialist Countries', in H. G. Heinrich (ed.), *Institution-Building in the New Democracies*, Collegium Budapest Workshop Series No. 7, pp. 167–200.

Krajnyak, K. and J. Zettelmeyer (1998), 'Competitiveness in Transition Economies: What Scope for Real Appreciation?', *IMF Staff Papers*, 45, pp. 309–62.

Krugman, P. (1991), 'Geography and Trade', *Gaston Eykens Lecture Series*, Leuven University Press.

Kyrkilis, D. and E. Nikolaïdis (2003), 'Regional Integration in South-Eastern Europe', in, G. Petrakos, A. Kotios and D. Chionis (eds), *International and Monetary Aspects of Transition in Southeastern Europe*, pp. 269–82, South and East European Development Centre, (Volos: University of Thessaly Press).

Kyrkilis, D. and E. Nikolaïdis (2004), 'Transition Implications for Regional Integration in South Eastern Europe', *Transition Studies Review*, XI(1), pp. 84–94.

Lankes, H. P. and A. J. Venables (1996), 'Foreign Direct Investment in Economic Transition: The Changing Pattern of Investments', *The Economics of Transition*, 4(2), pp. 331–47.

Lopandic, D. (2001), 'Regional Initiatives in South Eastern Europe: An Assessment', Paper presented in the SEED International Conference on *Restructuring Stability and Development in Southeastern Europe*, June.

Lougani, P. and N. Sheets (1997), 'Central Bank Independence, Inflation and Growth in Transition Economies', *Journal of Money, Credit and Banking*, 29, pp. 381–99.

Mackenzie G. and P. Stella (1996), 'Quasi-Fiscal Operations of Public Financial Istitutions', IMF Occasional Paper 142 (Washington, DC: International Monetary Fund).

Markiewicz M. (1998), 'Fiscal Policy and Disinflation in Transition Economies', CASE, *Studies and Analyses*, No. 127 (Warsaw: Centre for Social and Economic Research).

Markiewicz M. (2001), 'Quasi-Fiscal Operations of Central Banks in Transition Economies', BOFIT Discussion Papers, No. 2 (Bank of Finland: Institute for Economies in Transition).

Markusen, J. R. (1995) 'The Boundaries of Multinational Enterprises and the Theory of International Trade', *Journal of Economic Perspectives*, 9, pp. 169–89.

Masson, R. M. (1999), 'Monetary and Exchange Rate Policy of Transition Economies of Central and Eastern Europe after the Launch of EMU', IMF Policy Discussion Paper, PDP/99/5 (Washington, DC: International Monetary Fund).

Mazzaferro, F., Thimann C. and A. Winkler (2002), 'Stabilisation and Integration Views of Eurosation/Dollarisation Regimes: A Review of Some Specific Features', paper presented at the *8th Dubrovnik Economic Conference*, Dubrovnik, Croatia, 27–29 June.

Megginson L. W. and M. J. Netter (2001), 'From State to Market: A Survey of Empirical Studies on Privatization', *Journal of Economic Literature*, 39(2), pp. 321–89.

Michalopoulos, C. (1999), 'Trade Policy and Market Access Issues for Developing Countries', World Bank Policy Research Working Paper, No. 2214 (Washington, DC: The World Bank).

Mihov, I. (2001), 'The Economic Transition in Bulgaria, 1989–1999', in M. Blejer and M. Skreb (eds), *Transition: The First Decade*, pp. 401–40 (Cambridge, MA: The MIT Press).

Mundell, R. (1961), 'A Theory of Optimum Currency Areas', *American Economic Review*, 51(4), pp. 657–65.

Murrell, P. (1996), 'How Far Has the Transition Progressed', *Journal of Economic Perspectives*, 10, pp. 25–44.

Padoa-Schioppa, T. (2002), 'The Euro Goes East', lecture delivered at the *8th Dubrovnik Economic Conference*, Dubrovnik, 27–29 June.

Panagiotou, R. (2001), 'Foreign Direct Investment in Southeast Europe', WIIW 'Countdown' Project on *Regionalism and Balkan Integration* (Vienna: Institute for International Economic Studies).

Papazoglou, C. (1999a), 'Exchange Rate Policy and Output Growth: The Experience of the Transition Economies of Central and Eastern Europe', *Post-Communist Economies*, 11(3), pp. 319–36.

Papazoglou, C. (1999b), 'Exchange Rate Policy in Transition Economies: The Initial Choice and the Subsequent Experience', *Economia Internazionale*, LII(1), pp. 91–110, February.

Papazoglou, C. and E. J. Pentecost (eds) (2001), *Exchange Rate Policies, Prices and Supply-side Response: A Study of Transitional Economics* (Basingstoke: Palgrave).

Papazoglou, C. and E. J. Pentecost (2004), 'The Dynamic Adjustment of a Transition Economy in the Early Stages of Transformation', *Journal of Macroeconomics*, 26, pp. 547–61.

Petrakos, G. (2003), 'Trade Relations of the Balkan Countries: A Comparative Analysis', in, G. Petrakos, A. Kotios and D. Chionis (eds), *International and Monetary Aspects of Transition in Southeastern Europe*, pp. 15–46, South and East European Development Centre, (Volos: University of Thessaly Press).

Petrakos, G. and S. Totev (2000), 'Economic Structure and Change in the Balkan Region: Implications for Integration, Transition and Economic Cooperation', *International Journal of Urban and Regional Research*, 24, pp. 95–113.

Resmini, L. (2000), 'The Determinants of Foreign Direct Investment in the CEECs: New Evidence from Sectoral Patterns', *Economics of Transition*, 8(3), pp. 665–89.

Rosati, D. (1994), 'Output Decline during Transition from Plan to Market', *Economics of Transition*, 2(4), pp. 419–42.

Rose, A. K. (2001), 'Currency Unions and Trade: The Effect is Large', *Economic Policy*, 33, pp. 449–61.

Rose, A. K. and C. Engel (2000), 'Currency Unions and International Integration', NBER Working Paper, No. 7872 (Cambridge, MA: NBER).

Rutkowski, J. (1998), *Employment Adjustment and the Wage Structure in FYR of Macedonia* (Washington, DC: The World Bank).

Rutkowski, J. (2003) 'Does Strict Employment Protection Discourage Job Creation? Evidence from Croatia', Policy Research Working Paper 3104 (Washington, DC: The World Bank).

Sachs, J., A. Tornell and A. Velasco (1996), 'Financial Crises in Emerging Markets: The Lessons from 1995', *Brookings Papers on Economic Activity: 1* (Washington, DC: Brookings Institution), pp. 147–215.

Sargent T. and N. Wallace (1981), 'Some Unpleasant Monetarist Arithmetic', *Federal Reserve Bank of Minneapolis Quarterly Review*, fall, pp. 1–17.

SELDI (2001), *Background Document on Corruption in Southeast Europe*, Southeast Europe Legal Development Initiative (Sofia: Center for the Study of Democracy).

Selowsky, M. and R. Martin (1997), 'Policy Performance and Output Growth in the Transition Economies', *American Economic Review, Papers and Proceedings*, 87, pp. 349–53.

Slaveski, T. and P. Nedanovski (2003), 'Foreign Direct Investment in the Framework of Gross-Border Co-operation in Selected Balkan Countries', in G. Petrakos, A. Kotios and D. Chionis (eds), *International and Monetary Aspects of Transition in Southeastern Europe*, pp. 172–87, South and East European Development Centre (Volos: University of Thessaly Press).

Sonje, V. and M. Skreb (1997), 'Exchange Rate and Prices in a Stabilization Program: The Case of Croatia', in M. Blejer and M. Skreb (eds), *Macroeconomic stabilization in transition economies*, pp. 212–33 (Cambridge: Cambridge University Press).

Sonje, V. and B. Vujcic (2001), 'Croatia in the Second Stage of Transition, 1994–1999', in M. Blejer and M. Skreb (eds), *Transition – the First Decade*, pp. 193–258 (Cambridge, MA: The MIT Press).

Stubos G. and I. Tsikripis (2004), 'Regional Integration Challenges in South-eastern Europe: Banking Sector Trends', Unpublished manuscript, Bank of Greece, Athens, October.

Tavlas, S. G. (1994), 'The Theory of Monetary Integration', *Open Economies Review*, 5, pp. 211–30.

UN/ECE (1995), *Economic Survey for Europe in 1994–95* (New York and Geneva: United Nations).

UN/ECE (1996) *Economic Survey for Europe in 1995–96* (New York and Geneva: United Nations).

UN/ECE (1997), *Economic Survey for Europe in 1996–97* (New York and Geneva: United Nations).

UN/ECE (1999), 'Post-war Reconstruction and Development in South-East Europe', *Economic Survey of Europe*, No. 2 (New York and Geneva: United Nations).

UN/ECE (2001), 'Economic Growth and Foreign Direct Investment in the Transition Economies', *Economic Survey for Europe*, No. 1, ch. 5 (New York and Geneva: United Nations).

Uvalic, M. (2001), 'Regional Co-operation in Southeast Europe', *Journal of Southeast European and Black Sea Studies*, 1(1), pp. 23–40.

Weber, B. (2000), 'Institutional Reform in Transition Economies: How far have they Come?' (Washington, DC: International Monetary Fund).

Wei, S. J. (1997), 'How Taxing is Corruption on International Investors?', NBER Working Paper, No. 6030 (Cambridge, MA: NBER, National Bereau of Economic Research).

Welfens, J. J. P. (2001), *Stabilizing and Integrating the Balkans: Economic Analysis of the Stability Pact, EU Reforms and International Organizations* (Berlin: Springer).

Wolf, H. (1999), 'Transition Strategies: Choices and Outcomes'?, Princeton Studies in International Finance No. 85 (Princeton, NJ: Princeton University).

World Bank (2000a), *The Road to Stability and Prosperity in South Eastern Europe: A Regional Strategy Paper* (Washington, DC: The World Bank).

World Bank (2000b), *Trading Blocs* (Washington, DC: The World Bank).

World Bank (2002), *Transition – The First Ten Years: Analysis and Lessons for Eastern Europe and the Former Soviet Union* (Washington, DC: The World Bank).

World Bank (2003), *Trade Policies and Institutions in the Countries of South Eastern Europe in the EU Stabilization and Association Process*, Regional Report No. 24460, (Washington, DC: The World Bank).

Zinnes, C., Y. Eilat and J. Sachs (2001), 'The Gains from Privatization in Transition Economies: Is "Change of Ownership" Enough?', *IMF Staff Paper*, 48, pp. 146–70.

Index

The manufacturer's authorised representative in the EU is Springer Nature Customer Service Centre GmbH, Europaplatz 3, 69115 Heidelberg, Germany. If you have any concerns regarding our products, please contact ProductSafety@springernature.com

Printed and bound by CPI Group (UK) Ltd, Croydon, CR0 4YY

10/10/2026

02231221-0014